INDUSTRIAL EDUCATION
American Ideals and Institutions

INDUSTRIAL EDUCATION

American
Ideals and Institutions

Berenice M. Fisher

THE UNIVERSITY OF WISCONSIN PRESS

Madison, Milwaukee, and London 1967

Published by the University of Wisconsin Press
Madison, Milwaukee, and London
U.S.A.: Box 1379, Madison, Wisconsin 53701
U.K.: 26–28 Hallam Street, London W. 1

Printed in the United States of America
by the Heffernan Press, Inc.
Worcester, Massachusetts

Library of Congress Catalog Card Number 67-26626

To my parents

George Gottlieb Fisher
and
Elizabeth Ostry Fisher

Preface

As democratic and pragmatic as American education may be, it is remarkable how many high school students are only vaguely aware of what their comrades are doing in shop courses or in some distant vocational school, how many liberal-arts students have misty notions of what goes on in the technical departments of their campuses, how puzzled many white collar and professional people are concerning what industrial education is "for."

Perhaps this is part of the reason why, from the standpoint of scholarship, industrial education has remained a far more parochial area than other aspects of American education. There have been periods—ours is one of them—when one or another type of industrial education has been dragged into the light of public scrutiny. Yet this same impulse to subject industrial education to a thoroughgoing critique has its pitfalls; the most articulate critics are often members of groups by whom the wider picture of such education is only dimly perceived.

My aim in this book is to explore both the scope and the structure of the debate on industrial education, to develop an analysis which can serve as a propaedeutic to further study. The method which this investigation uses is historical and sociological, focusing on the temporal intertwining of social structure and ideology. Selected traditions in social historiography and sociology have contributed to such an approach; but my greatest and more personal debt is to Anselm L. Strauss, for the lessons I have learned through his lively tutoring and the example of his work.

I am also grateful to a number of other people for the help and advice they have given me: to Jack London, Geraldine M. Joncich, Martin B. Loeb, Stephenie G. Edgerton, and Howard S. Becker, who have helped me with their criticisms of one or another draft of the study; to Margaret D. Uridge, at the University of California at Berkeley, who helped to locate books from far-flung corners of the country; to the numerous people in Burbank and in the Los Angeles area who facilitated research there; to Joy A. Hussey and Annette E. Stiefbold, who have taken special pains in helping to prepare the manuscript; and to the Institute for Research on Poverty at the University of Wisconsin (through funds granted to the Institute by the Office of Economic Opportunity pursuant to the provisions of the Economic Opportunity Act of 1964), for aid in the final stages of manuscript preparation. The Institute, however, is in no way responsible for the conclusions drawn in this work.

Contents

Introduction

In order to explore a debate as complex as that which has surrounded industrial education in the United States over the last century and a half, it is necessary to develop a vocabulary which neither limits itself nor does violence to the perceptions of the disputing groups. Who these groups were and are and what their conceptions of industrial education involve must be the first topic of investigation; that is, rather than beginning with a definition, thereby immediately involving ourselves in the very debate we are seeking to explore, I propose to look at a wide variety of educational schemes which have taken industry or the consequences of industrialization as a central theme.

I believe that the advantages of such a diffuse approach far outweigh the disadvantages, for the idea that there has been or is one type of "industrial education" or a movement towards a single system in the United States dissolves readily on close inspection. It does not take long to discover that contemporary dichotomies between "liberal" and "vocational" or "general" and "industrial" education are themselves the product of one or another perspective in this debate. By leaving aside these concepts at the beginning, we have a greater chance of developing fruitful categories by which the whole spectrum of activities in industrial education can be analyzed.

xi

American ideals of industrial education cannot be neatly packaged; during the century and a half in which they have emerged, the groups which have advocated a given ideal have shifted; ideals have been blended and reconciled in response to particular situations; ideals which have been highly relevant to one group or from the standpoint of one period, become trivial or irrelevant to others. Yet given these often disparate, though partly overlapping, universes of discourse, it seems possible to find archetypes which can serve as tools in further investigation.

The purpose of the first part of this study is to uncover and explore these basic ideals and ideologies of industrial education —the ends toward which activities have been aimed and the imagery and argument which the various relevant groups have used. The first chapter is devoted to locating the major arguments in the context of a broader discussion of industrialization. The next three chapters move on to treat each of the arguments in detail. Although their exploration involves excursions into historical context, within which industrial-education ideals have evolved, these chapters do not constitute a history in its usual sense; rather, we shall move from group to group, asking what ideological and institutional responses each has given to the question of the relation of industry and education.

The second part of the study not only explores the scope of the basic industrial-education ideals, but seeks to use them as tools in analyzing situations which have diverged from the historical archetypes. The fifth chapter deals with geographical variations in the debate, and the final chapter asks how the terms of debate were modified to meet radically different economic conditions and to meet the current challenges to industrial-education goals.

It is important to keep in mind that, although the first part of the study explores and proposes a set of categories for the treatment of industrial-education discussions in general, the second part merely deals with the application of these categories (and, consequently, the development of new categories as well) to selected problems. Many more questions need to be asked about industrial education than this investigation can pretend to cover. The discussions of geographic variation in Part II are especially suggestive of further problems: we need to ask not only about the relation between industrial education and agriculture, but between industrial education and service or commercial occupations, whose evolving character is also changing the nature of this education in many areas. We need, also, to explore the question of industrial education for many special groups within the population and for many special settings—for the education of women or American Indians or residents of southern Appalachia, for example, or for the military services, for a wide variety of industries, for vocational rehabilitation.

The list of possible problems is unending, but it is not, I think, discouraging. The greatest problem is to bridge the gap which is so common in the discussion of education: the gap between those who are involved on a very immediate and pragmatic level and those who have strong commitments but only very general information. While this gap is often one between the educators and others, it can also be seen in the relations between various groups in the educational world.

PART I

INDUSTRIALIZATION AND
INDUSTRIAL-EDUCATION IDEALS

1

Industrial Education
and the Manufacturing Debate

Arguments about industrial education are, in an essential way, arguments about the kind of role industry should play in American life. This long-debated question has left a series of contradictory, though often blurred, assumptions in its wake, and industrial educators, like other Americans, have fashioned their own special views of the country partly out of such materials. Behind each of the major approaches to industrial education lies a central image of national development which shines through the educational rhetoric at many points. It is to these images, clustering around the problems of industrialization, that we may well turn first in order to understand the broader ideological setting for the industrial-education drama itself.

The chief argument in support of the development of industry has been the need to fulfill America's economic "destiny," and to use the richness of her "national resources." Although this argument has roots which extend as far back as pre-colonial days, its force first became evident toward the end of the eighteenth and in the early years of the nineteenth centuries, when national leaders began to debate the advisability of imposing

3

tariffs on manufactured products.[1] The issue of protective tariffs clearly involved conflicting economic interests; yet it also in-involved a choice between national styles of life: between that of an industrial nation and that of a nation of agriculture, handi-craft, and trade. Partisans of industry were well aware of the powerful imagery with which they had to contend. Their tactics were generally shrewd; by linking manufacture with the God-given land, with the nation's "natural" abundance, they could identify the destiny of America with that of industry, and make protection seem as natural an American policy as laissez-faire, manufacturing as natural an activity as agriculture and com-merce.

Tench Coxe, for example, the early Commissioner of Revenue and crusader for protection, was unusually adept at making such rhetorical identifications between the land and its industrial potential, insisting that the richness of soil, of sunlight, and of abundant "natural powers" (such as water and steam power) all indicated how much more fully agriculture might be devel-oped if manufacturing, and especially processing industries, were encouraged within the nation's boundaries.[2] Manufacture would also complement rather than compete with agriculture in the use of the laboring force, Coxe declared, for it was precisely those workers least useful to agriculture on whom industry would draw—immigrant artisans who were not interested in farming, city dwellers who sought work and were too poor to pioneer, and rural people who would devote part time to manu-facturing. Finally, he insisted, the country's shortage of labor would be compensated for by native mechanical ingenuity; with added inspiration from immigrant artisans, Americans would continue to invent laborsaving machines, relieving them-selves of the need to sacrifice agricultural workers to the build-ing of a manufacturing industry.

Inasmuch as they considered the quality of human resources an element in national economic progress, the protectionists implicitly raised the question of where Americans would acquire the skills necessary to the new manufacturing occupations. This was a difficult question to answer until a vision of the American labor force, more fully articulated than that of the protectionists, was formed. Coxe and other protectionist spokesmen were clearly casting around for a new perception of industrial workers; yet they were especially anxious to avoid adopting the image which their critics were most prone to attack, that of a permanent operative class. Instead, the protectionists argued for mobile, unskilled though literate, workers to run machinery, and for a skilled mechanic class to provide not only craftsmen, but inventors and "manufacturers." The protectionists considered the lack of special factory skills in the former group a positive factor, for it meant that such workers could move into industry easily and move out again; the best of them—the rural folk— would suffer little from the experience, and the worst of them— the city paupers—would be improved by the discipline of the factory. On the other hand, special tutoring for artisans was superfluous, for it was assumed that artisans would learn their work in the traditional fashion. With an improved tariff system, European craftsmen would immigrate in greater numbers, supplementing and improving the quality of native manufacturing: "Ours will be their industry," said Coxe, ". . . ours will be their skill. Interest and necessity, with such instructors, will teach us quickly."[3]

Although contemporaries of the protectionists were already questioning whether apprenticeship or apprenticeship-like arrangements were adequate modes of training for manufacture, it was not until the late years of the nineteenth century that a popular movement for formal industrial education developed which drew on the protectionists' national-resources argument. The delayed juncture of these ideas was due partly to the pace of institutional development within education itself, partly to the changed industrial scene which later political economists faced.* Simon Patten, a political economist writing in the 1880's, warned that workers were no longer either temporary machine operators or skilled craftsmen (of the north-European variety to whom the early protectionists had referred), but a mass of unskilled and ignorant new immigrants, men and women who were easy victims of the now gigantic industries. Patten contended that the old class of skilled labor was continually discouraged and driven from work by the vicious practice of employing the cheapest grade of labor; by these means capitalists were destroying their own businesses and the economic efficiency of the nation. On the other hand, he argued, it would benefit both industrial leaders and the country at large to give adequate wages and greater encouragement to skilled workers: "There are probably not five percent of the laboring population in any civilized country who would not willingly spend many years in preparing for their trade if thereby their future wages would be doubled."[4] To the question of how the masses of men in so civilized a country as the United States might acquire the skills of their trade, industrial educators attuned to the rhetoric of efficiency and economic progress provided the answer: the public schools, by a program of vocational education, would prepare American youths as skilled workers and prevent them from becoming a wasted national resource.

Patten's indictment of capitalists for undermining economic growth was part of an increasing, often harsh, critique of manufacturing leadership—the very leadership to which laissez-

---

* The question of why the trade-training movement (the subject of Chapter IV) came so late in relation to industrialization, why such training was not incorporated in the developing elementary schools of the 1830's instead of the developing high schools of a half-century later, is a complex one. The full answer, I believe, is dependent on a greater understanding of changes in apprenticeship and, especially, American attitudes toward that institution. See Marcus Wilson Jernegan, *Laboring and Dependent Classes in Colonial America, 1607-1783* (New York, 1960); and Paul H. Douglass, *American Apprenticeship and Industrial Education* (New York, 1921).

faire proponents of manufacturing had turned for a guarantee of continued economic development. The staunchest advocates of laissez-faire decried any protective policy, of course; but even those who conceded the need for certain tariffs parted ways with the political economists who considered national planning more important than the nature of individual men: "The principle causes of the rapid growth of national opulence," said Francis Bowen, "are moral rather than physical."[5] If so, it was reasoned, the development of an industrial leadership to promote economic growth would be assured when those with leadership ability were encouraged to realize their ambitions and were allowed to reap the rewards of their efforts.

Arguing the same case in its later Darwinian version, William Graham Sumner sought to establish a direct relation between untrammeled entrepreneurship and economic growth, and, sensing that his greatest competition came from those who used the national-resources rhetoric, Sumner shrewdly proceeded to unmask them. Imagine, he bid his readers, a dialogue between a contemporary statesman and an ambitious farmer. The farmer is trying to obtain an iron tariff so that he can exploit the mine which he has just uncovered:

Statesman— "You do not think what you ask. That would be authorizing you to tax your neighbors, and would be throwing on them the risk of working your mine, which you are afraid to take yourself."

Iron Man (aside)—"I have not talked the right dialect to this man. I must begin all over again. (Aloud). Mr. Statesman, the natural resources of this country ought to be developed. The American laborer must not be forced to compete with the pauper labor of Europe."

Statesman— "Now I understand you. Now you talk business. . . ."[6]

Though many political economists throughout the nineteenth century continued, like Sumner, to argue that the man who was willing to take risks was the key to national economic growth, the very process of industrialization began to exert pressure on the entrepreneurial ideal. Laissez-faire spokesmen faced a changing social structure. The growth of cities which accompanied industrial development was providing an environment quite different from that to which the champions of the rising industrial leader had attributed his leadership potential—a rural background, a stolid father and loving mother, a home-centered nurture, a basic education in the public schools.[7] In addition, economic organization and technology were developing and changing. The entrepreneurial ideal had flourished, in part, on a muting of distinctions between business, inventive, and technical skills, and all of these seemed to demand more and more precise definition as the nineteenth century drew on. Even in the heyday of the self-made man, it was becoming less clear that a youth who began as an apprentice should also learn business skills and develop the appreciation, if not the techniques, for invention.[8] Andrew Carnegie himself began to question the possibility, pointing out that boys from polytechnical and scientific schools were bringing an outlook and technical expertise to industry which the shop-trained manufacturers had difficulty in matching.

When opinion shifted in this direction, advocates of more formal business, technical, and scientific education could fit their own arguments to the manufacturing ideology. The self-made man was as much a hero to them as to the proponents of laissez-faire, but they argued that American economic development had reached the stage where neither apprenticeship nor the native catch-as-catch-can system of industrial training sufficed. More was needed to prepare the new generation of manufacturing leaders with requisite social, economic, or technical skills. This was the training which formal education could supply.

Like their national-resources adversaries, the proponents of the manufacturing-leadership argument assumed that America would move onward and upward, and the industrial educators whose ideals corresponded to these respective positions—the trade-training advocates and the partisans of higher technological education—were equally ardent believers in economic growth. It was difficult for either of them to account for the possibility that some members of the society would not profit from economic expansion, might decline in its face, or—worse still—sink into an economic, social, or moral abyss. The manufacturing boosters of Coxe's and Mathew Carey's generation had insisted that no group need suffer from industrialization; later national-resources spokesmen apologized for the poverty and degradation which they saw around them by showing how economic growth had not been properly fostered.[9] In similar fashion, laissez-faire spokesmen supported continued economic growth as a guard against developing a pauper class: "If," said Francis Wayland, "the increase of capital be so rapid as to allow the simple laborer sufficient wages to support and rear as many children as, under ordinary circumstances, form a human family, there will be no distress in any class; all will be well supported. There will be no beggars from necessity. . . ."[10] Or if by some chance there should be a pause in economic growth, the worker who had saved from his wages, by exercising the prudence and frugality characteristic of the entrepreneur himself, would avoid sinking into pauperism.

The original challenge to such sanguine interpretations of industrialism came from its opponents, the defenders of agriculture and commerce, who quite correctly perceived the profound shift in national direction which industrialization would involve. Foremost in the minds of these critics was the example of England, which, they said, had become a decaying land of "tenants, laborers, and mechanics panting for a revolution."[11] As alarming as the political consequences of industrialization appeared, its moral and economic costs—an end to agrarian virtue and the material prosperity natural to a nation of small communities, farmers, mechanics, and traders—seemed as great. The well-known critic John Taylor insisted that the English experience was not unique; American manufacturing proponents, he said, misleadingly pointed to the glorified factories of Waltham to prove that this country would never develop cities like Manchester. Yet if they would only look to the city of New York, they would see that the consequences of their ideal—pauperism, vice, and crime—were already afflicting America itself.

Some manufacturing proponents, though sure the agrarian prophesy would not come to pass, emphasized the beneficial aspects of industry and subtly laced their formula for industrialization with cautionary measures. Hence, laissez-faire spokesman Amasa Walker conceded that the division of labor which accompanied manufacturing progress tended to "enervate the laborer"; on the other hand, he argued, the development of the "sanitary arts"—including medicine, gymnastics, and the "manly sports"—made it possible for the workers to counteract such enervation.[12] Walker also admitted that manual workers could not utilize their full mental powers on the job, but claimed that their work would nevertheless foster their development: factory and city life offered a host of opportunities which the old, relatively isolated worker did not have; the churches, journals, lyceums, lectures, and debates in which the factory worker could participate would provide him food for thought and discussion during his working hours.

Walker's qualified optimism had much in common with the "onward and upward" arguments of pre-Civil War manufacturing proponents; like them, he went only a little way in meeting the charge that poverty and degradation had followed industrialization. Yet for over half a century, philanthropists, utopians, and social reformers had been proposing curative as well as preventive measures, insisting that either the manufacturing system or aspects of it must be modified. Whether the industrialized environment, or the man who constituted a part of it, was emphasized in these various prescriptions depended on the viewpoint of the diagnostician. "Misery," said economist and social reformer Edward T. Devine, ". . . is communicable, curable, and preventable. It lies not in the unalterable nature of things, but in our particular human institutions, our social arrangements, our tenements and streets and subways, our laws and courts and jails, our industry and our business."[13] The social illness which resulted from the malfunctioning of these institutions was not poverty in the ordinary sense, he argued (Devine remarked that he himself was poor at one time), but a poverty which so changed men that their state could be improved only through general reforms. The conditions which contributed to such debasing poverty had to be improved so that the "supreme aim" could be realized—that of "strengthening character."

Industrial educators who were sympathetic to this logic were quick to see the role which education could play. That educational institutions would help prevent men from ever succumbing to the threat which the new industries and the new cities posed; or that, once the laborer had fallen, education could help give him back the strong character he used to have—both seemed feasible prescriptions. Both also focused on the quality of the worker's life; it might be improved by a variety of educational programs—including the teaching of work skills—but the goal of such industrial education was, ultimately, the shoring up or the restoration of character.

The argument concerned with prevention or cure of industrialization's evils could, indeed, be blended with those which emphasized national resources and work skills; but the prevention-and-cure argument was not unique in this respect. When problem and perspective have so demanded, each of the major arguments for industrialization has been blended or reconciled with one or another of its alternatives. Spokesmen using the national resources vocabulary have sometimes focused on poverty, crime, and misery precisely because they have seemed a waste of national resources. Those arguing for laissez-faire have turned to the question of national resources and the relation between their exploitation and the opening up of greater opportunities for the rising man. And those concerned with the dangers and costs of industrialism have pointed to their proposed cures as prerequisites to national growth or individual opportunity.

Spokesmen for corresponding industrial-educational positions have also blended and combined arguments, adding to the overlapping and interweaving quality of the industrial-education debate. Yet, if we are aware that we must mute some of them in order to analyze others more fully, each of the major industrial education arguments can be treated in turn. Their treatment in the three following chapters is partly chronological, for the social-historical matrix in which each argument emerged— the social groups and institutions which gave it temporal shape and which it also molded—contributed to its special character. The industrial-education argument which emphasizes the prevention and cure of industrial evils became prominent before the Civil War; that which stresses success and industrial leadership began to attract widespread attention in the second half of the century; and the third which contends that industrial education should be aimed at training skilled workers as a key national resource emerged toward the end of the century and reached its climax in the Smith-Hughes Act of 1917. Each of these general positions has its own complexities which cannot be reduced, but I am going to use a shorthand which may at least help to clarify the inquiry. The image which has guided the efforts of the prevention-and-cure camp is dubbed the "philanthropic" ideal, or sometimes the ideal of the "honest workman." The image which dominates the rhetoric of the second major group is simply called the ideal of "success," or occasionally the "engineering" ideal. Lastly, the notion which pervades the industrial education argument geared to utilizing national resources is called the ideal of the "skilled worker" or sometimes the "trade-training" ideal.

2

The Philanthropic Ideal

For most pre-Civil War educators—and many who developed the same tradition in the latter part of the century—industrial education was viewed as a means for counteracting, or at least modifying, changes being wrought in American society. In occupational terms, the new order was marked by instability, a movement of people into unaccustomed geographic settings and unfamiliar kinds of work. For philanthropic industrial educators, the major threat which such upheaval posed was that of the loss of independence on the part of the worker. He would encounter new opportunities and would have to learn new ways of handling himself, but he might also succumb to the difficulties inherent in these challenges.

This traditional independence to which philanthropists turned their attention they felt had characterized not merely artisans, but small town and rural Americans in general. Hence the burden of philanthropic industrial-education programs argued the need to preserve, restore, or partly recapture that independence which all workers seemed to be in peril of losing. The manual-labor movement was originally developed to shore up the independence of a mobile ministry; the lyceum and mechanics-institute movement to strengthen the independence of professionals, merchants, farmers, and artisans. Another broad group of industrial-education schemes, forwarded by manufacturers, public-school advocates, and workingmen's leaders, focused on the even more threatened factory workers; they seemed by definition robbed of their independence and prone to sink to great intellectual and moral depths.

Lastly, some philanthropic industrial educators turned to the plight of the worker who had migrated to the city, and especially the plight of the worker's child. Far removed from traditional town or farm life, these folk needed an education which would both guard them from the greatest of urban dangers and enable them to carve out a decent life in city surroundings. To such ends, industrial-education schemes appeared as part of the movements for penal reform, kindergartens, playgrounds, and a host of social-work schemes which continued to present themselves through the end of the century.

Independence and Social Harmony

The Manual Labor Movement. If Americans of the old order were independent, Americans of the emerging industrial world interpreted that traditional independence as one which drew men together rather than tearing them apart. Most citizens pursued occupations related to agriculture and handicraft, and with such common work experiences it seemed inevitable that men would understand each other. But the simple yeomen and craftsmen of the early nineteenth century did not appear content; as they abandoned their work to climb to the heights of wealth, social critics began to sense that corruption was afoot: "The class of mouths oppresses the class of hands," said Theodore Parker, "for the strongest and most cunning of the latter are continually pushing into the ranks of the former, and while they increase the demand for work, leave their own share of it to be done by others."[1] The solution, said Parker, was for work to be "wisely distributed," so that all would share the burden of labor and all would receive its benefits. If the well-to-do did their fair share of work there would be no need to "exercise for the sake of health."

This fear—that an unwise distribution of labor would lead to an elite and unproductive class on one hand and a degraded and overworked class on the other—was part of the impetus behind the manual labor movement. Originally, the manual labor idea developed as part of a reform in seminary education, at a time when evangelical sects were engaged in an energetic recruiting campaign. Men were needed to fill the many positions which the early nineteenth-century crusades were creating, and schools were needed to train men for this enlarged ministry.[2] The moral aspect of evangelical schooling was particularly important. Since many of the students were to be sent west to serve, religious leaders felt that the young ministers should be equipped with a hardihood, a keenness and "perspicacious common sense" which would enable them to reach and cope with rough-hewn western men. Although the virtues of the frontier farmer closely resembled those prescribed for the minister, and many of the ministerial students were farm-bred, their evangelical teachers often feared that the students were vulnerable, and in need of further moral development. Like the religious movement which sponsored them, the evangelical seminaries reflected suspicion and fear of the shift from rural life.[3]

Sometime before 1820, Andover Seminary began to reflect this moral concern by incorporating gardening and wood-chopping as part of the student curriculum; a few years later, Maine Wesleyan Seminary began a self-conscious manual-labor program.[4] Other institutions soon followed suit, and their programs gained considerable support from the American Education Society. This group, dedicated to the promotion of ministerial training, especially for the West, looked upon manual labor as a sure way of dealing with problems of health, finances, and moral behavior which resulted from taking young students away from home. An article in the Society's *Quarterly Register and Journal*, for example, noted that one way to quiet down and sober up the boisterous students might be to set them to work, for this system had worked in prisons and reform schools.[5] Another contributor made a more subtle argument, pointing out that the Society's aid lifted "hundreds and even thousands of pious young men from their lowly occupations and gratuitously educat[ed] them for the gospel ministry."[6] Was there not a danger, the author wondered, that these youths, suddenly confronted with money, would be spoiled, would lose whatever virtue their previous industry had given them? Would it not be wise for them to continue to work in college to maintain their sense of proportion and, by the way, defray some of the cost of their keep? A third writer in the *Register* followed the argument to an even stronger conclusion, suggesting a rather different interpretation of manual activities.[7] Already noticing the decline of manual-labor programs, the author suggested that they be continued on an individual basis, each student minister taking himself off to a shop for regular hours every day. The young theologians, he said, needed to develop a worldly and independent spirit, for their future life would not be all study, and the spirit of inventiveness and enterprise would be invaluable.

The argument for manual labor was inclined to broaden as theological schools and colleges themselves were forced to expand their base.[8] Schools in the West had attracted some student ministers, but these institutions spent most of their energy training professionals and good Christian citizens, and it was not long before the manual-labor advocates adjusted to this broader student group. Manual labor, argued Theodore Weld, an agent for the Society for Promoting Manual Labor in Literary Institutions, would benefit each individual, as well as society in general; the mind and body, joined by divine purpose, would have to be cared for equally if society were to prosper. Modern medicine, he said, underscored the need of exercise for the college youth, whose unnatural idleness often led to either mischief or unhealthy and immoral outlets for "animal excitability." Manual labor would also serve a positive social function, by promoting an independent spirit and originality of thought in the student: "Instead of being a petty retailer of other men's wares, he would have a wholesale manufactory of his own."[9]

Not only the rising lower classes, but the upper classes as well, would benefit from this kind of education. Students from wealthy homes had little understanding of the working class, said Weld; the upper classes were so "wrapped up in the innumerable robes of ceremony" that they rarely knew what the rest of the country was doing; by putting himself in the place of a worker, the student would gain the understanding needed to penetrate social barriers. A manual-labor system, Weld concluded, was particularly suited to this country; the traditional system of education was "anti-democratic," separating men into disparate classes and arousing animosities between them, while manual labor was particularly republican, promoting the equality of men and emphasizing the independent artisan's and farmer's occupations. Manual labor stressed usefulness and productivity, raising the standard of living and promoting habits of industry in the nation.

Weld's concept of manual labor for the sake of democracy was intimately involved with the idea of manual labor for the sake of health; and ideas concerning public health were themselves in transition. In the early nineteenth century, American medicine was just developing its modern outlines; hospital and medical-school training were in the process of development, and doctors were becoming more interested in health reforms.[10] But although medicine of the 1820's and 1830's was becoming increasingly urbanized, it still had a strong rural cast. Like clergymen, the doctors looked to the country and cast a suspicious eye on the burgeoning cities. The medical advice books of the period and the profession's *Journal of Health* continually held up the countryside as the place for healthy living: the rural citizen provided the model for the wholesome, happy—and enterprising—man. Though the doctors admitted that country people had their illnesses, artisans, they said, were more plagued with occupational disorders, and the ambitious city people seemed the most unhealthy of all: "We have only to look around us, upon those engaged in the constant pursuit of wealth, or in the society of the dissipated, to see the dull eye and flabby corpulency of lethargic apathy, or the pinched features of fidgetty irritability."[11] The inequality of city men might be a good incentive for achievement, but the human cost, the doctors contended, was great. Given the excessive strain of modern life, parents should guide their children toward careers which would not encourage sickly constitutions; the weak child needed to be exposed to the outdoors, while the healthy child could better afford a sedentary career.

By the 1830's, American educators, too, were interested in matters of health. The American Institute of Instruction devoted a section to health, and Horace Mann included pleas for school hygiene and physiology lessons in his crusade for the public schools.[12] In addition, American colleges had pioneered in physical education from the early years of the century, and with the importation of European gymnastics, the emphasis on health education had increased. The German followers of Fredrich Ludwig Jahn were especially influential, founding private gymnastic clubs or, like Francis Lieber, starting public gymnasiums and swimming schools. The general public, as well as professionals, seem to have accorded this new system a hearty welcome—so hearty that Theodore Weld and the manual-labor supporters were forced to refute it as an alternative to manual labor. Some of their arguments were minor. For instance, the *Quarterly Register* pointed out that manual labor was more convenient, the shops were enclosed, and one could engage in it regardless of the weather. Weld himself declared that gymnastics were dangerous, unnatural, military, and unphilosophical, directing the mind inward instead of toward some "visible effect"; that is, manual labor produced something, and gymnastics did not. As this suggests, Weld saw a class bias in gymnastics: "The laboring classes, who make up nine-tenths of the community, are disgusted and repelled by the grotesque and ludicrous antics of the gymnasium."[13]

It is ironic, in the light of manual labor's democratic goals, that Weld's position also gained support from the seminaries, for they considered sports and playing undignified for the seminary student, for "a man of science."[14] Yet, even with this ministerial support, manual labor waned, while gymnastics increased in popularity. By the 1840's, gymnastics were moving into the colleges, and clubs were being established all over the country, but manual-labor schools were moving toward rapid extinction. Educational groups like the American Institute of Instruction had begun to question the value of manual labor: exercise was all very well, but the job of the schools was to make students and not laborers. The churches themselves were also changing. Revivalism had hit a peak in the 1830's, and, as ministers began moving back to a more orthodox position, there was a little less room for educational schemes of the manual-labor variety. Theodore Weld himself sensed the change, scanned the horizon, and threw his energies behind the growing abolition cause.

Mechanics' Institutes and Lyceums. William Ellery Channing, like his ministerial colleague Parker, was also concerned about the discontented and ambitious lower classes; but in Channing's view, the solution would be reached if each member of the working class remained in his proper place, improving his inward self rather than trying to improve his social position. "A trade," said Channing, "is plainly not the great end of his [the worker's] being, for his mind cannot be shut up in it," and a man at his work can clearly develop his many faculties: "Poems and systems of theology which have made some noise in the world have been wrought at the work bench and amidst the toils of the field."[15] If men would concentrate on "self-culture," divisive politics and economic ambition would fall to the background, and the honest pursuit of labor, both mental and manual, would be given its rightful place.

Channing's ideal worker, laboring at his bench and thinking great thoughts, might well have been found in the person of Elihu Burritt. By the 1840's the "learned blacksmith," Burritt, had captured the imagination of ministers and laymen alike. Despite his modest country background and his own limited income, Burritt taught himself so much and so well that Longfellow wrote him, suggesting that he move to Harvard to study. The blacksmith replied:

I thank you from my whole heart for your kind proffer of pecuniary assistance in prosecuting my studies. Having acquired the habit of regarding my literary pursuits as matters of mere recreation, and not allowing myself to expect from them anything but a species of transient gratification, I have long ago resolved to make them entirely subservient to the more necessary and important avocations of life. . . . With this view, I have always confined my "literary leisure" to those hours of the day *when no man can work*; . . . And I can assure you, Sir, that each of these two departments of my occupations gives a lively zest to the other. When I return in the evening to my little chamber, with the consciousness of having performed a full day's labor, I set down at my desk and commune with my little shelf of books with a relish that indeed makes for recreation. And in the morning, after having blown out my morning lamp, I resume my hammer with an equal relish, and ply it with such force and effect as give strength to my arm, make the coarsest and commonest fare more delicious than the viands of princes—and procure me all the gratifications of industry. But what is paramount to every other consideration is, that my physical constitution will admit of no suspension of athletic exercise, which, in whatever situation I may be placed, I never could resist my inclination to seek in honest and honorable manual labor. Then there is another thing: . . . everybody is ambitious, and I am particularly so to stand in the ranks of the workingmen of New England and beg and beckon them onward and upward, if I can, into full stature of *intellectual men.*[16]

Burritt never went to Harvard; he gradually moved away from full time smithing to become a leader in social reform, but as historian Merle Curti notes, his vision of the worker was always limited. He had himself been an artisan, and like many of his contemporaries did not see much of the industrial revolution which was taking place around him.

Although the occupation of the independent artisan was, indeed, still an important one, his position was changing. The rise of the merchant capitalist in the late eighteenth century had encouraged artisans to turn, as Channing feared, to the upward climb, and many artisans suffered rather than profited by the changing organization of industry. With the increasing division of labor, the master workman who could not merchandize his own goods might easily sink to the level of his journeymen and apprentices, who themselves were not faring well.[17] The early mechanics' organizations reflected this dual dilemma of master and workmen. Some of these groups, such as the Mechanics' Institute in Boston, established courses and libraries for mechanics and apprentices, with the avowed purpose of improving their skills. The Boston group, however, confined its efforts to those already in the trade, sensing the threat which unlimited encouragement might pose to the already endangered craftsmen. Other educational societies of the early nineteenth century, clearly representing the rising masters, as well as general proponents of manufacturing, sponsored loans to aspiring mechanics to help them become independent.

Mechanics'-institute promoters were particularly aware of the unsure and sometimes declining position of the independent artisans. The American variety of mechanics' institutes drew their inspiration from the original work of George Birkbeck, the Glasgow physician who had given such a vigorous start to British workers' education.[18] Birkbeck had promoted the scientific education of workers for the purpose of giving them an understanding of the principles which underlay their work—an understanding which would elevate the manual occupations, so that workers would find fuller satisfaction in their labors and the work itself would be improved. The Americans who harkened to Birkbeck's efforts followed his reasoning as well, but as we might expect, soon gave their own twist to the ideology.

Perhaps the most important of the American experiments was that begun by Samuel Merrick in Philadelphia in 1825. Merrick had originally embarked on a career in the commercial world, but the inheritance of a small manufactory had suddenly made him an entrepreneur.[19] He was surprised, he said, to discover how little esteem "mere mechanics" had, and how difficult it was to acquire a mechanical education. With these two problems in mind, Merrick went about organizing the Franklin Institute, the aim of which was to teach science to mechanics and to encourage invention and manufacture. A library was established, prizes were offered, and mechanics were kept abreast of improvements in their field through the pages of the Institute's *Journal*. Education, the *Journal* claimed, would be directed toward the improvement of mechanics, and even operatives, in the faith that science would expand both individual opportunity and national progress. The importance of scientific and mechanical enlightenment could be denied no longer.[20]

Despite the determination of mechanics'-institute advocates, however, the movement was not very successful in the United States, gaining none of the widespread support which it had excited in England. Significantly, it was the lyceums, the small town rather than the big city attempt to enlighten independent American workers, which drew the most plaudits; even the lyceums, however, ultimately missed the bulk of American artisans.

Josiah Holbrook, who initiated the American lyceum movement, shared that same faith in the modern science which had pervaded both the manual-labor and the mechanics'-institute efforts. He had studied and worked under Benjamin Silliman at Yale, had dabbled in a manual-labor experiment, and had finally turned to the lyceum crusade, appealing to the growing interest in scientific and public education. According to Holbrook, lyceums could bring the study of the natural sciences and a wide variety of other subjects within the reach of farmers, artisans, and teachers. Lyceum classes would probably stress subjects bearing on vocations, since these would be of great interest, but they could also serve the general purpose of elevating the moral tone of American communities, of giving citizens self-improving topics on which to converse, and of providing a "bulwark against vicious habits in the young."[21] Indeed, Holbrook felt that lyceums would prove a nostrum for the restlessness of the times, since an enlightened public would be less susceptible to the radical politics and political demogoguery with which the people were besieged.

Throughout the Jacksonian period, Holbrook's lyceums grew at a lively pace. The little discussion groups sprang up in towns of varying size and character. If the neighborhood contained many mechanics, the principles of mechanical science would be taught; but following Holbrook's ideals, it was this knowledge of principles, rather than mere trade techniques, which received the emphasis. In practice, however, it was not always simple to distinguish between knowledge for enlightenment and knowledge which might lead to an improvement in one's wordly position. Lyceum supporters found themselves forced to reiterate that education would not make the worker dissatisfied with his lot.[22] They noted that it was natural for men to rise and fall in the world, but argued that the lyceums would promote a harmony of classes. Holbrook extended the argument to envision a great national system of lyceums, harmonizing the entire country; yet even his more limited cause was in great part a lost one. As the century progressed, local groups came to rely less on discussion and more on traveling lecturers. The lecturers were most often literary men, who could feed assorted cultural dishes to a hungry and growing middle-class public. Artisans and operatives found little of interest in the lectures, and returned to their benches to await the next crusade.

The Worker and the Factory

The Manufacturing Viewpoint. While manual-labor advocates and lyceum promoters developed educational ideals which
cast the worker as farmer or artisan, as the independent man,
a new class of workers was emerging. Over them was a new
variety of entrepreneur, whose educational ideas were shaped
by his own position as well as that of the worker whom he was
responsible for bringing into being.

The prototype of this modern manufacturing leader was provided by the Boston merchants who moved over into manufacturing during the crucial era of the War of 1812. These were
wealthy, prestigious, commercial men, who were quick to see
the possible decline of shipping and eager to find other forms
of investment; it was the large-scale manufactory which caught
their imaginations, and it was on such an endeavor that Francis
Cabot Lowell, equipped with the usual textile machinery plans
stolen from England, convinced the Boston Associates to embark.[23]

As the opportunity for investment opened up, a broader group
of investors was needed. Parvenu traders like Nathan Appleton
were allowed to enter the fold, as was Kirk Boot, an engineer
from a well-to-do family who came to manage the Associates'
factories. Yet the owners of the new textile mills at Waltham
still saw themselves as an elite group of investors rather than as
"manufacturers." (That term, still associated with artisans, was
particularly distasteful to newcomers like Appleton, who, as
late as 1832 when he was one of the country's leading industrial
tycoons, still insisted that he was not a manufacturer but an
investor.)[24] From such heights, the first generation of Boston
manufacturers plotted out the shape of textile manufacturing,
larding their plans with a considerable dose of utopianism.

The first problem the manufacturers had to face was that of
finding labor, and the character of the laboring force they re-

cruited helped to shape their attitude towards it. Most of the area's manufacturing had originally been done in the country-side; as the putting-out system and cottage system replaced in-dividual work, the locale remained rural, and the family itself remained an important element. Early firms, such as that of Slater, brought entire families into the factories, the men with mechanical background becoming mechanics and overseers, while the women and children did the weaving. This Rhode Island family system had been preceded by an effort to use ap-prentices, but neither the family nor the apprentice scheme was highly successful; despite Slater's Sunday schools, the families and youths were hard to keep.

The Boston Associates needed an even greater labor force. With the increased use of power, their mills would be large. Their factories, too, would be manned by mechanics and over-seers (whose children, together with "poor" children, would add their hands), but the bulk of the labor force would be the region's young women. To recruit spinster labor, the manu-facturers had to establish living conditions acceptable to New England standards, and hence, the well-known boardinghouse system, with its matrons, literary activities, and spiritual facili-ties. But there was more involved in these plans than the desire to recruit labor. The early New England manufacturers were imbued with some of the lofty social ideals of their time; many were men like Amos Lawrence who believed in the stewardship of wealth, and their earliest plans for the factories acknowledged the need for schooling. If the manufacturers gave little support to the public school movement itself, it was not due to a total disregard for education. They expected and wanted an intelli-gent body of factory workers, and deplored the thought of de-graded English-type labor; but instead of looking to the schools, the manufacturers envisioned the factories themselves as the primary means for uplifting the masses.

The ideal of education through the factories was elaborated at an 1817 meeting of the American Society for Encouragement of Domestic Manufacturers. Like other pro-manufacturing groups, the Society grew enthusiastic over the potential of America for manufacture, but cast an anxious eye toward England. They insisted, however, that America already had manufacturing, and its consequences had been happy. Factories were being built in the countryside, by the lovely waterfalls and streams which provided the power, in a healthy atmosphere, ". . . where good instruction will secure the morals of the young, and good regulations will promote, in all, order, cleanliness, and the exercise of civil duties."[25] Apprentices, the Society promised, would be watched over with care, and the "beneficial clauses" of their contracts (presumably those relating to education) would be enforced. The factories would be uplifting for the mass of workers; indeed, the best-educated workers in the country were already the product of factories. Schools would be maintained, and many would have a chance for education which they did not have at present. Not only the individual worker, but the whole country, would profit as the wilderness was swept back, replaced by the garden—and the anvil.

These themes were elaborated upon by the New England manufacturers and their supporters. Nathan Appleton pointed out that labor was ubiquitous in America, respected and respectable. America, Appleton insisted, was not a land of inherited wealth, but a land in which "direct labor" reaped its reward and in which accumulated wealth soon dissipated without added effort.[26] American labor had never dropped into the "abject state" in which European workers were found, he insisted. Manual labor was respected in the United States, and therefore American workers were of high quality.

This concept of a labor force of high quality was basic to the manufacturers' ideology. American workers, wrote another contributor to the *Merchants' Magazine*, would always retain their high level. In a democracy, the people would be vigilant and not allow English conditions to appear. The religious background of America provided another bulwark, together with the integrity of the factory owners themselves. In addition, the New England workers lived near their own homes, and their friends and relatives would guard against their abuse. Finally, the writer argued, factory work was not a permanent job: "The young men and women of the country, in those places where the factory system prevails, employ their industry in these establishments, not as a main object of pursuit, but as a stepping-stone to a future settlement, or to other occupations."[27] The women could earn themselves a fine dowry and marry, while many of the young men would soon leave for the West.

There was no reason, according to the manufacturers, why factories should change into ugly, oppressive places. In fact there was no reason why the factories should change at all. Men of the first generation of Boston manufacturers, such as Amos Lawrence, clung to the ideal of intelligent workers as the basis for manufacture, and resisted the thought that innovation might make such a labor force less important. Yet it was difficult to maintain the early ideal. The New England mills of the thirties and forties were undergoing rapid alteration. Textile production was becoming more competitive; the character of the labor force was changing; and these two factors played into each other. New voices among the Boston Associates insisted on a more serious commitment to management (a commitment, it was said, which investors who were mere dilettante manufacturers could not provide!) including a more frugal concept of wages. The wages were reduced, hastening the flight of New England farm girls, who, unhappy with the changing factories, were moving to more attractive jobs. Irish immigrants rapidly filled the vacant places, providing a more docile and less literate labor force. The new managerial ideal had a new labor base on which to flourish, and the ideal of the factory for education, of the mill-by-the-stream, gradually dimmed.

The Public School Proposal. The movement of New England women into the factories had been a graceful one. Since early nineteenth-century Americans were accustomed to the image of the spinning housewife, it was possible for women to play a similar role in manufacture—as long as working conditions seemed tolerable and respectable. But with regard to children, the other major source from which the new factory owner expected to draw laborers, the picture was somewhat different. The image of the working child was certainly well established, but this very ideal of the child helping on the family farm, or apprenticed under a local tradesman, was meeting considerable challenge.

The challenge came in large part from advocates of public education who were struggling to reconcile the working-child notion with that of a common school.[28] A partial solution had been found earlier: placing the responsibility of educating apprenticed children on the masters themselves. Yet by the beginning of industrialization many American children either could not or would not be apprenticed. Humanitarians of the early nineteenth century were, therefore, faced with the prospect of rapidly expanding cities in which growing numbers of pauper children were left virtually without guidance. The reasoning of the New England manufacturers, that the factories could be used for improvement and education, seemed to offer hope for poor urban children. But it was difficult for many humanitarians to conceive of factories as a substitute for school; the entire concept of differential education, an education for the wealthy child at school and an education for the poor child in the factory, ran counter to American ideals of equality. For the same reason, the free schools which developed during the colonial era and the early years of the Republic did not offer a satisfactory solution to the problem of universal education. In order to advocate a genuinely common schooling, and at the same time take into account the changing character of industrial life, it was necessary to evolve a new educational ideology which complemented rather than conflicted with the ideal of the child as worker. This was the essence of Horace Mann's crusade insofar as it related to the industrial world.

Horace Mann himself had strong reservations about the consequences of industrialization, but he also saw in it a potential for good.[29] In his campaign for public schooling, Mann sought to form an alliance with the Massachusetts manufacturers, with whom he had certain ideas in common. Both represented a progressive middle-ground, stressing achievement and progress and lauding the old American virtue of industry. In his Annual Reports of 1839, 1841, and 1848, Mann made an extended argument for the public schools on the basis of their importance to an industrializing America. He began his argument by praising the textile magnates, from whom he was rather unsuccessfully seeking support.[30] Waltham provided a model for all, because the Boston Manufacturing Company had recognized its social responsibilities to its workers. Unfortunately, Mann added, this was not the case with smaller concerns; they operated on a fly-by-night basis, exploiting the resources of one community and then moving on to the next, careless of public opinion. "Vicious" parents provided the source of labor for such irresponsible firms, both parent and company violating child-labor and education laws.

Despite his praise for the larger concerns, Mann was also fearful of them. He predicted that factories would grow even larger because of the increased use of steam power, and that American factory communities might easily become Manchesters. Against this possibility, education could provide not only a guard, but a positive help to both the individual workers and to the factories. Although the people must not lose sight of higher values, Mann continued, the need for bread should not be scoffed at, and, practically speaking, some parents might only support education if the financial profit were spelled out. Since manufacturers were also keenly interested in the material value of education, factories would be truly the best places to assess this value. Manufacturers were too interested in production to make false distinctions between men; they would promote the best and most able men, and the best men would be those with the most education. Educated workers could also move into self-employment, survive the buffets of fortune and begin at the bottom again, if they had to. These workers, argued Mann, would forward industry itself through their keen minds and their inventiveness; the improvement of manufacture had just begun, and educated workingmen would help fulfill its promise.

Lastly, Mann, like so many others, insisted that an educated workman was a less dangerous workman; but, unlike the manual labor advocates, Mann did not expect education to bring about a great change in the attitudes of men. Displaying a bitter aspect of his thought, he noted that education would not necessarily make men so good that they became champions of the oppressed; however, he commented, ". . . it gives each man the independence and the means by which he can resist the selfishness of other men."[31] Mann was far-sighted in envisioning the development of large-scale manufacture. Moreover, his mixed attitude toward ambition foreshadowed an era in which ambition and individual progress would be the key issues in the debate on education for work.

The Workingmen's Indictment. The factory operatives of the 1830's and '40's still comprised a very small proportion of the manual-laboring force. When Mann's contemporaries spoke of "workers," they most often meant simply those who worked with their hands. The workingmen themselves had a diffuse conception of their ranks, and when the first workingmen's parties of the 1820's and 1830's were organized, they drew on not only journeymen and masters, but on farmers as well. All these independent workers saw themselves as producers, yet they suspected and to some extent feared the rising factories. On the whole, the operative fell outside the purview of these workingmen's groups, for he seemed a part of the new industrial system, chained to its machines rather than pursuing his own work.[32]

The workingmen's parties had broad goals which embraced

a wide variety of social and political reforms, including temperance, the abolition of imprisonment for debt, the extension of the franchise and, as the parties developed, the improvement of working conditions and wages. The workingmen also displayed interest in establishing stricter apprenticeship regulation, but they were wary of apprentice-training schemes; only common schooling received their wholehearted support. Although the workingmen did not always agree on the form which public education was to take, they did agree to the need for public schools, which might incorporate manual labor on the high school level, but would, above all, insure that lessons in reading, writing, and arithmetic would be available to all children.

Seth Luther, a leading crusader in the workingmen's movement of the thirties, was one of its most ardent advocates of public education. Like other humanitarian reformers, Luther's concern for education was grounded in an indictment of industrial poverty, and complemented by a hatred of the new money-makers and the idle rich. It was avarice, he declared, which was eating away at the basis of American society: "Urged on by the cursed hell-born principle of Avarice, men stake everything for GOLD. Any, every means, and all kinds of *meanness* are used to get rich. . . . The world is filled with ignorance, vice and misery, that men may gorge, if possible, an insatiate appetite for gold."[33] But the manufacturers could not see the increasing poverty, continued Luther, for they would never dream of associating with workers. The lauded lyceums of Waltham were no antidote, when workers spent their hours chained to machinery; they needed time for education, an education which would rectify social wrongs. Manual-labor schools would have to be established so that both rich and poor could learn the dignity of labor; only then would society improve, almshouses, prisons, vice, and bigotry disappear: "You will see less of people dying from excessive laziness, and others dying, as they do now, from excessive labor. . . ."[34]

Luther's plea for education contained still another note. He did not deny that rising and falling in the world was a necessary part of society; indeed, he supported his demand for improved working conditions by arguing that the manufacturer himself might someday find his sons reduced to working in a factory. Here, Luther not only suggested the growing creed of the self-made man, but hinted at that version which would undermine his very plea for education. He himself had only a poor common-school education, he noted, yet he had been able to learn by keeping his eyes open as he went through life; education might be vital, but no education would be of use if a man could not also learn to think.

The importance of education, however, continued to be a major theme for the workingmen's groups, especially when, after the panic of 1837, the reform and humanitarian elements came to the fore. Inspired by the educational and industrial experiments of Robert Owen and others, humanitarians had taken a keen interest in the workingmen's cause for a number of years; even the esoteric transcendentalists had gradually become more reform-minded, and their Brook Farm contingent was one of those which invaded the New England workingmen's association.[35] The workingmen's movement became a battle ground for Fourierists, Associationists and a variety of land reformers; it was not until the 1850's that the reformers and utopians left the field, making room for the craft-conscious element among the workingmen to build toward trade unionism.

The social utopianism which wound in and out of the labor movement of the 1840's was relatively moderate in its goals and its methods; even some of the most extreme critics upheld the right to private property, admitted that laborers were not the sole producers, granted that the position of American labor was relatively favored, and urged legislative reform before resort to force. The utopian communities which were established by such crusaders shared much of this spirit of reconciliation.

Of all these social experiments the Fourierist communities were perhaps the most widespread, or at least the most notable.

Fourier's major disciple in America, Albert Brisbane, published his first manifesto, *Social Destiny of Man*, in 1840. Within a few years Fourierist phalanxes had sprung up thick and fast, so fast and with so little attention to the wellspring of the movement that Brisbane had little control over their development. By the middle of the same decade, the leadership of American Fourierism had been taken over by the New England utopians, and the little hope that had existed that this would become an integral part of the workingmen's movement seemed to fade.[36]

Brisbane's (and Fourier's) plan had called for genuine workers, as well as for the cooperation of the intellectually interested; the ideal community was to be characterized by a just division of both profits and labor; work was to become a pleasure for all. His thought suggested that if only work were arranged in an efficient and reasonable fashion, men would take to it readily. Members of the phalanx were to be divided into classes and series, so that labor could be minutely subdivided; monotony would be avoided by allowing each person to pursue a variety of jobs. One might easily learn skills in related jobs, those connected with leather, for example, so that it would be possible to alternate one's occupations frequently. Individuals would also be able to choose vocations to which they were naturally suited; the smaller children would be encouraged to play around the various shops and fields, taking up little tools when a job caught their fancy. By the time they were physically mature, they would have determined their own natural bents and could embark on appropriate apprenticeships.

Brisbane had planned that profits would be split among the initial investors in the community, and the workers, who would become investors as well. It was the unequal distribution of property, he insisted, not private property itself, which made for a lack of social harmony. The system of phalanxes would remove this source of conflict, for men, being basically unselfish, would not naturally desire to be useless or unjustly rich.

There were, however, other dimensions in Brisbane's ideal of association, for he felt that investors would have to be attracted to finance the communities, and that association would, therefore, have to offer a decent investment. Children in the communities might also need more concrete rewards (Brisbane suggested honors for their work), although the adult workers would be spurred on by "emulation" and "corporate enthusiasm" alone. At some points Brisbane seemed to suggest that the incentive to honest labor is intrinsic, but he also stressed the need to make "INDUSTRY ATTRACTIVE." The jobs should not only be short and sweet, but the working environment should be a veritable pleasure: "The workshops and manufactories elegantly fitted up and decorated, and everything connected with them clean and perfect—the tools, implements and machinery of the best quality, labor-saving and convenient—the dresses tasty and comfortable—the workmen polite and well-educated, and united in their respective occupations by similarity of taste, by friendship, sympathy of character and identity of interests. . . ."[37]

One imagines that William Ellery Channing's ideal worker, dreaming of Plato at his bench, at least had the humanity to sweat, but Brisbane's problem was different from Channing's. Brisbane wanted to unite the rich and poor in work, and he saw some of the difficulties which might be involved. Polite, middle-class ladies and gentlemen might not want to work side by side with dirty, uncouth laborers. At first, admitted Brisbane, the upper classes would be loathe to mingle, but then some of the "favored" would take on the job of elevating these laborers. "The great body of Mankind are uneducated and coarse in body and mind; it will be the work of time to elevate them to a standard in Manners and Intelligence, that will fit them for refined social intercourse."[38] In a mere generation, Brisbane insisted, the crudities would disappear and a natural social harmony would be established.

Brisbane gained many followers in America, the most prominent of whom was Horace Greeley. While there is no end of indictments against Greeley for his philosophical inconstancy, this very inconstancy offers a fine example of shifting American ideals concerning work. During his climb from apprenticeship to editorial fame, his transition from Whiggery to Republicanism, Greeley discovered Brisbane. Greeley contributed little new to the doctrine of associationism, though his rendering certainly emphasized its inconsistencies. His creed revolved around the need of every youth to learn a trade and to acquire the ambition to exceed his born place. Toward such an end, Association seemed the ideal instrument; it provided opportunity combined with efficiency. According to Greeley, manual labor would create healthier, stronger men, who would be continually learning. They would improve the world rather than seek achievement at the expense of others, for an education which promoted the union of hands with minds would make men place the public good before their personal ambition.

Alongside this composite idealism of Greeley's ran another theme. He himself was an example of the self-made man who climbed by way of moving to the city; all around him he saw farm boys doing the same thing, and he was puzzled as to what to say to them regarding manual labor. The city exemplified one important associationist tenet—the diversity of occupations. This, Greeley noted, accounted for the superiority of city boys over country boys, regardless of the nature of their schooling. On the other hand, the city was a terrible place to come to without a job; rural folk did not realize how many more people than jobs there were in the city, how farmers and immigrants were flooding in. Teachers and lawyers and jacks-of-all-trades were a dime a dozen. But someone with "a thorough mastery of some good mechanical trade or handicraft such as is prosecuted in cities" would have a better chance, though he might not use his skill except in emergencies. Thus equipped, he would still have to be willing to start at the bottom of the ladder, not counting on friends but rising through his own efforts. It was a bitter struggle, Greeley concluded, and few really succeeded: "Scrutinize closely the lives of those who have made fortunes in the cities, and you will find that they were early risers, sharp dealers, and close calculators. Having obtained a good start early in life, the rest was easy. . . ."[39]

The cards seemed to be stacked against one in the city, even if he began with virtue and a trade, whereas the country, at least, seemed to offer the average man the promise of a comfortable, honest life. Indeed, Greeley reiterated the constant theme, implicit and explicit in so many of the manual labor schemes: the country, the healthy life, and the honest worker are wedded. If the country boy chanced into the city, he was admonished to bring his honest trade with him; yet as he embarked on city life, it was expected that he would leave that trade behind. It is, perhaps, implicit in this entire argument that the country boy's abandonment of his trade when he really began city life was the source of his new moral vulnerability.

Industrial Man and the City

With the growth of industrialism, cities underwent a rapid change, and Americans were forced to step back and evaluate their new urban environment. In the half-century before the Civil War, the countryside was relatively unquestioned as a place and source of the good life, while the city was seen in dual perspective.[40] On one hand, it was evil and seductive, and on the other hand, it was a great field for endeavor, the proper setting for the ambitious. Advice books and institutions like the YMCA came into being to guide the rural youth in his adjustment to city life. Guiding the city child, however, was seen as a somewhat different problem. Without a wholesome country background and faced with the lure of the city streets, the city child (the poor city child, but sometimes the rich city child as well) might easily succumb. On behalf of the child, therefore, the philanthropists went to battle with the city, looking to and developing institutions which might substitute for the natural bulwark of a country upbringing. In the course of this endeavor, the philanthropists considered a variety of solutions, some of which contradicted each other and some of which could be reconciled through a blurring or merging of ideals. Reformers debated over and over whether rescue should be accomplished through individual, or social, endeavors, through the family or through the community, through work in the city or work in the country, or even through play as opposed to work at all. Each of these arguments involved a concept of industrial education, inasmuch as ideals of the worker and work were bound up in conceptions of rescue.

The Remedy for Crime. In the contest between the philanthropists and the city for the soul of the urban child, it was more than likely that the city would win. Early nineteenth-century distinctions between poverty and crime were often vague, so that the very life-style of the impoverished urban child might easily lead to his being defined as a criminal. To some extent, the prison reforms which were begun in the latter half of the previous century had further confounded this distinction.

The penal system at the object of this reform was a harsh one, but it was a system which limited imprisonment to political and religious criminals; other crimes were punished by whipping and even harsher forms of punishment. The intention of penal reform, of course, was to eliminate such inhuman treatment. But by substituting imprisonment for corporal punishment and reinterpreting the jail as a reforming institution, the early reformers made it far easier to mute the distinction between penal and educational institutions; the jail might then be considered a proper option for the about-to-be-corrupted child.

Such logic was enhanced by the development of the Auburn penal system. The first penal-reform system, the Pennsylvania system forwarded by Quaker reformers, had stressed the virtue of isolating the prisoner in his cell, so that, deprived of criminal companions, he would come to see the light and the evil of his ways. The Auburn system, however, advocated a social form of rehabilitation; the most hardened criminals would be kept in isolation, but the rest would work together in the prison. This seemed a less harsh method for youths especially; it was consistent with the adage that those who eat must work; it had the added virtue of being less expensive; and it had the advantage of dovetailing easily with the aim of improvement.

The argument for the moral benefit of prisons was bolstered by the evolution of a prison contract system, by which prison labor was used to fill orders for outside firms. Such prison contracts and the additional practice of prison production for direct sale were strongly criticized, however, especially as organized labor grew; but the prison managers defended themselves against critics on the grounds of benefit to society. Prison industries, the managers said, gave the prisoners a chance to learn how to earn an honest living: "Want of trade is a permanent and potent occasion for crime. Three-fourths of our convicts make no pretense of having acquired a trade; and of the remainder more than a moiety have done so only in a very imperfect degree."[41]

Part of penal reform involved treating children separately from adults, and reformers had high hopes for the rescue of children through an education involving work. In 1823, a group of New York ministers and professional men formed the Society for Prevention of Pauperism, which would, they claimed, do the job which neither the public schools nor the prisons had done. The philanthropists projected a House of Refuge, to shelter young criminals from further contact with the city and to provide them with an education: "If it were possible, they should hear no clanking of chains; feel no restraint of bolts or bars: they should be made to think rather that they are in a place of instruction and WORK, preparing for their future support and usefulness."[42] The nature of the instruction was to be profoundly moral. The boys were to learn "simple mechanical arts," and some would be apprenticed after their stay in the school. The most important part of their training, however, would be in the improvement of their characters through learning the basics of literacy, through acquiring habits of industry, and through being exposed to moral and religious teaching. The New York reformers did not stress trade education, for they reasoned that the United States was a changing, growing country; with a fluid labor market, and a demand for even the unskilled, the best reformatory policy seemed to be to equip each boy with a general preparation which would enable him to enter the ranks of farming or manufacture:

> The object of a Reformatory is not to send forth a class of highly-educated and polished persons, but to raise up out of the dust hundreds now festering in sinful homes and vicious societies; to hold them near the truth until their minds shall be impressed with it; to teach them the use of personal implements with which, in most cases in the humblest walks of life, they will secure an honest living; and then give them a fair start, with hard labor and an honest purpose, to create for themselves a comfortable home.[43]

It was important that these ex-reformatory youths be able to establish "comfortable homes," for it seemed to many reformers that the lack of such homes had contributed to the youths' misdirection. Indeed, the argument for home life was often turned against the reform-school advocates themselves. Groups like the New York Association for Improving the Condition of the Poor sent "friendly visitors" into homes to help and guide the city family. Sometimes the New York Association counseled removal to the country, but the family itself was to stay intact: "No schemes of man's devising or systems of reform, should in any case supercede those divinely ordained, or relieve parents from the moral responsibility and obligation of supporting and educating their own offspring; and by this is meant such a training as will best fit them for the discharge of moral and social duties, and for a useful career in the relations to society."[44]

The reform school felt the force of these criticisms, for it was not easy to deny the traditional goodness of the American family. By the late 1850's, cottage-type reformatories were becoming more common, replacing the old dormitory system. In addition, many reformers pressed for increased use of foster homes, and men like Charles Brace lauded the rural home as an especially efficacious setting for reform. The reform-school directors did not, of course, stand idly by; Reverend B. K. Peirce of the New House of Refuge defended his and similar institutions by an implicit attack on the home: if home life were a sufficient guard against corruption, the House of Refuge would not have so many inmates from comfortable homes, where children had been "thoroughly indulged." If such respectable families could not raise their own children, how could one expect them to provide a reforming environment for the more hardened immigrant child, fresh from the streets? The reform school could provide such discipline, Peirce contended, and it also provided industrial experience; nor was such a school necessarily devoid of home atmosphere any more than the so-called "family-system," which was itself merely providing a "make-believe family."

Even if the reform schools offered a home-like atmosphere, however, it was not clear that they could provide all of the virtues needed to combat the city; the success literature of the day pointed out that one succeeded in the city, rather than succumbing, because of the virtuous upbringing bestowed by a rural mother.[45] The reform school advocates dealt with the mother issue in two ways: either by insisting that they provided maternal guidance for the delinquents, or by claiming that it was a father's care which these boys needed. The incorporation of women teachers into the reformatories, "carefully trained and well-educated Christian ladies," provided the uplifting guidance of a mother or a sister. The cottage system, too, gave women a position as matrons, and by the end of the century, these ladies were considered by some to be indispensable. The women, however, did not take over the reformatories. Some old-school disciplinarians opined that delinquent boys were far more in need of "fathering" than "mothering," for the youths required a strong hand to guide them. Other critics noted that the schools were filled with women, and the boy whose father was never at home had no contact with men except those of the worst sort who hang around the streets.[46] Indeed, many commentators noted that city life took the father away from home. The man whom they missed, of course, was the pre-industrial farmer-father or artisan-father, who combined work and home, or at least whose work was never far removed from home; the man who, above all, could teach his son a trade.

One further aspect of the reform-school effort should be noted. In the late 1840's, the young Reverend Charles Loring Brace embarked on a campaign to help the street boys of New York. Most of these boys were homeless, earning their living by street trades, if at all. Brace's Children's Aid Society, founded in 1853, promoted a system of lodging houses which complemented the Society's Sunday meetings and industrial schools. Brace, however, was sceptical about industrial schools and even more sceptical about reform schools. The latter seemed to teach nothing, neither marketable skills nor habits of industry, while his own schools suffered from obsolete machinery, union opposition, and the tendency to stultify independence. In Brace's mind the industrial schools had an immediate function: these boys were too poor to go to the public schools, and industrial schools could raise them to a decent level. Once at that level, they were ready for the real cure, a change of environment. They would be placed in western homes, where the boys would have a chance to improve themselves, unhampered by city corruption and competition.[47]

As we have already seen, reform school supporters felt menaced by the foster-home system, and many of them were no more happy with the country solution, even though reform schools were often located in the country. Critics of the rural reform-schools pointed out that city boys ought to learn city skills, for this was where they would inevitably spend their lives—they had "town fever in their veins." And critics of the rural reform school also picked up the attack on rural life which had been developing since the end of the Civil War. Not only could boys not learn appropriate trades in the country, but the farm itself had become a dangerous and sordid alternative to the city.[48]

Social-Welfare Solutions. In the latter part of the nineteenth century, there was a change in the character of philanthropic thought which helped to modify concepts of the child in the city. The city was being accepted for good or for evil, and philanthropists, seeing that they must operate within its framework, took two courses. On one hand, they intensified their drive to get to the child before the city did its worst. On the other hand, they developed a variety of prescriptions for reforming the child's environment—the family, industry, schooling. These two approaches were interwoven, as reformers now sought to carve out not only a better but a new life for the urban child.

One of the most colorful programs which they evolved was the kindergarten movement.[49] Inspired by European pedagogical experiments, philanthropically-minded ladies had been founding kindergartens since the middle of the century, and the idea began to flourish in the last two decades of the century. There was more than a tinge of religious mission in the work of the new kindergarten advocates. Well-dressed ladies searched the slum streets for infant recruits and went to their homes to convince doubting parents of the need for such schooling. This put them in the ambiguous position of lauding motherhood as a major force in genuine education and at the same time challenging the adequacy of their charges' own mothers: the kindergarten teacher, while teaching mothers how to truly perform their roles, was also to be a loftier type of mother—one who, not unlike the Virgin Mother, was to uplift all little children.[50]

Clearly, it was not difficult to reconcile themes of social harmony and equality with the kindergarten ethos. But one might imagine (especially having seen these themes played against each other by reform-school advocates) that it was more difficult to reconcile the maternal role with the ideal of preparing the child for a specifically industrial environment. Yet this was not the case. During the 1880's and 1890's, when manual-training and trade schools were receiving increased public attention, some of the kindergarteners began to claim that their system could also contribute to industrial education. Kindergarten exercises, it was said, not only improved the moral nature, but could lay the "foundation for successful industrial skill"; such "pretty play," could "constitute a most real education by and for work." In addition, kindergarteners (who had always seen their classes as more democratic than the public schools) now claimed that kindergarten made industrial education more democratic by bringing it within the reach of more children. Industrial education would begin in the kindergarten, and the kindergarten would gradually extend itself into the public school system.[51]

The kindergarten penchant for blending work and play increased as the movement turned in the direction of progressive education. Meanwhile, other philanthropists and reformers were turning to play itself, as opposed to work, as a way of saving the child from the city. In the 1870's, playgrounds for older children were being established in public parks, and by 1886, Boston, under the urging of Dr. Marie Zakrzewska, had established the first playground for the little folk. The playgrounds were to provide the healthy and moral outdoor activities of which city children seemed to be deprived, giving them the background necessary to success in the city. "The boy without a playground," said Joseph Lee, the chief advocate of the movement, "is father to the man without a job." Yet the world of play and the world of work were totally distinct; the change from one to the other world was a change in the "aim and conception of life, not merely in occupation but in point of view. The boy in his playground days belongs essentially to the pre-industrial or barbaric age."[52] The painful transition to the world of work,

Lee argued, could be softened through gardening and handi-craft activities, which would help to develop a love of crafts-manship. Then, when the child was fully matured, he would be ready to enter a genuine trade school.

This playground concept of childhood as a period of growth and freedom from adult (work) responsibilities was supported by a growing criticism of child labor. Child-labor reformers were especially concerned about the timing of childhood experience, and crusaded for a bulwark against children going into the fac-tory world too early. Florence Kelley and others argued that legislation was inadequate, home life was paltry and impover-ished, and even the elementary schools had betrayed the children by adopting industrial values.[53] The industrial education pro-grams were no better, she claimed, for while they kept children out of factories, the children were taught nothing to broaden their lives. Even the factories, cried another critic of child labor, did not profit from the children. Each child or group of inef-ficient child-workers who replaced an adult only crippled in-dustrial efficiency and slowed industrial reform and innovation. In addition, the influx of immigrants had made labor competi-tion so fierce that the duller child, the first to be rejected by the schools, could not last long in the factories, while the abler child was soon incapacitated for the working world: "The child who is forced to be a man too soon, forced too early to enter the industrial strife of the world, ceases to *be* a man too soon, ceases to be *fit* for the industrial strife."[54]

Taken together, then, the arguments of the social reformers and philanthropists posed a series of alternative solutions to the problem of the city child. The home, the street, the factory, the playground, and the school—each became a locale weighted with meaning, but each with a different meaning. While some reformers stressed the need for industrial legislation to keep the child at home and in school, others insisted that the home, because of current industrial conditions, could no longer fulfill its educational function, and blamed the school for relying on it.

While some argued that the child was better off in the factory than on the street, noting the positive function of factory experience, still others argued that the street itself could teach lessons in hardihood.[55]

The real problem for the reformers was how and where, given the industrial character of the nation, the child was to be made into a man. And neither child-labor legislation nor a host of other reform causes could solve the question simply. The developing profession of social work, however, was leading in two directions: the first, toward casework; the second, toward community reform.

The casework approach shifted the focus of reform, again, to the family, which had indeed been the focus of much earlier philanthropy; not only the family, however, but its major breadwinner was of particular importance. Josephine Shaw Lowell, whose pioneer "scientific" charity work presaged later casework techniques, stressed the importance of determining the character of the wage earner: was he a hopeless case, or could he be helped by carefully planned financial aid?[56] It was to a great extent on his competence that the fate of the whole family rested; and one of the main jobs of his wife was to help manage this income with the greatest efficiency. Since without the parental bulwark the main battle for the child would be lost, caseworkers often felt that they were helping the child in the most effective way by helping the family. Hence some casework leaders deplored overemphasis on the child at the expense of the family as a whole. It was the proper family environment, they contended, which would give the child initiative, and keep him from drifting into idleness when he came of working age.[57]

Despite similarities between this family-centered conception of social work and the settlement house movement, which was developing at the same time, the two interpretations of philanthropy came into partial conflict. Both groups emphasized the plight of honest working people, but while Mrs. Lowell hoped to prepare the family for industrial society, Jane Addams stressed the disintegrating impact of this very society, which she hoped to counteract. Miss Addams's approach, keyed to the problems of new immigrants, was dominated by her goal of social harmony. The gap between immigrant parents and their children seemed to her one of the greatest sources of social tension; and to the end of lessening such tension, Hull House established a Labor Museum, where immigrant parents could display their handicraft skills, preserving their fine work and teaching their children the meaning of old-world labor. The immigrant children, Jane Addams felt, needed a special education for the new industrial world. They were absorbing a set of values which stressed social status, and middle-class Americans showed little understanding when they condemned such immigrant girls for spending their incomes on elegant clothes. Yet these girls knew perfectly well that the way for them to rise was by hiding their origins, dressing well, and if possible moving away from their families.[58] The real problem, Jane Addams argued, was to reform a set of values which placed so much stress on financial achievement by climbing a commercial ladder. Too little attention was paid to the idea of success in the factory world, a success of self-fulfillment as well as income; contemporary industrial education, too, busy training inventors and superintendents, placed little value on the ordinary workers. Education for working youth needed to stress the meaning of industrial life, so that the worker could find a harmonious place within it: "To give the child industrial training in its historical implications and scientific foundations; to make the child understand that his work has little meaning unless it is attached to social development about him; to give him to feel that he is taking no great part in the world unless he is doing his work worthily and understandingly, such an education would not only make over the whole school, but the future generations of such children might begin to modify industry itself."[59]

By the time Jane Addams made this statement in 1908, philanthropists were moving toward support of the growing movement for public vocational education. Their interest in the reintegration of work with modern industrial and urban life had been increasing steadily during the Progressive era; yet the Progressive strain of philanthropists was never geared to the teaching of trade skills per se. For them, the goal of philanthropy and all the institutional reform it might engender was the preservation or shoring up of character.

Despite their innovation and the pioneering quality of their efforts for industrial education, it is hard to deny that the philanthropists' concentration on morality gave their ideology a genuinely conservative cast. They looked with concern at the consequences of industrialization and urbanization, phenomena which seemed especially injurious to the laboring classes and which seemed to rob them of the pre-industrial virtue and well-being. Yet, fearful as these changes seemed, the philanthropists accepted the fact of change, parrying those thrusts of industrialization which appeared to foretell the greatest social conflict. Education was to be one of their greatest weapons in the duel; education was to be a bridge between the past—the old American work-world virtues—and the changing and threatening present.

Their ideal for the laborer was generally modest; the new decent life was to have much of the stable quality of the old farm or artisan life. Like the old life-styles, the new were to be good, but appropriate to the worker's position, and therefore minimally disruptive of the already confused social order. William Ellery Channing's ideal was the most extreme in this respect, though in various ways the other philanthropists shared his fear or distaste of mobility which was too rapid or too great. At the same time, the theme of mobility did weave in and out of many of their discussions; the manual-labor and mechanics'-institute advocates, the early manufacturers, labor leaders, and public-school promoters, the social reformers and urban rescuers, all saw opportunity arising from industrialization. They could not, however, fully exploit this theme, for other aspects of their ideologies conflicted with the ideal of untrammeled mobility. It was not until after the Civil War that industrial educators took change as the keystone rather than the counterpoise of their ideal, and insisted that men could succeed only if they made that change a part of their own lives.

3

The Ideal of Success

The American ideal of individual success through the leadership of industry waited for spokesmen and heroes, and for a stage of sufficient proportions for their performance. Although the ideology and the opportunity for success had been developing since the early years of industrialization, the burst of industrial activity which followed the Civil War thrust the self-made man into the limelight. The image of this man—who had succeeded at first by cutthroat competition and later, as the century approached its end, by a shrewd amalgamation of enterprises—was as important to the post-Civil War ideal for industrial education as that of the honest workman to the first half of the century.

It is important, however, to see that the new ideal overlay the old rather than replaced it. For despite the fact that large businesses became increasingly dominant after the War, not all manufacture was booming and expanding; some small businesses grew only slowly, and the size of the average shop in others actually decreased.[1] There were settings in this complex industrial world in which several ideals could thrive, that of the honest workman no less than that of the self-made man.

50

Independence was an important element in both of these ideal figures; but whereas the concepts of social harmony and well-being within one's own group had shaped the philanthropic interpretation of independence, its limits were less rigidly defined in the new social climate. Yet the belief in a "self-made" man was to an extent ironic, for even the most independent efforts toward success took place in a social setting and with the activities of other men. The ambitious youth who disdained formal schooling still had to accept or wrench his manufacturing education from the men around him in the shop or factory, and the proponents of self-education had to acknowledge the role of the setting as they evolved their formula for success.

Many proponents of the self-made man admitted that—at some time and for some purposes—education might take place in a formal setting (evening or correspondence schools were the favorites), and some even suggested that a certain amount of full-time schooling might supplement education in the shop. Industrial educators simply adapted this shifting logic to their own purposes. The new breed of post-Civil War industrial educators also wanted boys to get ahead, yet insisted that at particular junctures in the youths' careers they must undertake formal education. The educators did not, therefore, discard the ideal of the self-made man; rather, taking its outline as a starting point, they constructed a new formula for success, with different concepts of career timing and educational setting.

The members of one such group of educators combined their interest in mobility with a commitment to scientific education. Their interpretations of mobility varied with their conceptions of scientific study: Daniel Coit Gilman, at one extreme, thought in terms of membership in a scientific research elite; Andrew White, at the other, interpreted scientific education in terms of technological progress and the raising up of industrial leaders who could build a better country.

A second group, the engineering educators, followed White's style of thought, conceiving of an industrial leadership nurtured on science and technology, one which would lead the nation. They had to refine this ideal, to decide whether science alone could prescribe the qualities for leadership or whether equally powerful business ideals would have to be taken into account. Then, once the engineers had evolved their own ideal, they turned to the problem of education for the lower orders of the industrial world, for whom mobility was not always deemed desirable. As the engineers were thus abandoning the image of the rising youth, however, certain secondary-school educators were making the ideal of the socially mobile engineer part of their own concept of industrial education. The most notable of these educators was Calvin Woodward, who, with his manual training scheme, is the last subject of this chapter.

Scientific Education

Not long after the Civil War, American scientists and their supporters began a concerted effort to bring science into greater prominence in the nation's educational institutions. In part, this effort rested on changes which were already taking place—the development of full-time scientific occupations and the articulation of scientific activity with the goals of developing higher education. Yet the transition was not a smooth one. Many of the emerging universities faced state governments and a public to whom the purer forms of scientific research were difficult to interpret; an interpretation in terms of the country's growing technological needs was often the result, so that the advocates of scientific education had to find a way of coming to grips with conflicting ideals.[2]

The difficulties involved in promoting scientific education can be seen in the words of John Tyndall, the renowned English physicist who was invited to America not long after the Civil War. "It is never to be forgotten," the physicist told his American audiences, "that not one of those great investigators, from Aristotle down to Stokes and Kirchhoff, had any practical end in view, according to the ordinary definition of the word 'practical.' " Pure scientists, Tyndall continued, worked only for intellectual gratification, yet it was only the practical application of their research which received public acclaim. The pure scientist was ignored in the cry for technical education, ". . . a cry in which the most commonplace intellect can join, its necessity is so obvious."3

Tyndall's devotion to science was shared by many American educators, but his creed of pure science was variously interpreted by them. Perhaps Daniel Coit Gilman, in his ideal for Johns Hopkins, came closest to Tyndall's own meaning; but before Gilman came to head that pioneer institution, and even during his presidency, he had to cope with the question of technological education. In fact, he began his career as an administrator of Yale's Sheffield School in the 1860's and at that time was an enthusiastic supporter of the new land-grant colleges. These new "National Schools of Science," he wrote, had an important function in training leading scientific men, superintendents of public works, and surveyors. He insisted that the new colleges ought not to be used for training mere workers, men who would "go back and labor with the hoe or anvil," but he did expect that the schools would develop qualified teachers for a lower order of industrial schools where elementary and practical instruction could be provided.4

Gilman went from Sheffield to the University of California where, in a turbulent term as president, he struggled with the demands for a practical education in that state. He was called then to head the new Johns Hopkins University. Even though Gilman's ideal for Johns Hopkins was that of a genuine research institution, training scientists and scholars, there is no reason to think that he was particularly hostile to practical education. In the 1880's, he was endorsing everything from kindergartens to grammar school carpentry, trade schools, higher training for engineers and technological leaders, and advanced research in technology. In the 1890's, he reiterated the need for a hierarchy of schools and noted that deserving students would rise, while each could find "enjoyment of work," if he were well trained for his appropriate occupation.⁵ Yet, with all his respect for technical and practical training, Gilman was most anxious that Johns Hopkins should not be pushed in this direction. As a result of his commitment he was forced to fight running battles with a few disgruntled trustees, with unhappy Baltimorians, and especially with the Baltimore and Ohio Railroad.

Johns Hopkins' fate was intimately tied to that of the B. and O., since the university was a principal stockholder in the company; for this reason alone, the railroad people felt that the university should take an interest in technical education. The B. and O. had developed a corporation school to train and upgrade its own employees to meet the railroad's needs, but the school had its difficulties, and the management felt that the backing of the university would help enormously. Gilman's attitude infuriated the B. and O. educators, who accused him of creating a medieval retreat, an undemocratic institution which was blind to its civic duty. We hear, said the railroad men, that there is much research going on in those laboratories, but "The beneficial results of these discoveries have not yet been seen or felt in Baltimore."⁶ Baltimore's trade was, indeed, in the doldrums, and it seemed perverse that the city should become the setting for such a university.

The problem of the relationship between the study of pure science and the need for technological skills was also being tackled by Charles W. Eliot, who had become Harvard's president in 1869. Eliot, himself a chemist, was wholehearted in his acceptance of science, but he insisted that applied science should be pursued in an institution separate from the college. For him, the purpose of a college was to train leaders for the nation, and he did not equate the qualities of manhood needed for leadership with the skills needed for technological competence. The college should emphasize study for its own sake in an environment free from commercial consideration: "The

poorest and the richest students," said Eliot, "are equally welcome here provided that with their poverty or their wealth they
bring capacity, ambition, and purity. The poverty of scholars is
of inestimable worth in this money-getting nation. It maintains
the true standards of virtue and honor."[7]

Eliot willingly granted that America needed specialists; yet he
criticized the American reliance on self-education and mechanical cleverness. Because of this, he said, the country had failed
to develop the special kinds of education which an orderly
division of labor demanded. He insisted that students being
trained in technical work should attend their own schools, for
despite the fact that breadth and thirst for knowledge could be
as important in a technical school as in a college, the ultimate
end for the technical student was an understanding of natural
processes in order "to turn them to human uses and his own
profit"; the proper technical school would lay "the best foundation for later work; if well organized, with a broad scheme of
study, it can convert a boy of fair abilities and intentions into
an observant, judicious man, well informed in the sciences which
bear on his profession; so trained, the graduate will master the
principles and details of any actual works, and he will rise
rapidly through the grades of employment. . . ."[8]

Ability, society's needs, and the division of labor, were the
bases on which Eliot divided the prospective students. The
cream of the cream would struggle up to (or if fortunate, simply
enter) the colleges, and then proceed with whatever further
professional training they might need. The boys of "fair abilities
and intentions" could make the grade in the technical schools,
and come out as technical experts or industrial leaders, constituting a middle rank in society. Technical specialists, however,
were not to be confused with artisans. For this reason Eliot insisted that shop work was out of place in a technical school:
"The fact is, that, in training his brains, a young man cannot
have his cake and eat it too."[9]

Eliot's interest in building a relationship between science, technical competence, and national leadership was reflected in many contemporary discussions of scientific education, but some educators were more eager than he to bridge the gap between these activities. President Andrew White of Cornell, at a farewell dinner given at the end of John Tyndall's tour, proposed a way for Americans to reconcile and blend these differing forms of leadership. After Tyndall had spoken on the ideal of pure research, White rose to add his praise of science; however, his reasoning took a sharp turn away from that of the English guest.

The burden of White's message was that America needed scientific education badly because the country was beset with an indifference, scepticism, infidelity, and materialism, which were pushing the nation to the brink of total decay. The atmosphere of corruption which pervaded political life was merely epiphenomenal; the real problem lay deep in the character of national leadership. Such deeprooted ills, White contended, could be combatted only if the best men were brought to the fore; the encouragement of scientific education would inspire such men: "The reverence for scientific achievement, the revelation of the high honours which are in store for those who seek truth in science . . . all these shall come to the mind of thoughtful men in lonely garrets of our cities, in remote cabins on our prairies, and thereby shall come strength and hope for higher endeavor."[10]

White was not alone in this argument. Edward Youmans, who in the 1860's had launched an all-out attack on the classical curriculum, made substantially the same point. And when the astronomer Simon Newcomb summarized the state of science in America in 1876, he underlined the same need for education of the talented, and bemoaned the presence of ignorance and confused thinking in high places.[11] These post-Civil War statements bore the hallmark of a new era, for despite the fact that in earlier discussions the enthusiasm for science was sometimes linked with opportunities for success, the primary objective of pre-Civil War industrial educators was to make workers virtuous after their own station; it was assumed that political, social, and industrial leadership would come from the upper classes, while intelligent cooperation would come from the lower classes.

When the scandals of the Grant administration, to which White alluded, came to the attention of the articulate part of the American public, a challenge was thrown out to such assumptions. Some of the blame could be and was placed on the inequalities of society, on the dissatisfied (and therefore unvirtuous) lower classes, or on the upper-class leadership which had abdicated its responsibility; interwoven with this old complaint, however, was the call to discover and to train a new leadership.[12] If that leadership were, as White conceived it, to be expert, and recruited from all classes within the society, institutions of higher education would have to be developed which the "men in lonely garrets of our cities, in remote cabins on our prairies" might attend.

The new land-grant colleges seemed to fit such a purpose perfectly, for they were to be schools of advanced practical learning and schools for the ordinary people. Yet to become a training ground for leaders, the land-grant colleges, unlike Hopkins or Harvard, had to dissociate themselves from some of their own roots.

The land-grant college movement had grown out of a great dissatisfaction with the traditional classical curriculum of pre-Civil War colleges, and out of a feeling that science and modern languages, together with practical training, were more suited to the demands of a democratic and growing country. Before the Civil War there were a variety of attempts to meet these demands: colleges began to incorporate work in theoretical and applied science; engineering and private agricultural schools appeared. But, on the whole, the number of practically oriented institutions was small. By the 1850's, the public interest in educational reform increased, and a number of organizations, particularly agricultural groups, began to press the legislatures for action.

The Illinois Industrial League, with erstwhile professor Jonathan Baldwin Turner as its spokesman, was especially articulate and on the ground floor of the state-college movement. Much of Turner's rhetoric had an earlier, Jacksonian cast; he lauded education for the "development of a TRUE MAN-HOOD" and condemned any system which would separate the classes, generating "clans and castes" and spoiling the God-given harmony of men. Turner pointed out that men would have to be trained for the occupations they would pursue, and that the industrial classes thus far had lacked the chance for elevation "to that relative position in human society for which God ordained them." State universities could offer practical training, and could also prepare teachers for the lower levels of education, and writers who would produce a literature appropriate to the needs of the laboring classes.[13]

Within ten years of Turner's statement the Land-Grant Act had been passed, but despite the popular interest which had engendered the legislation, the schools were slow to develop. With little institutional machinery to begin with, and an Act which gave them no clear model, most of the land-grant colleges went through a period of groping. Since the schools were bound only by the obligation to offer practical and liberal studies, every variety of educational debate was invited. The new faculties included classicists and modernists, pure scientists and old manual-labor men.[14] Those who stressed the "practical" aspect of manufacture were quick to establish workshops. The workshops, it was felt, could serve the needs of those many land-grant students who, in the 1870's and 1880's, were coming to college directly from the elementary schools.

Although the workshop phase of the land-grant colleges left a lasting mark, it was relatively brief. One reason for the brevity seems to be that the college workshops modeled themselves on two conflicting educational experiments: on the one hand, the manual-training system of the Massachusetts Institute of Technology, which stressed the development of basic skills for boys who would move into higher technical fields; on the other, the training method of the Worcester, Massachusetts, polytechnical school, which strove to simulate genuine shop conditions and to produce saleable articles. This latter system appealed to many who, thinking along the manual-labor lines, felt that the land-grant colleges should offer opportunities for students to support themselves. While the advocates of the two different systems battled with each other, the entire concept of workshops in the colleges was also under attack. By the 1880's, the land-grant colleges were beginning to raise their educational goals, to focus on industrial leaders rather than the industrial classes.

The experience of Cornell University suggests how this newer state-college concept came to overlay the old. The founder, Ezra Cornell, was a self-made man who pictured himself as an honest workman at heart, "a mechanic and farmer" who had become a millionaire through hard work in his chosen occupations.[15] When Cornell came to the point of aiding New York in establishing a university system, however, he was far from sure what kind of university to support. Here, Andrew White, according to his own account, stepped in, won over Cornell to the concept of one great state university, and moved the philanthropist toward a more modern view of education.

White, who soon became the university's first president, stated his educational philosophy in no uncertain terms: first, the university was to exemplify the "union of liberal and practical instruction"; second, it was to be a non-sectarian institution; third, it was to strive for cooperation with the state school system, for the purpose of elevating the latter; and finally, it was to promote itself as the state's major institution for higher education. White's goals were democratic, but when Ezra Cornell, honest workman that he was, suggested university-connected factories in which students could support themselves, the president demurred. The public schools, said White, could give young folk "an elementary education while making shoes and chairs," but the universities' job was to ". . . send out into all parts of the

State and the Nation thoroughly trained graduates, who should develop and improve the main industries of the country, and by their knowledge and example, train up skillful artisans of various sorts and in every locality."[16] Shops and farms, he said at another time, had their place on the campus, but not for the purpose of training "a few more intelligent farmers or artisans." Rather, such places should be laboratories, where the application of science to practical wants could be explored.[17]

White followed Charles Eliot in refusing to use the university to train workers, but parted from Eliot on the question of training industrial leadership. White would not allow the industrial sciences to be separated from the rest of the curriculum because, he insisted, industrial leaders needed to be well-educated citizens and well-rounded men. Indeed, White did not separate industrial leadership from other forms of leadership: leading manufacturers and engineers were to be among the leading citizens. No longer was leadership to be confined to professional men and men of independent means, but industrial captains were also to be included.

Engineering Education

The Professionalization of Engineering. Unlike the land-grant colleges, the higher technical schools had a full commitment to practical studies from the first; yet the path of the technical schools was not self-evident either. Despite the need for engineers to build roads, build bridges, do surveys—and by the 1830's, to build railroads—engineering schools were not established quickly.[18] Until the founding of Rensselaer Polytechnic Institute in 1824, the only engineering course available was that given at West Point. Before the Civil War, only three other engineering programs had come into existence; those at Sheffield, Lawrence (Harvard), and the University of Michigan. It was only with the Land-Grant Act that engineering schools really multiplied; in 1870 there were seventeen, while by 1880 there were eighty-five.

The history of Rensselaer illustrates the movement from the ideals for mechanical training of the Jacksonian era, to those of modern engineering. In 1824, Stephen Van Rensselaer planned a scientific school which had as its goal "to qualify teachers for instructing the sons and daughters of farmers and mechanics, by lectures or otherwise, in the application of experimental chemistry, philosophy, and natural history, to agriculture, domestic economy, the arts and manufacture."[19] Classes at the Institute were to include both laboratory work and demonstrations at nearby farms and shops: but "demonstration" did not imply work in the shops. Rather, it involved visits, followed by laboratory experiments. The demonstrations soon ranged much farther afield than neighborhood industries, so that by 1830 students were being taken on long summer tours, to acquaint them with engineering progress. At the same time, their classes were becoming more specialized. Rensselaer began to offer general courses in civil engineering and surveying, and in 1835 the first civil-engineering degree was awarded. Standards were raised even higher in the 1840's, and at mid-century Rensselaer was reorganized as a polytechnical institute on the model of the great French technical schools. The school's new goal was "The education of architects and civil, mining, and topological engineers, upon an enlarged basis with a liberal development of mental and physical culture."[20]

The stress on "liberal development of mental and physical culture" suggests that although the engineering educators began to promote greater specialization and a high level of competence, their goal for the engineer was more than that of technical expert. Indeed, their problem was that of creating a new alternative between the earlier informal and eclectic modes of technical training and the established modes of higher education. If, as Andrew White had implied, the training of technical leaders was also to be the training of leading citizens, it was necessary to define carefully what bearing various kinds of education had on the training of an engineer. Francis A. Walker, who became head of the Massachusetts Institute of Technology in 1881, made a determined start toward such a definition.[21]

When Walker took over the presidency of M.I.T., the school was in considerable difficulty. Since 1870, it had been under intermittent pressure from Harvard to become the technical school for the university, and the Institute's financial difficulties made such an alternative increasingly appealing. Neither the earlier leaders nor Walker wanted to take this step; M.I.T. had a planned program, in contrast to Harvard's elective system, and the Institute's leadership believed that its prestige and purpose would suffer in the event of annexation. Walker felt that technical students would be looked down on in a university setting, yet he felt that it was very important for engineers to have a liberal education. The problem of technological education, declared Walker, was many-sided; many of the entrants to engineering schools were not college graduates and would have to be provided with several kinds of education. First, they would have to receive a technical education of high quality. Walker insisted that students should not be offered mere "knacks of a trade," for they had chosen not to enter trades, but to put off immediate financial reward and aim for higher positions. The engineering education which would best prepare them was in no sense narrow: "We assert that the disinterestedness of study does not depend upon the immediate usefulness or uselessness of the subject-matter, but upon the spirit with which the student takes up and pursues his work. If there be zeal in investigation, if there be delight in discovery, if there be fidelity to truth as it is discerned, nothing more can be asked by the educator of highest aims."[22]

In making his plea for engineering as a science, Walker resembled earlier spokesmen who identified science with moral virtue; yet at the same time he did not see scientific training alone as sufficient. If engineers, said Walker, were going to become industrial leaders, they would have to be fully developed human beings. A liberal education was necessary, not only for the sake of happiness, but also in order to obtain genuine business success: "A great lawyer generally is a great man but he need not be. . . . But a great engineer must be a great man," for he takes on tremendous moral responsibilities when he captains the country's technological development.[23] In addition, Walker cautioned, the very course of the engineer's personal career depended on the liberality of his education. The "conservative influence of culture" gave the educated man the advantage over the self-made man. The former was bound to make mistakes near the beginning, the latter was more likely to make mistakes once he had reached the pinnacle of success; the self-made man was apt to overestimate himself or to underestimate the complexity of the problems which he faced. The solid scientific technological education, Walker concluded, would go far to insure that the engineer always understood his work, while a complementary liberal education would provide the additional discipline necessary to leadership.

Walker's prescription underlines the duality emerging with the professionalization of engineering, and discussions in the early meetings of the American Society of Mechanical Engineers suggest the implications of this duality. Engineers were looking in two directions, toward science and toward business.[24] Their struggle to define the relation of their activity to science, of their own education to scientific education, was intimately connected with the effort to establish formal education as a substitute or supplement to scientific talent or inventive genius. Critics had been taking the "amateur engineer" to task for some time, for it was easy to point to mistakes made by untutored men.[25] Until the wider development of engineering schools, however, it was difficult to recommend alternatives for the self-taught inventor.

In addition, those who proposed to substitute formal for self-education had to face a powerful belief in the efficacy of intuition and inborn genius.

The popular literature of the late nineteenth and early twentieth centuries shows how long the belief in the primacy of innate talent lasted, and with what the engineering educators had to contend. The inventiveness of manufacturing heroes showed itself in a variety of ways. They had revelations of new machines; they were "handy," and incessantly tinkering; they combined innovation with marketing insight.[26] In short, they had so many qualities that it seemed unlikely that engineering education could be an improvement. Yet in 1884 Robert H. Thurston, a key figure among the mechanical engineers, did his best to refute the popular prejudices. His argument began with the insistence that science must lead art, rather than art lead science. "The blind, scheming ways of the older inventor will give place to the exact determination, by scientific methods, of the most direct and efficient way of reaching a defined end—methods now daily practiced by the engineer in designing his machinery."[27] The spread of scientific knowledge to all levels of society was necessary for mechanical progress, for even mechanics did not yet know the most fundamental principles on which their practice was based. On the professional level, pure science was needed to make mechanical science possible. If scientific schools were established, the entire country would be rewarded by the progress in applied science; such progress would eliminate much of the unskilled work of industries and open up new domains, raising the whole level of the society.

Thurston's sanguine outlook encouraged a program for an engineering education that would go hand in hand with scientific research, since both would replace the old inventive genius. The engineers, however, were in the process of shaping their own activities, and, for better or for worse, differences between themselves and scientists were beginning to be defined. One answer was simply to draw the line: since the scientists were concerned with "pure" problems, and the engineers with "practical" ones, their respective laboratory or "shop"-oriented educations were appropriate preparation for what they would actually do. But for many engineers, the argument about differences was also an argument about priority. Thus, according to one engineering spokesman, the best men of each age were drawn into its dominant activity; the major work of the current age was that of production; therefore, the "mechanicians" were the ones who were headed for industrial leadership—while the more contemplative, more basic, but more remote operations of science were pursued in the background.[28]

Even though such engineering spokesmen were sometimes themselves anxious to remain in touch with the scientists, others were clearly expanding their identification with the business world. While the scientifically interested (if sometimes hostile) engineers spoke to meetings of the American Association for the Advancement of Science, fellow professionals were taking part in the meetings of the American Society of Mechanical Engineers. Here was an organization of businessmen and engineers, many of whom were businessmen-engineers, and their president, the ubiquitous Robert Thurston, stressed the many interests they had in common: engineering would help business to mechanize; business would finance experimental work and engineering study.[29]

Yet despite Thurston's attempt to unify engineering and business ideals, increasing technological specialization brought their identity into question. During the 1880's and 1890's the engineers were struggling to define their relation to business, asking whether engineers made good businessmen, or how engineers should relate to business in their developing roles as managers or consultants. Not surprisingly, some engineers drew the same distinction between engineering and business that had been drawn between engineering and science: namely, that the skills involved in the fields were quite distinct. Such a line of reasoning was particularly applicable to certain emerging professional roles. For instance, if an engineer were to be a consultant, he would have to stress his separation from business interests, otherwise he would not be trusted by his clients.[30] At the same time, the engineer would still need to acquire sufficient understanding of the business world to gain the esteem of the men with whom he would deal.

Technical competence, as Francis Walker had explained, would not be enough, and the mechanical engineers exhorted themselves to gain polish. In his address on "The Engineer as a Scholar and a Gentleman," President Oberlin Smith of the ASME remarked that although college-trained engineers tended to be a bit rough, having a "natural distaste" for the social and intellectual amenities, "No standard of gentility, no patent of nobility, can be too high for a profession which leads the civilization of the world. . . ."[31] Engineers, he continued, have yet to realize what other professionals have long known, that the "social aspect of professional work" was necessary to success.

Smith's speech illustrates the complexity of establishing an ideal for the complete engineer. At one moment the president was berating the "big-brained young men who are full of scientific zeal" but who could not comport themselves properly at a social event. At the next moment he was asserting that, inasmuch as engineering education dealt with "pure truth" and "the resistless logic of nature," engineers would be precise and upright men. In fact, engineers like Smith wanted the best of both the business and scientific ideal; each, in its way, seemed to contribute to an honorable and noble success.

The Engineers and the Secondary Schools. Oberlin Smith and his colleagues often spoke as though the engineering schools would have to bear the entire burden of the education of their students, since, though some students would come from fine homes, many would come from "poverty or geographical isolation," from "orphan asylum, from factory, from distant farm."[32] Yet other members of the engineering organization did not make this assumption. They were well aware that, at the same time that they were shaping their own profession, the nation was in the process of developing and refining its secondary school system; engineering schools would be recruiting fewer and fewer students from the elementary schools and the shops, and more and more from the high schools. At the same time, the secondary system was becoming more complex, and the engineers might have something to say about the way it was to be rationalized, how its various kinds of training might relate to engineering education.

Among the engineering educators who were concerned with secondary education was John Runkle, a mathematics professor and head of M.I.T. during the 1870's. At the Philadelphia exhibition of 1876, Runkle had discovered the Russian system of workshop education, which had been pioneered by Victor Della Vos, director of the Imperial Technical School of Moscow. When that school was reorganized in 1868, Della Vos had introduced training in which instruction was separated from actual construction of products; that is, the basic skills, such as drawing, were taught before construction was attempted. The real import of the system was its separation of learning skills from production, a separation which struck at the heart of the apprenticeship method. In the Russian school the students followed a system of carefully graded projects, with the understanding that they were not in training to be mechanics, but rather engineers, draftsmen, and foremen.

No sooner had Runkle discovered the Russian experiment than he reported it to the Massachusetts Board of Education, arguing to its members that manual training could help restore the dignity of labor to manual occupations, satisfy the demand for skilled labor, ease the conflict between capital and labor, and aid the development of industries.[33] Runkle also contended that the ordinary high schools were turning out students who were neither cultured nor able to make their way in the industrial world. Manual training could give them both skills and discipline by "making the arts and not the trade fundamental." In addition, the system of graded shopwork would enable the school to adjust the program to the goals of various kinds of students, whether they planned to become machinists or engineers.

Runkle's report, and his own actions in introducing shopwork at M.I.T. and starting a manual-training high school in connection with the Institute, dovetailed well with the engineers' growing interest in the problem of shop training. During the 1880's, the ASME was presented with several alternative methods for teaching shopwork in the polytechnic or high schools. At the 1884-1885 meeting, George Alden of the Worcester Institute outlined his school's plan. The main feature of the Worcester system was the reproduction of actual shop conditions. Boys worked under a journeyman-teacher and spent their time in construction of commercially saleable items. It was a "business shop," and the fact that it was geared to the needs of a real market imposed a standard of workmanship which, according to Alden, could never be maintained in a merely academic shop. The boys who graduated from Worcester were fully prepared to enter a trade, although mere trade training was not the goal of the school. The shopwork training, Alden claimed, provided just the foundation needed for higher endeavor: "The draftsman, the designer, the inventor, the engineer, must go to the shop for the perfection, embodiment, and execution of his designs, inventions and projects."[34] Without an understanding of the potentialities of the shop, more advanced work could not be pursued.

The major alternative proposal to that of Alden was the scheme developed by Calvin Woodward. Woodward, as the dean of O'Fallon Polytechnical Institute of Washington University and the head of its Manual Training School, was concerned with training engineers in a more direct sense than Alden, and saw manual training as an intimate link in a series of steps leading to this end. In the year following Alden's paper, Woodward tried to sell his conception of a total system of engineering education to the engineers. What Washington University offered, said Woodward, was a three-stage course leading to the professional degree of Dynamic Engineer. Boys entered the Manual Training School at the age of about fifteen, and for three years they were given work in shop, mathematics, science, language, literature, and drawing. Through shopwork, the boys were familiarized with the basic processes and procedures in areas such as joinery, founding, and machinery: "The aim is to master the range of every tool and to cultivate the habit of analyzing complicated processes into simple elements."[35]

Woodward next described the Polytechnical Institute's engineering course which followed the manual training studies. The Polytechnical students moved from two years of a general engineering and literary program, to two of specialization in civil or mechanical engineering, to a fifth year in which they did laboratory research and writing. But overall, Woodward insisted, their studies and experiments were founded on an understanding of the nature and limitations of materials and mechanical processes. This is why the shopwork background was indispensible: ". . . a mechanical engineer is *first* of all a machinist; *secondly,* a draughtsman; and *thirdly,* he is a more or less (generally rather *less*) familiar with mathematics and theoretical mechanics."[36] Alden's view, Woodward concluded, was mistaken because he did not understand the educational role which shopwork played —that its basic goal was education rather than production. A school could not be both business and a place of learning. Nor, Woodward added, could a technical school be a place to learn business, though some proponents of the quasi-real shop claimed that it taught students the value of materials and labor. As far as understanding labor went, the skills involved in handling men could only be understood by practice; and as far as learning costs and wages, these, too, had to be mastered in concrete situations. The Polytechnical Institute, Woodward affirmed, could give a good background in the principles of political economy, but it could not and should not aim to make business-men, instead of turning out first-class engineers.

In their discussions of the Alden and Woodward papers, the engineers took four basic positions. First, there were those who rejected either system, reiterating the old claim that the "men who have made their mark in this country have risen through the shop."[37] Night classes and such additional aids were ap-proved, but the idea of a secondary-school system in connection with industrial careers was simply not meaningful. Second, there were those engineers who were particularly interested in manual training. They were willing to grant that systems like Worcester could turn out fine journeymen, but insisted that if one really wanted engineers, one had to train them in principles rather than the knacks of any given trade. Third, some partisans of the Worcester system brought out the point that the trade training given at schools like Worcester aided the would-be engineer, for it not only gave him the shop experience he needed, but gave him a trade to fall back on if he found himself unsuited to engineering or unable to succeed in the upward climb. These three viewpoints had one element in common; that is, they all saw a ladder, and they were trying to prescribe the best for-mula for climbing it.

A fourth position put forth in the discussions was that of Robert Thurston, and Thurston looked at the problem in an entirely different light. After Calvin Woodward had read his paper on manual training to the engineering society, Thurston remarked that both manual training and the Worcester method had their places, but that there was no real substitute for the genuine shop. Here we have what sounds like the opening lines of a speech on the self-made man, but Thurston was the last to espouse this ideal, for he was an ardent fighter for engineer-ing education and an equally strong opponent of the self-taught inventor. In a sense he was both too old-fashioned and too modern to accept the idea of widespread mobility. His con-servative political economy contained just the elements necessary to link him with the emerging trade-training ideal: "The great problem which confronts the educators of this country is thus to so organize the school systems that the sons and daughters of the well-to-do people may pass by a regularly graded course from primary school and on into college, and if they choose, into the higher work of the university; while the children of parents less favored by fortune may similarly pass from the secondary school into the professional or the trade school, and even, in the case of the poorest, from the primary school into trade school; the latter, in this case, becoming the secondary or high school, beyond which these students cannot afford to go.[38]

Although Thurston's language offers a rather startling contrast to the ideas we have been discussing, he was not as out of step with the rest of the engineers as it might at first appear. As one reads through the transactions of the ASME in the 1880's and 1890's, it becomes clear that the manual-training movement never found a home there. It had advocates, but on the whole it was treated with reservation. When educators at large began to swing towards trade-school education in the late 1890's, the engineers were among the first to support the new system. There were unquestionably many reasons for their attitude. As the century drew to a close, the engineers were becoming more and more interested in the idea of industrial management, an idea in which the concept of opportunity was rather elaborately circumscribed. In addition, although engineers were still fighting well into the twentieth century to establish the need for formal engineering education, they were, by the twentieth century, a distinct professional group. Whether they saw themselves as managers, entrepreneurs, or experts, they knew that in order to do a good job they must have a corps of well-trained men below them. How much mobility these men in the ranks were to have was not a matter to be dismissed, but at the same time, it was not the matter of greatest importance. What the engineers wanted were the competent mechanics and superintendents who could help to realize an engineer's industrial dreams.[39]

Manual Training

The Manual-Training Approach. Although the growing engineering profession may have been less than enthusiastic toward Calvin Woodward's manual-training proposal, the engineering ideal itself was the key to his educational position. Like the engineers, he assumed that his students would move onward and upward; manual training was to be the secondary-school step in their climb. Although Woodward recognized that his boys might move into many kinds of careers, his architectonic goal for them was an engineering career.

Woodward was born in Fitchburg, Massachusetts, in 1837, and apparently his origins were humble, for the town aided him in going to Harvard.[40] There he became a prize student in mathematics and, on graduation, went into high school teaching. After serving in the army he returned to be a high school principal, and it was from this post that Washington University in St. Louis called him to become a mathematics professor. This was in 1865. By 1870, he had been given the endowed professorship of mathematics and applied mechanics, and the next year was made dean of the polytechnical school, a post he held for twenty-five years.

Washington University had been founded in 1853, and within a few years had established the O'Fallon Polytechnical Institute. The Institute was originally planned on the model of European mechanics institutes, so that in its early years the O'Fallon school not only taught the common branches, together with such subjects as drawing and algebra, but offered classes for working boys. Within the university proper there was also a growing interest in mechanical work. Not long after the Civil War the university carpenter had established a shop, which gradually turned into a workshop for the students. Woodward took advantage of the shop by sending his own students there, for in the course of laboratory teaching he had discovered that few of the lads knew even the rudiments of shop work. As the shop grew in importance, it was moved to its own building, where classes were developed for the students of the university preparatory school; and by 1879, Woodward's ideas were sufficiently crystallized to begin a campaign for a new school with a program based upon manual training.

Woodward, accompanied by the Chancellor of the university, presented his idea to a group of St. Louis businessmen, who obligingly agreed to donate to the new school. Its primary purpose would be to prepare youths for the growing industrial world, an aim to which the business community could readily assent; the students were to attend the Manual Training School and then move on to the since upgraded Polytechnical Institute. These plans were quickly realized. The novelty of the venture, together with Woodward's enthusiasm, drew educators and interested spectators from all over the country; in 1884 the school held its first exhibition before the National Education Association, and by the early nineties Manual Training was "the most popular secondary school in St. Louis." Yet within a few years the prestige of the school had begun to wane. The manual-training idea had reached its peak, and despite the proliferation of manual-training schools, the entire movement had taken on a new cast. The system had been not only assailed and rejected in many quarters but, worse still from Woodward's viewpoint, reinterpreted into extinction by the new progressive educators. Woodward's biographer reminisced that he would "never forget the sad look which spread over Woodward's face and the words he uttered when, in 1903, a prospective teacher of grade [school] manual training presented for his inspection a series of useful models . . . prepared as a part of a teacher's course surreptitiously conducted at the Manual by a progressive and enthusiastic teacher. . . . Words fail when an attempt is made to give here the inflection he placed on the phrase, 'Has manual training come to this?'."[41]

Woodward's ideas about the meaning of manual training had evolved only gradually. His early goal was to use exercises to develop in the students an "alphabet of tools."[42] The program he spelled out in the early seventies emphasized the vocational aspects of technical training; young people were to have both "theoretical and practical training . . . in some one respectable trade or profession." Woodward acknowledged the danger of too narrow a technical education, which seemed to him to be characteristic of European trade schools, but he also stressed the nation's concrete need for trained persons; "general culture" was often a mere excuse to learn "a little of everything and nothing deep," although there might be considerable benefit in offering manual training to children—to insure them "a wholesome intellectual culture."[43]

For about ten years Woodward continued to focus on trade training, appealing, like many later trade-school advocates, to the fear that native American boys were being prevented from becoming artisans. However, by 1882, when Woodward presented his ideas to the National Education Association, his trade-training ideas were undergoing subtle elaboration: "Now," he said, "if indiscriminately we educate all our youth away from certain occupations and into certain others, as is very clearly the case, some employments will be crowded and consequently degraded; in others, the choicest positions will be filled by foreigners; and the lowest posts, wherein labor is without dignity, must perforce be filled by those who have neither taste nor fitness for their work. The result is broils and social disorders."[44] The proper kind of education, he continued, would enable each to find his "true calling": "I have no sort of doubt, however, that the grand result will be that many who would otherwise eke out a scanty subsistence as clerks, book-keepers, salesmen, poor lawyers, murderous doctors, whining preachers, abandoned penny-a-liners, or hardened 'school-keepers' will be led, through the instrumentality of our school, to positions of honor as mechanics, engineers, or manufacturers."[45] With this end in mind, the new and "splendid crop of millionaires" ought to contribute generously to the support of manual training schools, using such accumulated fortunes, not to spoil individual sons, but to raise up the sons of the nation.

It is worthwhile to give closer scrutiny to Woodward's message. To begin with, he saw many avenues of achievement blocked; the professions, he said, were already filled and therefore degraded, while the mechanical pursuits still allowed for success on many levels. At a period when commercial educators were beginning to cry out for trained office help, Woodward was treating the commercial world as a land of little opportunity. It is clear that for him other pursuits simply did not have the dignity, the nobility, of the mechanical ones. In this respect, his rhetoric echoed that of the pre-Civil War spokesmen, who were so involved with the idea of the noble artisan. However, Woodward's thought went further. He was not solely interested in training artisans. His earlier writing suggests that he saw manual training as a system allowing youths to leave school at any level and become dignified and competent workmen. Although he continued to say that artisans with manual training were far better off both in skills and as men than those without, a distinct suspicion, perhaps dislike, for artisans began to play a more and more prominant role in Woodward's thought. He gradually became less concerned with the threat of foreign artisans, and more concerned with moving American boys up to a level at which they would not have to compete with artisans at all. Woodward's use of the phrase "the lowest posts, wherein labor is without dignity" marks his move away from the position of the pre-Civil War utopians.

Woodward's concept of manual training as a background for ambitious youth was an important part of his campaign, begun sometime in the early 1880's, to convince professional educators that all children should have manual training as a part of their "general culture."* Like the engineers of the 1880's, Woodward

* The accounts of Woodward's thought typically interpret his interest in "general culture" as an ideological shift, made in the 1880's under the pressure of NEA criticism. But from the standpoint of the present study,

was concerned with developing industrial leadership for a new age, and his concept of general culture, therefore, included precisely those qualities which were held to prepare for such leadership. One such quality was discipline in the pursuit of innovation, for the current age was a "dynamic" one; invention was "in its youth, and manual training is the very breath of its nostrils."[46] Manual training, he claimed in this 1883 speech, would keep the youths in school longer and would steer them away from those jobs which were not only unintelligent, but were also being eliminated by continued mechanization. Mechanization, together with proper education, would eliminate unskilled work altogether, Woodward prophesied: "If there are more machines, there must be more makers, inventors, and directors."

Another quality which Woodward's "whole boy" would acquire through manual training was the ability to comport himself as a social being—an ability so vital to the aspiring youth. Woodward proudly quoted the remark of a visitor to the Manual Training School: "The difference between the ordinary, stupid, dirty mechanic's-apprentice and one of these intelligent, handy, clean, gentlemanly lads is as that between night and day."[47] Woodward's own description of his manual-training classes further underlined the high seriousness of the boys' preparation, the moral and dignified nature of their mission: "While boys are at work in a shop I would allow no whistling nor playing nor idling. There is no objection to such conversation as may be necessary to the prosecution of their work. The essential thing is to keep the boys' minds on their work. . . ."[48] Yet the point of such discipline was not moral reformation, according to Woodward, but to discover those boys with ability who had been ignored by the classical school system, and to facilitate the

Woodward's development is seen in terms of a shift in audience. Whereas Woodward had excited little interest among the engineers, he found himself engaged in a lively dialogue with the public school teachers. In the course of this dialogue, the style of his rhetoric underwent some modification, but his argument was broadened rather than changed.

development of bright boys whom that same school system served ill. These boys with hidden or obvious ability, though not "bad," still needed guidance and a moral model, for which reason their teachers would have to be men trained in pedagogy, rather than artisans. The manual trainer molded as he enlightened: "While in shop our teacher dresses as he expects his pupils to dress, appropriately. He sets no bad example; his language is correct and pure; his manners those of a gentleman."[49]

In Woodward's thinking, the boys who had gone to manual-training school were better prepared for the upward climb than those who either had gone to trade schools or who had served a regular apprenticeship. If a boy left the manual-training school to go into a trade, the work itself took on new dimensions: ". . . those who enter mechanical pursuits after a course in a manual [training] school are to raise those pursuits from the level of mere trades, and to make them take on some of the characteristics of professions. . . ."[50] The youth who went on to an ordinary college, Woodward noted, would be an apter, more disciplined, and better educated student. And for the one who went to technical school, his manual training, together with the general education he had received, would make him a superior student. To support his claims Woodward gave an account of the positions which Manual Training School graduates were holding, but the account contained much that Woodward himself was unwilling to discuss, and much that his opponents found significant: bookkeepers, general assistants, and accountants, 153; draftsmen, 100; merchants and manufactures, 90; higher schools (obviously others had gone on to higher schools, but had already finished) 75; technical engineers, 65; superintendents of manufacture, 44; salesmen and agents, 41; teachers, 39; lawyers, 30; and an assortment of trades and professions, each claiming smaller numbers of graduates.[51]

The Battle of the Public School. Despite the continuing interest in manual training by some engineering educators, most plaudits for Woodward's system came from the lower-schools contingent—kindergarteners, progressive educators, rural educators, and normal-school people.[52] The popularity of manual training was undoubtedly related to the fact that so many different teacher groups could find it of interest, but the system's flexibility was not sufficiently great to save it from attack within the very walls that had given it shelter—the National Education Association.

For the professional educators, the question of manual training was intimately connected with the question of secondary schooling, the function of which was being increasingly debated throughout the nineteenth century. During the 1880's and 1890's, advocates of a better-developed terminal high school education argued in much the same fashion as supporters of the land-grant colleges; the democratic commitment of the public schools was stressed, and the need for "practical" education was reiterated. The secondary school curriculum had been undergoing modification continually, as Latin or English schools, academies, and finally high schools became more and more popular institutions for the training of the middle-class youngsters. Now, once again, it came under review when the question of workers' children was raised. Debates over the difference between terminal and college-preparatory curricula were crosscut by debates on the classical versus the modern science and language curriculum, or the modern curriculum versus an even more specifically occupational training. What was regarded as a "practical" curriculum differed from group to group. Proponents of the modern curriculum, who stressed education for the white-collar occupations, often found themselves allied with the proponents of education for the trades, against the champions of classical studies.[53]

As the NEA began to discuss industrial education in the 1870's, arguments about the land-grant colleges were interwoven with arguments about the place of manual work in the secondary schools.[54] High school educators seemed to have had special difficulty in dignifying the idea of manual training, for industrial training of youngsters was closely associated in the public mind with the rehabilitation of youthful criminals, with poverty and corruption, rather than with the wholesome, solid, middle class from which most high school students were drawn. If the goal of industrial education was reform, the educators would have to decide how such a goal could be articulated with the growing high school system. Again, if industrial education was a "modern" form of schooling, educators would have to decide on the relationship between shop work and the newly emerging scientific studies. Runkle's introduction of the Russian training system in 1877 presented one answer to these questions and caused a considerable stir among the industrial educators. When this theme was presented in a different form by Calvin Woodward, the members of the NEA were all ears. By 1891, the Association's industrial department had become the "Department of Industrial Education and Manual Training." Manual training had made itself a place, but the security of its position was another matter.

Not long after Woodward had presented his own scheme of industrial education, he found himself fending off attacks. In 1887, Woodward devoted a good part of his NEA speech to criticizing an article by Edward Everett Hale. Hale, in a piece for the *North American Review* on the need for half-time schools, had bemoaned the passing of the old-time school, in which students were prepared for life by teachers such as Daniel Webster or Harriet Beecher Stowe.[55] Yet now, he said, children were not only given a poor general education, but one which mistakenly tried to substitute itself for the home education of which the children had been deprived. Rather than try to teach children the skills they used to learn at home, Hale recommended that class time should be limited, and children given time to gain that experience which comes only from the world—like wisdom gained by the country child.

Woodward was equal to any such argument: "I am as familiar with the fortunate circumstances of the farmer's boy as Mr.

Hale. I have tried the school winters, and farm summers. I know the value of a country training, when a fond father is never tired of giving sound instruction and encouraging high aspirations. But the evils of which Mr. Hale complains are chiefly found in the city school; they have a small foothold in the country, now. Not one percent of the fathers in a great city can command the facilities for teaching what he says every boy ought to learn at home during vacation."[56] Even for those fathers who had the skill—and the time—to teach their sons, Woodward continued, the family system was not the best. The atmosphere of the school was more stimulating and the school system far more democratic. Instead of learning "petty details" which craftsmen-fathers might teach, and instead of being confined to the trade of his father, a boy would be free to choose his occupation. Manual training, Woodward concluded, freed boys for just such a choice, prepared them better for the trades, or for anything else they might choose. Manual training was not merely an education for orphans and Negroes, as some critics had contended; when they place "the unfortunate between truants and paupers on one hand, and freedmen and Indian youth on the other, I cannot avoid the conclusion that it is not respectable to be an orphan."[57]

While Woodward was protecting one flank from the advocates of home life and philanthropy, he faced a far more formidable adversary and a far more subtle argument. The most powerful educator to criticize manual training was William Torrey Harris, a contemporary of Woodward's. Although Harris' career resembled Woodward's in many respects, Harris' work as educator and administrator was linked to the study of philosophy rather than of science or technology, and he devoted much of his energy to discussing the philosophic bases of his educational position. In 1889, Harris' unique combination of theoretical and practical experience gained him the post of United States Commissioner of Education, and during the eleven years in which he held this position he was an indefatigable speaker before the NEA.

Harris' social philosophy, although far more elaborately articulated than that of Woodward, had much of the same bent.[58]
Harris, too, was vitally concerned with maintaining respect for
the rights of property in an orderly society, and had a strong
faith in progress. For Harris, however, progress was not merely
that of material well-being and innovation, but, ultimately, the
progress of intelligence. The social corollary to such progress
was the upward movement of the entire social hierarchy.
Whereas, Woodward's concept of class was blurred in precisely
the way necessary to support his ideas of mobility (a vast number of average American boys constituting the worthy classes,
with some discounted Negroes and Indians below), Harris conceived of a distinct property-holding class, a distinct working
class, and a dangerous element below, into which the working
class might fall if its members were not properly tutored. From
the standpoint of industrial education, then, Harris' problem
was to insure the upward movement of the working classes, an
upward movement which would be intellectual rather than
merely material.

Harris rejected European-style trade training and, to some
extent, manual training, because they did not, in his mind, contribute to the development of intelligence.[59] The problem with
trade schools was that they wanted to begin too early, cutting
off the students' general intellectual development. With the increased use of machinery, jobs were going to depend more and
more on the understanding of machines and less and less on the
actual running of them. Men needed to be trained to supervise
and repair machinery, and even operators would have to have
sufficient flexibility to move to new work when their machines
became obsolete. For this reason, Harris continued, science was
important in the public schools, for science gave the workingman
an understanding of principles, an understanding to which at
least the scientific aspect of manual training could also make a
contribution.

To the extent that he assigned this role to science, Harris took a position similar to that of the pre-Civil War proponents of scientific education for the laboring classes. For Harris, however, science could not fulfill the double purpose of knowledge and morality, since, with the exception of evolutionary science, he saw such studies as tending to materialism.[60] What one needed in addition to science, he reasoned, was an education for leadership which cultivated qualities of directive ability—qualities which the traditional high school and college programs had always cultivated by opening the "five windows of the soul" to the wonders of nature, and training the "three departments of the mind" to control the natural environment. If manual training too could play a role in the development of discipline, the strengthening of the will, there was no reason why it should not be a part of the curriculum. But manual training was in no way essential; the classical subjects did more for discipline, and the sciences themselves offered the best way to develop the intellect. Vocational training was important, but it had to come last, when the language and scientific studies were understood. If educators wished to have manual training serve as a finishing-off course and as an introduction to genuine trade-training, there was no reason, Harris conceded, why it should not.

This was a rather grudging admission on Harris' part, and Woodward was understandably unhappy with it. To a great extent the two men missed each other's thought entirely, rather than contradicting each other; both of them saw a changing industrial world in which men would have to be equipped to swim with the tide, and for this reason both rejected the trade school idea, claiming that it limited flexibility. Both saw a country in which mobility was the key feature and in which special attention needed to be paid to students who were moving up in the world. The point of contention was how scientific and mechanical training could contribute to such mobility. This is illustrated nicely in the discussion which followed one NEA report on manual training which Harris presented. First, a delegate from Colorado remarked that mechanical drawing should be taught in the public schools, but that manual skills themselves should be reserved for the trade schools. Woodward countered that the two were inseparable. Harris, then, began to take apart manual training in another way. Wasn't the scientific work done in manual training really the most educative part? Harris asked. Again Woodward said that the two were inseparable: "The study of science has its eminent value; we do not omit it; but mere scientific training leads to futile attempts in invention. The inventor must be familiar with mechanical processes, and mechanical skill is necessary to practical success."[61] Harris demurred: it wasn't so. Then the two educators proceeded to match inventors: Whitney and Morse were pitted against George and Robert Stephenson.

Harris' whole attitude toward invention was a mixed one. For him, Americans were an inventive breed, but for that reason especially it was necessary to emphasize discipline in education.[62] Flashes of inspiration were no more in his line than in Woodward's, but Harris' ideal always tempered innovation with tradition. For Woodward, discipline had appeal if it were the discipline for invention and success, but tradition was hardly his favorite topic; he was looking almost exclusively forward.

Ironically, as far as their industrial education ideas were concerned, Harris and Woodward were to be run over by the same juggernaut. Around the turn of the century, the NEA meeting began to give more and more time to the idea of public secondary schools, and the trade-school partisans quickly gained a devoted following. They did not treat kindly of either manual training or Harris' occupational ideal; to the trade trainers, both men seemed aristocrats, more interested in educating the few than in educating the many.[63]

These changes taking place in the discussion of public education had much in common with changes within the general industrial education debate—and changes in the American attitude toward industry itself. The concept of leadership on which promoters of scientific and technical education had founded their efforts in the three decades after the Civil War were no longer unquestioned, for land-grant college and engineering educators in particular had interwoven their ideal of national-cum-industrial leadership with an ideal of untrammeled mobility. Two emerging factors posed special threat to these ideals—the changing character of the laboring class and the increased specialization within industry. The advocates of an industrial education for mobility had paid little heed to the problem with which the philanthropists had early begun to struggle—that of a permanent working class. Nor, for a long time, did the advocates of mobility deal with the problem of how scientific or technological expertise, once it was the rule rather than the exception, would affect mobility itself.

Toward the end of the century, the waxing profession of mechanical engineering began to take such problems into account, and the trade-training spokesmen among the public-school educators began to forward their complementary ideal. The era of enterprise seemed to be over, and although leaders were still needed, it appeared time to become interested in the education of the ranks. In the minds of the trade-training advocates, neither the high schools nor the manual-training schools were looking after the country's need for skilled labor. Some educators urged that manual-training schools be converted into trade schools, and this, indeed, was happening. Others insisted that trade courses be incorporated into the public schools, a pattern already begun. Still other spokesmen for trade training demanded that separate trade schools be established. This, too, was under way.

4

The Ideal of the Skilled Workman

After the turn of the century the notion of trade training was adopted by professional educators with relative rapidity. About 1900, trade-school advocates began a concerted assault on the NEA, and by 1910, that group had come out with a program which, though retaining a form of manual training for the elementary schools, gave a clear endorsement of trade training for the secondary level. The triumph of the trade trainers was built in great part on the growth of private experiments in trade education, some sponsored by philanthropists, and others by trade-school advocates who rejected the philanthropic approach.[1] Such experiments, despite their different and even contradictory rationales, were founded on the concern for growing manufacture which characterized the Progressive era; the problem around which the trade trainers organized their efforts was how that growing manufacture could be best—most "efficiently"—promoted.

Like the Progressive movement as a whole, the concept of industrial efficiency involved conflicting elements.[2] To some Progressives, industrial efficiency through the growth of manufacture and the increased division of labor promised the ultimate prosperity and well-being of each member of the republic. To others, the dangers of giant manufacture loomed foremost, threatening the sacred tenets of democracy and equality. Both those who hoped for and those who feared the growing manufacture felt that it was resulting in circumscribed mobility; the goals of the rags-to-riches era, of the ambitious and unencumbered climber, would or should, it seemed, have to be abandoned. Trade-school advocates, and even those who opposed them, groped for a new ideal which would combine the virtues of the pre-Civil War honest workman with those of the mobile worker, whose mobility now could only be realized in part.

One aspect of this circumscribed mobility and its relation to efficiency is brought out in the pioneer work on industrial management; here planning was analyzed, and the educational problem became one of reconciling training with an industrial world which was broken down into a series of minute occupational niches. Yet the division of labor was not the only conceivable basis for efficiency; even partisans of industrial management admitted that, past a certain point, the division of labor might actually become an impediment to efficiency. Those critics of industrial management who inherited the philanthropic tradition in industrial education tended to place that point close to the image of the honest workman. They interpreted efficiency in terms of the philanthropic notion of "character," which suggested that the complete workman, the whole and happy workman, was also the most efficient workman.

Business groups and organized labor turned to both interpretations of efficiency in developing their educational goals. Although opinion varied within the business and labor communities there emerged enough of a common ideological base so that, violently antagonistic as parts of each were towards parts of the other, they could agree on a federal program of trade education.

Education and Efficiency

The Management Ethos. One of the pressing problems which big business articulated during the century was that of management—of enabling all the parts of a large organization to function together for the utmost efficiency of the whole. The professionalization of management took place late in the century as demands for capital investment became greater and the base of stockholders broader. Yet the same concerns for greater efficiency had been building since the advent of large-scale manufacture; the early textile mill owners had gradually come under attack for their absentee and spendthrift management; stockholders in the erratic mid-century railroad industry had moved to rationalize its procedures; the growing iron—and later steel—industry struggled with new styles of dividing labor, of reconciling older artisan skills with changing shop conditions.[3]

The role of the foreman or supervisor was particularly crucial here; shop supervisors could be recruited either from among independent artisans outside the company, or from the ranks of the workers. It was difficult to adjust these various career patterns to each other, for changing conceptions of supervision were also involved. The early foreman, like the independent contractor, had had broad responsibilities.[4] It was up to him to keep the shop producing, to supply the material for work, to hire, to assign jobs, to teach men their work or any special techniques which they might not know, to see that the goods were delivered, and to do much of the clerical work of the shop. Although patterns varied in the different trades and industries, the growth of large-scale manufacture and the development of unions tended to reduce the foreman's original role. As companies grew, they divided jobs more finely, assigning clerical work, ordering of materials, and so forth, to separate departments. As organized labor grew, men tended to take their grievances and questions about shop efficiency to the shop

steward, who thereby pre-empted another aspect of the foreman's role. Foremen, like the workmen they supervised, began
to feel the effects of the division of labor.

Frederick Taylor's systemization of these various problems in
management first brought them to public attention. His own
career illustrates the vagueness of routes to supervision; when an
eye injury interfered with Taylor's law studies, he took up machinery work, and despite what his biographer calls "a strong
distaste for manual labor" completed an apprenticeship in machinery and pattern-making.[5] He then began at the Midvale Steel
Company as a common laborer, from this position rose to a clerk-
ship, then became a machinist, and finally was made foreman. In
the meantime, he completed his formal education by home studies
through Harvard and the Stevens Institute, earning a mechanical
engineering degree from the latter.

His scientific studies bore fruit in several inventions, but Taylor was as yet very much out of the mainstream of professional
engineering. In the middle eighties he joined the American
Society of Mechanical Engineers, and before long had become
an active member of the organization. He spoke to the engineers
not as an inventor, however, but to tell them of his supervision
problems at Midvale and how he had solved them through time
and motion studies; he spoke to his colleagues of the need to
separate and coordinate the manufacturing and managerial
aspects of production, and to effect a fine division of labor
within each realm.[6] Three images of the worker emerged in
Taylor's system; the average laborer, who was the raw material
for scientific management; the trained average worker, who had
benefited from scientific management; and the mechanic, the
man with ability who (beginning at the bottom like Taylor
himself) would rise to a supervisory position. Educating the
average laborer by scientific management, teaching him the
easiest and most efficient way to do his job, posed few problems
for Taylor, but the question of educating the potential supervisor was not so simple.

At the end of one of Taylor's key speeches to the society, one ASME member remarked that Taylor did not differentiate between education and production—a telling comment, for in scientific management the two activities blended, at least with respect to educating the average workman. This is evident in Taylor's testimony before a special congressional committee, where he described how shoveling could be made scientific. When one of the shovelers in a gang was having trouble or producing below par, said Taylor, a "teacher" was sent to show him how to do the job most easily and quickly. "Now, gentlemen," Taylor continued, addressing the committee, "I want you to see clearly that, because that is one of the characteristic features of scientific management, this is not nigger driving; this is kindness; this is teaching; this is doing what I would like mighty well to have done to me if I were a boy trying to learn how to do something."[7] This kindness, however, was not "philanthropy"; it was helping a man to earn an honest living.

For Taylor, the mechanic who started out shoveling with the intention of rising to a better job posed a different problem, because here the energy of the firm was really being used for education as opposed to production. Taylor argued the importance of not keeping talented men in jobs below their capacity, where they were wasted and disgruntled; "On the other hand, this policy of promoting men and finding them new positions [in other firms if there were no room in one's own] has its limits. No worse mistake can be made than that of allowing an establishment to be looked upon as a training school, to be used mainly for the education of many of its employees. All employees should bear in mind that each shop exists first, last, and all the time, for the purpose of paying dividends to its owners. They should have patience. . . . And no man should expect promotion until after he has trained his successor to take his place. The writer is quite sure that in his own case, as a young man, no one element was of such assistance to him in obtaining new appointments as was the practice of invariably training another man to fill his position before asking for advancement."[8]

Taylor was groping with a complex issue, though he did not face it openly: the men who would work for money alone posed little problem, but the men who were working for advancement were costly to the company—at least in the short run. Yet, despite the fact that the question of mobility remained unresolved, both the engineers and many others saw scientific management as a happy solution to labor-management conflict; the theory offered enough scope for one to preserve an ideal of mobility by focusing on the managers, and at the same time incorporate an ideal of improvement by focusing on the managed. The question of bridging the gap between the two groups, however, tended to become blurred.

Guiding the Worker. While Taylor's ideas were gaining currency, several other movements were in the making which also stressed the importance of individual satisfaction within the broader framework of industrial efficiency. A key point in scientific management was the need for suiting the man to his job, but Taylor had relied for this on wise supervisory choices and individual initiative. Americans, however, had never been left to their own devices in finding proper positions in the industrial world. Career-advice books grew in popularity all during the nineteenth century, and by the early years of the twentieth they abounded. This was the time at which Frank Parsons began to develop a more formal system of vocational guidance.

Parsons, a reformer of the social gospel variety, was an ardent opponent of what seemed to him the contemporary money culture, the defects of which he felt might be remedied through a system of basic annuities. These were not to be so great as to stifle initiative, for Parsons proposed only a fair start for each worker, one which would minimize the accidental element in his career. At the same time, workers would be guided to the right jobs; industrial efficiency would be assured; and the social class system, though still allowing for mobility, would reach a sort of equilibrium. The better and more intelligent men would rise to leadership in the New Republic; there would be dignity in labor for all and room for both "mobility and adaptivity."[9]

In the early 1900's, Parsons began to give lectures on vocational guidance, and his talks prompted many young men to come to him for advice. The questions led him to ask educators and employers about training and job opportunities, and by 1908, to open the Vocational Bureau of Boston. Parsons died not long after the Bureau was started, but his disciple Meyer Bloomfield continued the work. In a speech to the engineering educators, Bloomfield emphasized the bond between guidance and scientific management which educators themselves were quick to sense: ". . . in the field of efficiency engineering I find an analogy for what vocational guidance regards as the true function of the school and of education. The teachers are the functional foremen, the courses of study are the planned and routed tasks."[10] The end of training, said Bloomfield, was efficiency, "economy of effect," and the understanding of human relationships.

Yet the teachers themselves were not to be the sole promotors of efficiency. Youths needed to be kept out of blind-alley jobs, to be kept in school, and to be directed to the kind of school most suited to their various potentials. Informed and experienced people—educators, social workers, businessmen, and labor leaders—could all help develop guidelines for these young folks, while trained vocational guidance personnel, who had experience in many areas, could provide individual advice. At present, Bloomfield noted, vocational guidance people had to rely on common-sense methods of determining the job for which an individual youngster was fit; it was to be hoped that the psychological laboratory would develop more scientific ways in which to handle cases.

The psychological laboratory was hard at work, in the form of Hugo Münsterberg, a Harvard psychologist who had studied in Wundt's laboratory and had helped to bring experimental psychology to the United States. About 1911, Münsterberg became interested in the application of psychology to industry, experimenting on job efficiency and visiting a number of large plants, with an eye to evolving methods of job selection. The professor's experimental and consulting work was only the barest beginning in industrial psychology, but a few more pioneers cropped up before the first World War. In 1915, the California Institute of Technology began a division of applied psychology, in which research on vocational guidance was included, and, with the War itself, psychological testing techniques received their first major boost.

Not long after he began his work in industrial psychology, Münsterberg began to examine psychology in the realm of vocational choice. Glamour and immediate satisfaction, said the professor, played too great a role, masking the true nature of vocation: "The vocational life is . . . the real center of all endeavors toward happiness which man can know. It is service to ideal goods and therefore an abundant source of satisfaction, but superior to all other strivings because it is best adjusted, best prepared, best focussed."[11] From the standpoint of the lower pleasures, he continued, all work involved "drudgery," but there was no job which, "seen from that higher point of view," was not "a source of inspiration and happiness." The acquisition of knowledge and technical skill were vital, but valuable only after the correct choice of work was made. Both the individual and the society as a whole would suffer if the choice were not correct; efficiency and "joy" were bound together, and the industrial psychologist, "in the service of civilization," could promote both by suiting men to their jobs.

Münsterberg clearly took issue with the complaint that industrial psychology abetted modern industry in making work monotonous. The charge of monotony, he said, was usually connected with the fact that workers did not produce a whole product. Wholeness, however, was only relative; a small portion of a product could have its own completeness, its own intricacies.

One worker might see many fine points in a seemingly simple job; another could tell how satisfying it was to do an apparently repetitive motion. And the worker had "every reason" to prefer uniform, simple work, since in that way he could produce more and earn higher pay; people with seemingly complex and interesting work were often unhappy. Even the most involved job could become monotonous to a given individual, Münsterberg insisted. Monotony was obviously a matter of perception rather than an inherent quality of given occupations, and the goal, therefore, was to put an individual in the job which was interesting *for him.* Then profits would be increased, wages would go up, hours would be reduced, and all the ugliness and drudgery associated with work would be "replaced in our social community by overflowing joy and perfect harmony."[12]

Art, Craft, and Democracy

The proponents of industrial efficiency, especially reform-oriented men like Frank Parsons, sensed the implications which efficiency might have for individual well-being and the shape of the social order. Their image of the skilled workman who had found or was placed in just the right industrial niche was open to attack (as Münsterberg's defense illustrates) on the grounds that the workman was robbed of pride in his product. In the same way, the ideals of democracy and equality, or equality of opportunity, seemed threatened by the apparently rigid hierarchy which efficiency would impose. Admirers of art and the crafts, and crusaders for a new social order, rose to bring such charges against industrial efficiency and against the trade schools which made industrial efficiency part of their creed. Ironically, however, both defenders and critics of industrial efficiency contributed to the very ideal of the skilled workman which was basic to the trade school movement itself.

The Craftsman as Artist. Although the skilled workman of the new era differed from his Jacksonian counterpart because of the increased division of labor and the greater use of machinery, many Americans felt that the old-fashioned virtues and quality (if not type) of skill could still be brought to a man's work. If one could not make a complete product, at least the act of making could be complete, not only in skill and honesty but in a sense of beauty. As early as the 1850's, when American artists and art lovers discovered the English Pre-Raphaelites, the reborn ideal of medieval craftsmanship began to receive an American formulation; artists like John La Farge struggled to embody Pre-Raphaelite concepts in their paintings, and experimented in bringing greater beauty to traditional crafts.[13] Toward the end of the century, another craft revival wave began: in 1897, the American Society of Arts and Crafts was founded in Boston; by 1907, there was a National League of Handicraft Societies of America, and at the beginning of World War I, the Art Alliance of America was formed. None of these later craft revival groups, however, invoked the spirits of Ruskin and William Morris more ardently than the United Crafts of New Jersey.

The United Crafts, "a guild of cabinet makers, metal and leather workers," was organized by Gustave Stickley along the line of William Morris' firm. The goals of Stickley's guild were three-fold: to produce a useful and agreeable art, suited to "the needs of the century"; to unite the designer and workman, thus ". . . raising the general intelligence of the workman, by the increasing of his leisure and the multiplication of his means of culture and pleasure"; and finally, to stimulate the movement for cooperation (the optimal way to reunite the workman with his product), but at the same time encourage individuals and private businesses to help develop a national art.[14]

Stickley reasoned that, since a democratic society needed an art which came from the people rather than one which was imposed by the leisured classes, America's art should be dictated by its national resources and its national character. In furniture, for instance (Stickley himself was a carpenter), wood was the natural material, and design should be dictated by "structural" principles, since structure was the peculiar American genius: "A simple, democratic art should provide them [the people] with material surroundings conducive to plain living and high thinking, to the development of the sense of order, symmetry and proportion."[15] (Think, for a moment, of the role which scientific education was to play for the Jacksonian workman.) The public schools would have to teach art "practically," art practiced for its own rewards, rather than filling the students full of information on the history of art.

Stickley insisted, however, that the craft revival should not be a simple rebellion against machine production, not the rejection of the machine, but the promotion of thought and care on the part of the workman. Many handicraft advocates, he said, fell into the same error which manufacturers themselves made, that of turning out attractive but useless items. The whole purpose of craftsmanship was to relate production to man's total needs; if machinery could aid in achieving this goal, as it clearly could in the hands of competent craftsmen, there was no reason why it should not be used: "The invention of modern machinery is in itself a notable achievement of the true spirit of craftsmanship."[16] The only threat which the machine posed was the threat of mastering man, his work, his leisure, and his tastes. If the workman were in control of all phases of production, industrial slavery would be avoided.

The pages of *The Craftsman*, of which Stickley was the editor, reflected some of the difficulties which the arts and crafts people faced in realizing their ideal. One lady, a rug maker, pointed to the problem of financial return: "The modern craftsman is not one who can exist on a few cents a day, and make up the deficit with the purple light which is supposed to irradiate his work. On the contrary, he is an *artist who works*. He is a man with cultivated tastes and many requirements. He has exceptional gifts, and represents long years of artistic training. He cannot use the laborious methods of medieval craftsmen, and—live."[17] The craftsman would not only have to use modern techniques and machinery, but also learn sufficient business methods to sell his work: "But let me not be misunderstood to commend a commercial spirit in these industries! Still . . . ."[18] Still, the lady's image had drifted far from Stickley's ideal; the craftsman was forced to become a specialist—separated from the run-of-the-mill workers—and a businessman to boot!

Another article in *The Craftsman*, by Mary Simkhovitch, suggested the problems which social reformers might face in applying the arts and crafts ideal: "Although the handicrafts extremist insists upon designer and worker being the same person, there seems to be no reason why in many of the handicrafts the two functions should not be separated, though the worker must be able to appreciate good design and the designer know good work when he sees it."[19] Miss Simkhovitch, like Jane Addams, saw that despite the desirability of preserving native crafts, the immigrants would have to make their way in an industrial world in which the division of labor was an accomplished fact. Most workers would be able to do handicraft only as a vocation or an income supplement; possibly, for those unable to work in the factories, it could provide a means of livelihood. One needed to be careful in encouraging handicraft, for the very conditions in which most hand work was found—the impoverished home and the vile tenement—displayed the evils against which reformers were struggling.

According to Stickley, one of the major ways to transform the worker into a craftsman was through the study of drawing, the "basis of all the manual arts and . . . one of the essentials of a primary education which shall be worthy of the name."[20] By the turn of the century, this pronouncement was far from radical. In his *Art and Industry* volumes, for example, Isaac Clarke reflected the excitement felt about drawing in the 1880's. Art, Clarke argued, had a special role in democratic countries, as one could see in the development of industrial art: "In this wedding of Use to Beauty, there is no inevitable disparity; for true democracy seeks not to drag down the highest, but only to lift up the lowest.

So Art, entering the world of work is not thereby degraded but stooping to the lowly, lifts them to her own high level; giving to homely uses divine significance.["]21 The public might be more interested in the fact that art education paid dividends, yet profits were only secondary; art would elevate consumer taste and give the honest workers the kind of education which would "make their work a joy," their lives happy rather than "dark, gloomy, and wearisome."

As Clarke's study demonstrates, the movement for art education was not new; in 1838, Henry Barnard had urged the introduction of drawing in the public schools for the sake of improving manufacture, and attention to the progress of European schools had increased the appeal of such a suggestion. It was difficult for art training to gain a firm foothold, however, for drawing was associated with culture or engineering rather than with basic studies. Under continuing pressure from educators and manufacturers, Massachusetts finally enacted permissive legislation, and in 1870 passed a law requiring that free evening drawing lessons be offered in every town above 10,000; but it was not easy to realize the new legislation. Massachusetts and the city of Boston made a start by importing Walter Smith, head of the Art School at Leeds, to serve as head of the Boston Normal Art School and supervisor of the state's art programs. His creed of art education matched the public service character of his duties; he stressed the ability of all to do drawing, and spoke for both its general and industrial education functions—promoting individual development and work skills.

These two themes, art for education and art for vocation, were elaborated by others. Many saw the evening schools as the beginning of technical schools; some were delighted at the thought of a more cultured public. As drawing instruction spread through the northeast states, the NEA began to pay attention to the movement. In 1884 the Association formed a Department of Art Education, in which discussions of art for use and art for individual development took on interesting elaborations. Certain of the educators stressed the importance of art for the development of skilled labor to meet the competition of foreign skilled labor; others spoke of the moral effect of art on uncouth laborers— manual training and drawing would not only teach these men skills but keep them out of the rum shops.[22]

Although advocates of drawing had difficulty in separating the question of developing skills from that of improving the morals of the laboring force, many began their arguments by appealing to the need for individual development. Drawing teachers often stressed that "the moral nature" was "stimulated by the cultivation of taste, and truthful expression of form."[23] Art seemed to offer a means of self-expression, a way to develop the creativity in an otherwise stifled life. Art educators who stressed the moral aspect of drawing also tended to be interested in manual training. In 1886, for instance, the president of the NEA art department noted that the drawing teacher was also paving the way for manual training, giving the student such a "love for mechanical pursuits" that he would want to go on to manual training school: "any course in drawing, sufficiently broad to be termed industrial, should provide for three lines of work: construction of objects, representation of objects, and decoration of objects."[24]

This argument needed only one further step to become a positive threat to manual training, and that step was taken by Charles Carter, industrial-drawing agent for the Massachusetts Board of Education. The purpose of both manual training and industrial drawing, he declared, was to teach children to think, to help them to discover the world through the "Forms of Things." "The world of things" was not limited to shops and tools, nor to the products of manufacture; for that reason, one had to be careful about the tendency of American manual-training to specialize in the direction of vocational needs: "It is interesting to note, in this connection, that some persons believe that the industrial-art school offers all that is needed in the way of manual training."[25] Of course, Carter noted, what was really needed was to bring the two together, although (he could not resist adding) the interest in drawing was booming while the question of workshops in the schools was still under debate.

There were a number of other interesting elements in the overlapping area between industrial drawing and manual training. In an article in *Century*, in 1888, Carter made an extended argument about the cooperation of drawing teachers and parents; he felt that shops would never be incorporated into the public schools, but that shop work could be revived in the home with the help of the teacher. The child could learn mechanical drawing in class and, armed with a few hints on construction, work on projects at home, asking help from his parents "who thus unconsciously become teachers of manual training."[26] The illustration accompanying Carter's article says almost more than the article itself. There is the earnest child, seated next to a table, working under the lamplight. There is his manly father seated next to him, and hovering close by is that true guardian of the American home. This is the image with which Woodward was struggling when he insisted that manual training be done in the schools.

Another article in *Century* suggests why many people were more happy with the idea of crafts in the home, rather than shopwork at school. Commenting on his own system of decorative art, the writer remarked that it was better for little girls to begin with fancy sewing and learn plain sewing afterwards: "There is another reason for not putting plain sewing strongly forward: of late years in every ragged school and drunkards' children mission, such work has been given so much prominence that the parents of pupils in the public schools have a not unnatural aversion to having it said that their children are taught it gratis."[27] Thus, the argument implied, while crafts in the home had a warm and traditional glow about them, crafts at school had an unpleasant aura. But if one added the component of art, that very moral and most genteel activity, to construction at school, perhaps such work would be acceptable.

With the American adoption of sloyd, the confrontation of art-and-craft education with manual training reached its climax.

Sloyd was a Norwegian and Swedish revival of rural handicraft, originally aimed at remedying the ills of urbanization. By the time John Ordway of M.I.T. brought the system back to the United States, sloyd had taken on the rhetoric of general culture —the love of labor, the training of the hand and eye, the development of moral qualities. In response to American enthusiasm, a number of Swedish instructors came over, most notably Gustaf Larsson, who under the aegis of Mrs. Quincy Shaw started a normal school in Boston to train American teachers in sloyd and to propagandize the method to the public. Educational circles were receptive, for the growing attention to the arts and crafts had helped to intensify the critique of manual training, and Woodward's system ignored the aesthetic element in construction. Larsson and Woodward battled over the merits of the two systems, Woodward seeing little difference, Larsson stressing the usefulness of sloyd objects.[28] Woodward was once again up against the homelife image, for Larsson claimed that by making real objects rather than doing exercises, the child recaptured the character-forming work experience he once might have had on a New England farm.

While Larsson and Woodward argued, the social and developmental aspects of their theories were being adopted and recast through an emerging concept of art education. By 1901, when the NEA manual training and art departments held a joint session, the progressive approach had hit its stride. Clara I. Mitchell's talk on "Textile Arts as Constructive Work in the Elementary Schools" pointed to a new function for the arts and crafts—helping to provide social experience for children analogous to that which the "great world" provided.[29] Construction activities, manual training, and the "industrial arts" were now seen as "representative forms of the great type of industries." By "struggle with the world's work" the child could come to understand labor's historical dimension and to feel his relation to all men as workers. Mitchell did not expect children to merely bow to the social order through understanding work, for the child was also to be an explorer and an innovator, developing "originality, freedom, and taste" through playful creativity. In short, the child would not only learn the world's work, but also bring his talents to it.

Clara Mitchell was a member of the School of Education at the University of Chicago, where John Dewey had taught and conducted an experimental school from the middle to late nineties. Dewey, like Larsson and so many spokesmen with whom we have dealt, was concerned with the loss of that education which the pre-industrial family had provided—the family in which the child had been a helper. To recapture this kind of learning, he urged that the school itself be considered a kind of community and an introduction to the community at large. Through an education which stressed the social significance of work, it was hoped that man would recover that understanding of, and fusion with, the productive part of his life. The shop-in-the-school was to symbolize a part of man's real-life activities, be a symbol through which the child could gain an understanding of those activities.

So far, Dewey had much in common with the pre-Civil War educators, who were interested in shopwork activities as a way of understanding the meaning of work. But Dewey added a distinctly new dimension. In addition to the "social instinct," the child brought the impulse to construction, the instinct of investigation, and the "art instinct" to his activities; art work would have to be free and flexible, with a social motive and a message. This was not art in the sense of high culture; this was art in the sense of making, of completing, of understanding a socially meaningful work: "I think everybody who has not a purely literary view of the subject recognizes that genuine art grows out of the work of the artisan."[30] When shop work in the school took its true form, as a way of unifying and perceiving human activity, it became art. Art then, ". . . is the living union of thought and the instrument of expression. This union is symbolized by saying that in the ideal school the art work might be considered to be that of the shops, passed through the alembic of library and museum into action again."[31]

Dewey was perfectly willing to accept manual training as part of school work, but such exercises now had a meaning far from Woodward's; they were symbolic of the occupational aspect of life, a way to develop motor skills while coming to understand the meaning of such skills in the contemporary world.[32] And educators interested in manual training were receptive to such a new interpretation, Woodward's grief notwithstanding. In 1904 Dewey took this new interpretation to Columbia, where Teachers College provided fertile soil.

In the course of twenty years, Teachers College had moved from a philanthropic effort to train children in work skills to a teachers' college stressing manual training, to a broad and advanced teachers' preparatory school. Both Nicholas Murray Butler and James Earl Russell, who succeeded Butler as the College's head, stressed the training of well-rounded professionals, so that even as the school raised its sights, it was considered important to maintain a place for the manual activities. When Dewey joined the faculty of education, adding this position to his philosophy appointment, the "social" direction of the College's manual studies was assured. The establishment of the College's School of Practical Arts in 1912 merely symbolized the changed meaning of manual training.

By 1909 Russell was already noting the uselessness of manual training, except insofar as it taught design. The real need, he argued, was to teach industrial arts with an understanding of social use and beauty: "In all industrial processes, wherever man transforms material into things of greater value, he employs a technique peculiar to the situation, and gives to the product a touch which pleases his aesthetic sense."[33] And Frederick Bonser, one of the College's leading spokesmen for industrial arts, gave even less credit to manual training; it was, indeed, mere skill as opposed to genuine education.[34] Nor was he convinced that the purpose of the schools should be trade training. In this opinion, Bonser followed out the logic of his Deweyan commitments.

When, by 1914, a movement for federal aid to vocational education was well underway, Dewey was concerned. He cautioned the public to note that the movement for industrial education had been the work of the business community; if businessmen wished to supply industrial education, that was their privilege, but if they wanted the state to underwrite such education, the people should take exception.[35] Justifications for industrial education, Dewey noted, turned to the example of Germany, where industrial education served the state through bettering its position in international competition. America's problems were different; the country needed to keep its children in school, to develop industrial intelligence, not mere trade efficiency. In any case, the trades for which American vocational education was preparing the youth were those very trades, the skilled ones, where training was least needed, where strong unions could always recruit members. Americans should be worrying rather about the displacement of workers by machinery, Dewey warned, and on this issue the vocational schools seemed to have little to offer.

Dewey's remarks in the *New Republic* did not go unanswered for long, for a few months later David Snedden, Commissioner for Vocational Education in Massachusetts, wrote a rejoinder.[36] There was both irony and logic in the fact that Snedden, a sometime professor at Teachers College himself, was also an interpreter of Dewey's thought. How, cried Snedden, could John Dewey, of all people, have joined the opponents of a broader curriculum? Vocational education, he continued, was simply the traditional procedure of education for work; there had been continuous progress in educating youth for medicine and law, and there could be no reason why education for industry should not be of the same quality. It was "incredible" to Snedden that anyone with an awareness of modern economic conditions could suggest that industrial education would benefit employers alone.

Dewey rebutted immediately: "I object to regarding as vocational education any training which does not have as its supreme regard the development of such intelligent initiative, ingenuity and executive capacity as shall make workers, as far as may be, the masters of their own individual fate." And trade schools and faulty industrial education programs did all they could to defeat this end: "The kind of vocational education in which I am interested is not one which will 'adapt' workers to the existing industrial regime; I am not sufficiently in love with the regime for that."[37] Rather, one should work for a system of vocational education which would gradually "alter" and "ultimately transform" the existing industrial system.

Craft and Social Conscience. There were two aspects of Dewey's thought which led to his suspicion of trade training and his rejection of separate vocational schools. For one thing the artisan-artist image was basic to his thinking, and closely related to this was his ambivalent attitude toward industry and industrial efficiency. Although Dewey argued that industry had been the "chief factor" in the development of modern democracy, he felt that industry had a distinctly destructive tendency: "To counter the soulless monotony of machine industry, a premium must be put upon initiative, intellectual independence, and inventiveness . . . . The imagination must be so stored that in the inevitable monotonous stretches of work, it may have worthy material of art and literature and science upon which to feed, instead of being frittered away upon undisciplined dreamings and sensual fantasies."[38] Dewey warned Americans not to move so quickly in their technological progress that workers could not adapt themselves, yet at the same time he noted the need for workers to have great "self-command." The goal was a rewarding place for all in the working world, where "good workmanship" would be pursued for "public ends."

Dewey's effort to reconcile the philanthropic ideal of the honest workman with the ideal of mobility, the ideal of mobility with that of industrial efficiency, and the notion of industrial efficiency with that of democracy, was indicative of the struggle through which socially-conscious progressives were going. Beginning with the renaissance of social reform in the 1880's, partisans of equality and democracy had taken a new interest in the question of industry; proponents of various socialist doctrines were looking to new industrial forms; and religious leaders, imbued with the "social gospel," were bending their attention to the working classes. The developing American universities and their new social-science departments also were opening many doors for social reform.[39] The Midwest in particular was the setting for such academic innovation; Lester Ward's theories were taken up by Albion Small, who headed the pioneer Chicago department of sociology; Richard Ely and John Commons at Wisconsin set the sights of economics toward social betterment. Wisconsin-trained Frank Tracy Carlton reflected the concern which some social scientists felt toward industrial trends, especially the increasing division of labor.

Contemporary America, Carlton suggested, needed an education that not merely served but improved the industrial order. Education was now in a "factory stage," with students turned out by the educational machinery to fit predetermined roles in the factory system. This, however, was neither economically nor psychologically sound: "as students are dissimilar units and must fill dissimilar roles in the economy of the world, artistic, rather than interchangeable, products should constitute the true output of the school."[40] The school needed to become a "studio, rather than a factory."

Although Carlton called on the artisan imagery, he explicitly rejected traditional craftsmanship as unsuited to modern society. Given the modern division of labor, it was necessary to find the appropriate specialty for each worker; education properly was "an organized attempt to put the right man in the right place." Indeed, Carlton came perilously close to Hugo Münsterberg's position—proper placement leads to individual satisfaction and social efficiency. Yet he also saw education as part of the gradual realization of cooperative society. He lauded the kindergarten (a favorite of many socialists), stressed the importance of manual training for self-expression and culture, and refrained from attacking the trade schools on the grounds that, though narrow now, they were gradually expanding their curricula; broad technical education would be vital to an improved society.

More militant socialists were impatient with the kind of gradualism which Carlton espoused. Education, they claimed, would always be a product of those classes which ran the educational machinery, and education would, therefore, be suited to the needs of the rulers rather than the governed.[41] Edward Bellamy, in his socialist scheme, rejected trade education as the product of an insidious industrial system: "If every boy learned a trade, none of them would be better off, because under the present industrial system there is always and necessarily a large margin of unemployed."[42] If a man were unemployed, it didn't matter whether he were skilled or unskilled; in fact, if more people were skilled, the greater would be the chance that skilled or no, men would be unemployed. Again, if workers in the United States were trained, they might have an advantage against the rest of the world, but workers elsewhere would be still more miserable. Under nationalism, Bellamy concluded, the nation would test youth, to find out for what work each was really suited, and the public ownership of industry would guarantee that work would be available.

The contradictions into which Bellamy's argument led were resolved by neither the more sophisticated and orthodox socialists, nor the social gospelers who often admired Bellamy's nationalism. C. Hanford Henderson, for example, found little room for trade education in that hoped-for "Kingdom of Heaven on Earth." For Henderson, contemporary industrial education was only a final step in industry's conquest of the "human spirit." To reverse this trend, it would be necessary to reincorporate the humanizing aspects of education, the cultivation of those feelings for which industrial efficiency had no use. Yet Henderson was not willing to dispense with trade training altogether. He insisted that children ought not be given such education too early, but that ". . . no system of Education can be socially complete or acceptable unless at the proper time it *is* vocational and unless in the end it *does* produce efficient labor power."[43]

If Henderson wished to have the prosperity on which his kingdom on earth was to rest, he had to provide for a modicum of efficiency. As Taylor's scientific management sacrificed a little education when it began to conflict with efficiency, Henderson sacrificed a little efficiency in his Educational Industry scheme. Indeed, what he proposed was a utopia very close to that of the American Fourierists, in which the curriculum of work would be a curriculum of education, in which vocations would be rotated to avoid monotony. In the end, Henderson sounded like an earlier utopian, bringing to mind the philanthropic aspects of such conservative socialist thought. Democracy and cooperation, said Henderson, were really aristocratic creeds; they stressed the love of the finer things, of opportunity combined with self-discipline: "Democracy is too often thought of as a social ideal of a less excellent sort; a shirt-sleeves, standardless world of uncouth speech, loutish manners, unbeautiful dress. . . . But happily Democracy does not mean this or anything like it. It is not the open door *into* this sort of thing,—it is the open door *out* of it."[44]

Some Business Ventures in Education

For the businessman, the problem of industrial efficiency was a no less perplexing one. His dilemma was much like that of the professional engineer: success routes were changing; the boy who could once use the office or factory as an educational setting now, it seemed, had to turn to formal modes of education. Turning to such alternate routes disturbed the continuity of the success route; the "gap" between worker and manager increased; and the new set of industrial conditions necessitated new notions of education for both kinds of men.

The self-image which late nineteenth- and early twentieth-century businessmen were developing was important to the education they envisioned for themselves. As Taylor's influence grew, the literature on management concerned itself with division of labor among managers: between the businessman and the engineer, for example.[45] Some texts stressed the need for financial insight and understanding, but there was also a great concern that the "human element" be understood. The ideal business leader might be pictured as anything from benevolent dictator to charismatic figure, but in all cases he was seen as both strong and dignified. Ruggedness might have done well for the self-made man, but the new situation called for less coarseness and demanded more princeliness. The businessman, then, needed a princely education, one of breadth and cultivation.

Edmund J. James, of the Wharton School of Finance and Commerce, developed just such an educational ideal in his reports to the American Bankers Association in the 1890's. In the first of these reports he pointed out that boys who wished a higher education before entering business had few ways to turn, and usually chose the collegiate literary course or a business or commercial college. These so-called business colleges were fine, but they were really schools for training clerks: ". . . they do not touch the essence of successful business management or tend to develop the higher sides of business activity; they bear little relation to those broader views characteristic of the business manager as distinct from the business clerk and are of course next to useless as a means of liberal education."[46] The literary course had produced successful businessmen, James granted, but it had often subtly wooed the would-be businessman away from his original goal, changing his tastes and ambitions.

James continued his report by recommending a special curriculum, combining the "liberal and practical," which would train the cultivated and public-minded business leadership the nation required. Self-made men may have developed the virtues of cultivation and public spirit, but they (and he clearly had in mind that many members of his audience were self-made men) didn't want their sons to have to go through the struggles that they had had. It was necessary to find a way to give these youths the "right sort of higher education," "the right spirit" with which to take up the job of managing. Many of these boys would have to guard and improve fortunes already acquired, and only the right education could prevent the old American adage—"from shirtsleeves to shirtsleeves in three generations"—from being fulfilled.

James also noted the need for commercial high school courses to replace inadequate private business colleges. If business education at the college level were reformed, colleges could then help to develop business courses in the secondary schools. Secondary commercial education and higher business education, James thought, should both be geared to mobility. In this respect, his ideal for commercial education had much in common with the earlier manual-training ideal and, especially, the industrial-arts ideal of progressive educators. Note how close James's prescription comes to Dewey's concept of industrial education: "It [commercial education] would include a view of the rise, development, and present condition of the great branches of human industry. It would consider not only the actual facts of industrial life, but also their relations and the reason for their existence, thus rising from the level of a more empirical observation of phenomena to a philosophic and scientific study of their connection."[47]

This plan was far ahead of contemporary high school courses. In 1892, the NEA began a Department of Business Education, but commercial education was still mostly concerned with such things as penmanship and accounting. Yet the broader ideal slowly penetrated the discussions until, by the beginning of the century, supporters of commercial education were suggesting a program that would parallel industrial education. In some discussions, the parallel between secondary commercial education and a manual-training course was made explicit, and the general education aspects of manual training attributed to commercial education as well.[48] Yet the relation between secondary and higher education which James suggested failed in precisely the same way that Woodward's manual-training scheme had failed. Businessmen, like engineers, did not want a secondary school training designed solely for mobility; they looked to the secondary schools for a corps of trained commercial people who could fill the lower positions in business.

As a result, commercial education, as it was systematized, stressed the limits of both vertical and horizontal mobility. Terminal education was needed for commercial students, and such education should be entirely distinct from industrial education. In 1890, Andrew Carnegie had written about the informal education needed for commercial and mechanical roads to business success. In 1907, the Hart Schaffner and Marx Company awarded their essay prize to a treatise on industrial education which outlined two distinct educational routes for commerce and technology; each route had a series of terminal points from which one could move upward with only the greatest difficulty.[49] Such ideal divisions and hierarchies did much to shape the educational goals of large businesses, where the subtle differentiation of jobs was becoming important.

The Corporation Educators. With the growth in business size and capital investment after the Civil War, larger concerns began to consider more formal training for their own workers: in 1875, the R. Hoe Publishing Company established the first corporation school in the United States; ventures like the Baltimore and Ohio training program of the 1880's were tried by many companies. By 1905, the interest in training employees began to mount, and in 1913, a group of companies which had or were interested in establishing corporation schools was formed. The roster of members of the National Association of Corporation Schools was impressive: American Locomotive, American Telephone and Telegraph, Brighton Mills, Brooklyn Union Gas, Burroughs Adding Machine, Cadillac Motor Car, Carnegie Steel, Commonwealth Edison—and so forth.

These NACS members had many interests in education; they were concerned with selling, with office work, and with manufacturing skills. With regard to manufacturing, the programs fell into three categories.[50] Special training programs focused mainly on college graduates and the most skilled technical workers, priming them for managerial positions. The techniques for such training varied—sometimes including instruction in theory, sometimes quasi-apprenticeship under foremen, sometimes study in a cooperating school—but always the programs stressed a broad view of the work. Second, manufacturing firms developed courses for unskilled workers, programs aimed at their Americanization rather than the direct upgrading of their skills; they argued that non-English speaking unskilled workers were a menace, first to production and later to national security, and that companies themselves needed to remedy the situation. Third (and most important for our discussion) companies established trade apprenticeship programs. It was common for the company to provide the mechanical training involved in the specific job, while the apprentice attended either special company classes or classes in a cooperating public school, where he studied basic subjects related to his work and continued his general education.

The Lakeside Press in Chicago, for instance, had an apprentice school which took boys at fourteen years of age. The first two years were divided between academic work (one and three-quarter hours a day) and shop lessons. At sixteen the youth became a regular apprentice in the factory itself, where his learning would also be productive for the company. It was the Press's Thomas E. Donnelley who argued before the NACS for private rather than public-school industrial education. The latter, he said, was only a "dream of the schoolmaster and the professional or dilettante social reformer."[51] The American school system, unlike that of Germany, was "democratic" and therefore "politics ridden," subject to pressure from groups such as organized labor; it was better for corporations to run their own schools, which they could tailor to the real needs of industry.

The response of NACS members to Donnelley's speech was revealing. For some, the separate teaching shops of the Lakeside system seemed a fine way to separate learners from jealous journeymen; for others, discounting the importance of public schools was a mistake, since they could contribute not only supplementary education but vocational guidance. Indeed, the NACS managers and corporation-school educators found themselves wrestling with the same problem that had faced other industrial educators: was industrial education to be offered in a quasi-classroom setting, a normal factory setting, a general school setting? And given one or another of these choices, how was it to relate to general education?

NACS educators also had to face the question of mobility, as General Electric's experience in training college graduates[52] indicates. Charles P. Steinmetz, in discussing this, explained that they spent a year in the laboratory, followed by either the company's commercial or engineering course. There was no point in giving them shop classes, Steinmetz argued, whether they specialized in design, laboratory work, research, or general engineering, for many of them had had shop experience. The non-college men who were taken into these programs were generally "not on equal terms" with the graduates, for they lacked basic course work; and the same was true with less skilled workers from the company's own shops. Thus it was difficult to create a continuous ladder for engineering education within the company. If the company wanted to promote the able few, it would have to supply the general and scientific education which these workers lacked, and those left behind would feel that their training was incomplete, would feel resentment toward the system.

The NACS members differed over Steinmetz's statement on

promotion and education from the ranks, but all seemed to agree that something must be done with the less skilled workers. Since the NACS represented giant industries, the members were particularly aware of the nation's vast pool of unskilled labor, the immigrants, and the growing number of Negro workers. To make these workers efficient, it was felt, a basic education—literacy at the very least—was needed. Some workers would also profit from industrial education; but the relation between general and industrial education still had to be decided, along with the proper setting for each.

Most corporation educators agreed that, if the public schools would provide a solid (and industrially oriented) fundamental education, with adequate vocational guidance, the industries themselves could supply the job training. There was some doubt, however, that public schools would provide even these minimum services to industry. Members of the NACS committee on public education noted the mutual distrust between businessmen and "schoolmen," and some urged that businessmen might improve the situation by becoming more active in their local school boards. But other corporation educators seemed to have given up the hope that the public schools would educate a satisfactory working force. A number of the large firms were already running what were virtually elementary schools, with courses in English, citizenship, mathematics, and science among the most popular. One NACS member even remarked that by offering lectures to all employees, rather than the apprentices only, jealousy of apprentices diminished, for all were members of a learning community.[53]

When the corporation school people spoke of basic education, they meant not only language and mathematics, but an entire educational outlook which they felt the public schools should be giving. As an ideal, at least, they were prepared to offer a curriculum broad enough to insure both "vocational efficiency" and "an insight into the social and moral needs of community life, cooperative action and civic responsibility."[54] Clearly, the NACS members used much progressive rhetoric in their discussion of education as well as in their general approach to employees. They gave serious consideration to welfare questions, matters of health, of working conditions, of recreation and culture. When the question of labor trouble came up (and it rarely did), their answer was typically progressive—understanding, and cooperation were needed.

The corporation schools were far from simplistic in their attitudes toward education, but they had one rather astounding blind spot; until 1917, when the Smith-Hughes bill was passed, they hardly mentioned federal aid to vocational schools. Of course, given their attitude toward public education and the fact that they weren't likely to receive any aid, it is hardly surprising that the NACS did not go to battle for the Smith-Hughes bill. What is surprising is that the organization didn't discuss the considerable impact which large-scale federal aid to vocational education would have on the corporation programs. Members sometimes admitted that the corporation school idea wasn't catching on as quickly as they had hoped, yet the general feeling was that federal legislation would not make much difference. Even after the Smith-Hughes Act was passed, the NACS was sanguine: the legislation would give them better trained boys, but not competition for the corporation schools.[55] In their consideration of education, as well as other matters, their discussions were smooth, almost gentle; there was rarely any strong dispute on matters of education, and little strong criticism directed at anyone during such discussions. Occasionally the philanthropic tone had a tinge of righteous indignation, but not anger.

Smaller Businesses and the Public Schools. By the 1890's, small businessmen had begun to see themselves as a group with interests distinct from those of the ever-growing holding companies and trusts. Whether opportunities actually diminished in the age of the trusts is a matter of question, for business as a whole had been increasing since the Civil War, small business as

well as large. Yet contact between the smaller and larger concerns was limited; the National Association of Manufacturers was
composed of medium-sized businesses which were inclined to go
their own way.[56] They were angry: angry with their own dis-
senting members and angry with other sectors of the economy,
with labor and with big business.

This was not the case in the NAM's early years. In the 1890's,
an atmosphere of relative geniality pervaded employers' organizations. The trade agreement seemed to offer a solution to industrial conflict, and the NAM could devote itself to questions
of tariff rates and foreign trade. By the turn of the century, however, the peaceful solution was coming into question. Unions
were being accused of bad faith in the agreements, and a new
crop of employers' groups, distinctly belligerent, were being organized. Many NAM members shared this belligerent attitude
and found a spokesman in their president, David M. Parry.

In his 1903 "Annual Address of the President," Parry lashed
out at the unions, claiming that no group could change the harsh
realities of economic life and that the unions were injuring the
economy, the growth of which provided the only hope of alle-
viating poverty.[57] Against the wishes of some of his members,
Parry recommended a new organization, specifically geared to
fight the unions. The fight between the conciliatory group, with
their faith in intelligent labor and rational management, and the
belligerent group, with their own version of class warfare, was
short; the NAM formed a committee, out of which the anti-union
Citizen's Industrial Association was to come, and threw their
weight behind the open shop movement. If the NAM were preparing for war, one of the biggest weapons in their arsenal would
be trade education.

The early NAM had paid some attention to the question of
commercial education, since the group's original interest was in
the promotion of trade. In his 1903 report, Parry alluded to the
importance of training in languages, financial methods, and the
details of transportation, and he also urged that the NAM sup-

port expanded technical education. In the following year, the first report of the NAM's Committee on Industrial Education was given. Committee chairman Anthony Ittner, an all out supporter of Parry, charged that the trade unions had made apprenticeship "obsolete," that hostility had replaced the cordial master-worker relationship, that entrance to the union was limited, and that foreign dominated unions not only kept American boys out, but even kept a father from teaching his son a trade. The solution, Ittner concluded, was the establishment of trade schools—not polytechnical schools, not manual training schools, but "trade schools, pure and simple."

To this prescription he added the familiar mobility theme: the young man who had to go to work "should be encouraged to study the common school subjects at a night school and to acquire a knowledge of bookkeeping and other business branches at a commercial college at the same time he is learning to be a skilled mechanic at a trade school. Thus equipped he will be better able to battle with the world and to forge his way to the front than were at first a large proportion of successful business-men of the present day. . . ."[58] The fact that Ittner omitted the element so important to most proponents of mobility—a flexible general education to prepare the student for a changing environment—was pointed up by his lack of great interest in the teaching of "principles."

Ittner, like many others, was groping with both the ideals of the honest workman and of mobility for the workman. His reports combine references to "honorable employment," the "honorable citizen," the development of "manhood," and the need for physical and mental fitness for "the battle of life." The goal, said Ittner, was to ". . . train the free-born American boy to the end that he may have a fair field and an open path, to work onward as a free American citizen. . . . Do our duty to the boys, and from them will come the high-class mechanical men we are looking for."[59] Here, of course, was the rub. If the "free-born American boy" got going, was he going to stop with being a "high-class" mechanic?

A 1907 article in the NAM's periodical clearly reflects this dilemma. "The Dearth of First-Class Mechanics" describes a retired workingman "of the old school," who was meant to be a model for the modern workingman. This old gentleman was raised on a farm and took up shopwork in his youth:

He first became a blacksmith's assistant. . . . In three months he had mastered the secrets of the craft. . . . Before half a year has passed, my friend—we will call him Smith—was satisfied that it would be a waste of time to continue at the anvil, and he started again as an apprentice in the molding room. Slowly he worked up from the drudgery of this department until the intricate mysteries of sand cores and cooling metal were his, and then he again started at the bottom, this time in the pattern shop. Such was his proficiency that the foreman offered him an increase to three dollars a day. The amount tempted the farmer boy, but he firmly declined, and the following week found him in the machine shop, with an initial wage of seventy-five cents a day.[60]

At every stage the worker improved himself, adding the finer points of machine work, drawing, and a host of other skills to his background, making himself the very antithesis of a machine "hand." His integrity of workmanship became so complete, his understanding of processes so comprehensive that he could have stepped into the shoes of a top executive without blinking an eye. Yet he did not become an executive. Indeed, the NAM writer stressed, this fine old gentleman became a consummate workman because he *had* resisted the temptation to become a supervisor, to specialize in one phase of the work and rise through it.

The NAM was also concerned about the timing of training: that the mechanic's career should not begin too early, nor be postponed too long. The 1912 report of the Industrial Education Committee emphasized the importance of an elementary education, including pre-vocational and manual training, to introduce the child to "real things" and prepare him for leadership. At the present time, the Committee noted, there was no point to remaining in school after the age of fourteen, for the high schools did nothing but train wretched little clerks. However, youths who went directly into industry needed to continue their education, so that they would not end up in "blind alley" jobs: "We all love the little newsboys, busy, efficient, honest little businessmen. We have little realized that their earlier efficiencies offer no hope of later success but the reverse."[61]

Soon after they had rejected both regular public schooling and self-acquired education, however, the NAM members discovered the Munich educator Georg Kerschensteiner and his continuation-schooling work. The businessmen carefully picked out those elements of the German system which appealed to them most—cooperation between manufacturers and educators, the combining of trade and general education—and became far more enthusiastic about this divided scheme than they were about the full-time trade school. The trade schools were expensive and ineffective, according to H. E. Miles, who took over the chairmanship of the Industrial Education Committee. They had been in existence for more than thirty years, yet only a handful had been established, and they were "not reaching the millions and millions of children who become our mechanics, our common working people. . . ."[62] Miles and his Committee especially admired a system of industrial continuation-schools which Wisconsin had developed, schools separate from the general high schools. In this way Wisconsin provided for those who never reached high school, and kept them off the streets and away from the paths of juvenile delinquency. Those who did reach high school could also avail themselves of the continuation-school facilities, so that additional trade-school programs would not be needed. All students would remain in school longer under this system, and more would have the opportunity to rise to higher positions, take advanced commercial and trade training.

Indeed, as had Ittner, the NAM Committee still envisioned a combination of common school, continuation school, and perhaps commercial and trade courses, to shape a new kind of self-made man, superior to the man trained in the standard course of public education: "Sixty-five per cent of the men in the technical and managerial positions, in the foremost industries of Germany, came from lowly places through the continuation schools and higher secondary school as here indicated. As a rule the men of the strictly professional all-day technical and engineering schools are serving under and not over the self-made men who were helped in connection with their work by the continuation and special schools."[63]

The remaining question for the NAM was how to finance such elaborate programs when small communities might not be able to carry the load. State or federal aid was one obvious solution which the National Society for the Promotion of Industrial Education was already exploring, and with some reluctance, the NAM joined this growing group. The reluctance stemmed from the fact that the NSPIE included representatives of organized labor, which the NAM feared would dominate the movement. Yet the businessmen were more or less forced to accept the presence of labor men in industrial education groups. Labor was not going to stand idly by while the NAM planned a public trade-school system, and the businessmen of the NAM, unlike the giant firms of the National Association of Corporation Schools, could not afford to establish separate school systems of their own. So the manufacturers made a limited truce with labor; the federal government would establish a board on which both groups were represented. (Other interests, such as agriculture, too, would be represented, but these did not so much concern the business leaders.) Vocational boards would also be established on the state level, so that everywhere business could have a voice and maintain a vigilant guard against the encroachments of its arch enemy.

Industrial Education and Organized Labor

When the NAM mounted its industrial education offensive, organized labor, particularly the craft unions, was put in a difficult
position. The NAM had taken up industrial education with the
two-fold purpose of educating skilled workmen and combatting
the trade unions. The American Federation of Labor was as devoted to the skilled-workman image as the manufacturers, but
the AF of L had committed itself to fight for the skilled worker
on an economic level and had its reservations about education
as a path to social reform. The NAM's anti-union interpretation
of industrial education made it even more difficult for the craft
unions to develop an industrial education ideal of their own.

Labor's early educational goals, formulated in the Jacksonian
era, had remained important as long as labor considered social
reform of first importance; elevating the honest workman, ultimately establishing a cooperative society in which the meaning
of labor would be changed, were themes which had continually
played through the National Labor Union of the 1860's, the
Knights of Labor in the seventies and eighties, and the writings
of socialist dissenters and academic partisans of labor, who still
looked to educational means for social change.[64] Yet when the
craft unions were organized, they had struggled to shed their
utopian brethren, and the advent of the "bread and butter" ideal
had meant the end of much of the union movement's educational
ideology.

The irony of the AF of L's position, then, was that their new
conservatism, which enabled them to participate as labor spokesmen on matters of industrial education, had been made possible
only by the gradual elimination of the very element within organized labor which had a well developed educational philosophy.
In harmony with the Federation's new approach, Samuel Gompers joined the National Civic Federation, and he and United
Mine Worker president John Mitchell sat down with its business
tycoons, men like Marcus Hanna, to ponder the solution of such

national problems as that of industrial peace.[65] Although voluntary conciliation soon became a less fruitful approach, Gompers kept his affiliation with progressive organizations, and, in 1907, joined the new National Society for the Promotion of Industrial Education. Here again, business and labor would sit at the same table with educators and social reformers to develop a national program beneficial to all groups. Gompers' own ideas on education, however, were far less carefully articulated than those of many NSPIE members, and hardly of a pioneering variety. In his autobiography, where Gompers painted a portrait of his years as a cigar maker, the early nineteenth century themes in his educational perspective become apparent. The cigar workers, said Gompers, would talk as they worked, sometimes discussing articles which were read out loud. The discussions were stimulating: "While working in the shop, if any thought came to me as a result of reading or any current of thought, I would stop and make a memorandum on slips of paper which I kept for this purpose."[66] Although Gompers' account is remarkably like William Ellery Channing's ideal worker, the man who mused on Plato while he toiled at the bench, Gompers of course was musing on neither Plato nor the principles of cigar-making science, but, like the literate and articulate German immigrants with whom he worked, on socialism and the questions of labor's future.

Gompers' image of himself as a worker was not purely political, however, despite the fact that the shop furnished him and many others the opportunity for an informal political and economic education. He loved, he said, the work and good workmanship. Nor was he opposed to broader learning: "For me, as for many another boy of New York City, Cooper Union was a university that gave me access to stores of information and an opportunity to know something in the realm of science. I found many extension courses in the discipline of life."[67] Yet one suspects that if he had had to choose between education through labor fellowship and education through outside educational institutions he would have chosen the former. For him, the trade union had an educational function; it made its members aware of the social issues in which they were intimately involved; indeed, education was a necessary function of trade unions, since they were voluntary, and it would be impossible for them to reach their ends except through the education of their members.

Gompers was at first suspicious of the trade schools and noted that union men in general were opposed to such schools, although they were not able to give "technical reasons" to back up their opinion. Gompers complained about "botched workers," not scabs, though that was clearly on his mind. Perhaps it was this distrust, and an essentially older conception of industrial education, that kept him from adopting much of the trade-school rhetoric. For despite his willingness to work in the NSPIE with advocates of trade schools, Gompers' own educational goals had much in common with those of trade school critics: "Give to the masses of the people, those who perform the mechanical work, which is of its very nature monotonous and may became also stultifying, an imaginative understanding and such a wide comprehension of the wholeness of life that no vocation need be to them a rut. Enable such to see up and beyond with a vivifying grasp that shall interpret labor in values of human service, and to do the day's work with the joy of creative labor."[68]

The AF of L still had to cope with the trade education problem and in 1903, the same year that the NAM inaugurated its fight against the unions and chose trade schools as a weapon, the labor organization resolved to pay closer attention to workmanship and the apprentice system. Some members felt that a national policy on industrial education should be formulated, but the organization's education committee decided against such recommendations because of "the diversity of conditions and differences in skill required." The committee could only suggest that individual unions consider instruction in the "higher branches of the respective trades," the improvement of working efficiency, and adapting the apprenticeship system to encourage youths to find work for which they were fit. At the same time, the education committee censured the public schools for their bias against labor, for their neglect of the dignity of labor, and for forwarding "the shameful doctrine that the wage-earners should be content with their lot, because of the opportunity that may be afforded a few of their number rising out of their class. . . ."[69]

The AF of L was far more at home in the question of common schooling than that of industrial education. Indeed, as the education committee report reflected, national labor unions had long talked of unified requirements for apprenticeship, but efforts to standardize qualifications had inevitably fallen back on the individual unions.[70] These had made their own attempts at educational solutions, but, though the AF of L was to point with pride to these individual ventures, the local groups also faced problems. The long struggle of the New York Local of the International Typographers Union to initiate an education program is illuminating in this respect.

During the 1880's, the New York printers began to face a radical mechanization of their trade. At first it was not entirely clear that the machines would work, but with the introduction of Linotype in 1890, a committee of the ITU local recommended that the union acquire keyboards so that printers could learn the new skill. All during the nineties the printers played with the idea of an industrial education program, of beginning their own school. One Linotype company made several offers of machines for practice, with the sole stipulation that the printers not do work in competition with the company's customers. The Linotype company was not anti-union, in fact preferred that the union men conduct a program, but the union still hesitated. In 1900 they sent still another committee to investigate the possibility of setting up a school and decided against "this heavy expenditure":

It seems impracticable to establish a free school for the reason that perhaps not more than 100 men could be taught properly in a given year, and the selection of those to be given first opportunity is not a pleasant matter to anticipate in itself, while on the other hand a great number of our members quite likely would be opposed to paying $2,300 each year until all our members became efficient operators. Nor does your committee deem it wise to recommend that the union establish a school and charge tuition, for in such a venture there is a considerable amount of risk and responsibility.[71]

The New York local took no further step toward classroom industrial education and continued to concentrate its energies on apprenticeship. Other printing locals, however, had started their own programs, and by 1907, the International established a correspondence course. Significantly, this course was advertised as an antidote to specialization, an opportunity for compositors to learn "the principles of display and decorative typography." On the national level the course was a great success; almost 2500 journeymen and apprentices enrolled. But the New York local's own committee reported apathy among its membership. The committee could only urge the importance of such studies for the well-rounded worker, as well as for union strength based on the "esprit de corps" of a "scientifically educated body of craftsmen."

The unions were in a complex bind. The logic of their bread-and-butter program led to the concept of a trade education which would preserve jobs and strengthen craft unity. Individual unions could as ill afford such programs as the individual members of the NAM, yet a general suspicion of the public schools and of the employer's role in making school policy prevented the unions from turning in that direction. The same bread-and-butter approach gave the older honest-workman concept a limited appeal, despite its long history in the labor movement. Indeed, the NAM and the formation of the National Society for Promotion of Industrial Education seemed to have forced the craft unions into a national policy for which they were ideologically unprepared.

When Gompers joined the NSPIE in 1907, discussion of industrial education in the AF of L conventions began in earnest. One convention resolution, though noting the workers' traditional fear that trade schools would turn out strikebreakers and half-trained working men, still expressed willingness to endorse ". . . any policy, or any society or association having for its object the raising of the standard of Industrial Education and the teaching of the higher technique of our various industries."[72] In the same year, the AF of L Committee on Education reported itself "in favor of the best opportunities for the most complete industrial and technical education obtainable for prospective applicants for admission into the skilled crafts of this country, particularly as regards the full possibilities of such crafts, to the end that such applicants be fitted not only for all usual requirements, but also for the highest supervisory duties, responsibilities and rewards. . ."[73]

As opposed to the 1903 report, in which social mobility for individuals had been looked on with suspicion, the educational committee of 1907 incorporated equal opportunity for mobility into its industrial education aims. In this, the AF of L saw itself joining the progressive advocates of industrial education in opposition to those anti-union forces who sought to train men for one skill alone, to bind them to closer dependence on the employer. And Gompers' 1909 statement on industrial education linked it closer with labor's fight for democratic schooling: "Industrial education, the raising of the age limit of child workers, and compulsory school attendance are necessarily a part of our great beneficial scheme. Organized labor has always stood for, aye, has been the pioneer in, the demand for free schools, free text books, compulsory education in the elementary grades and for the fullest and freest opportunity in all lines of learning, technology included."[74]

In the same year, the union's Committee on Industrial Education, headed by John Mitchell, reported the results of its lengthy study. The gist of the report was that every effort should be made to keep children in school until sixteen years of age, so that they might develop more fully and be given the kind of training that "will help them to advance after they are in industry." The report stressed the necessity of keeping industrial education under public control and recognizing the limitations of classroom industrial education. The Committee recommended, first, the support of supplemental training programs, presenting ". . . those principles of arts and sciences which bear upon the trades and industries, either directly or indirectly. . . ."[75] Unions, the report suggested, should continue and improve their own supplemental programs, such as the one sponsored by the typographer's union. Second, the AF of L was urged to support separate "Technical Industrial Education" schools, for youths from fourteen to sixteen years of age, where they could be taught "the principles of the trades." The programs, the report explained, should be broad, including English, mathematics, physics, chemistry, elementary mechanics, and drawing; and shop instruction should be offered for given trades, with the drawing, mathematics, and sciences applicable to those trades included. In addition, each student should study the history of his own trade, with special emphasis on "the philosophy of collective bargaining." Lastly, the public should establish and support advisory boards for vocational education, which would include representatives of both labor and business.

During the next few years the AF of L watched the progress of federal legislation closely, and reported its own efforts to achieve a satisfactory act; the NAM was merely talking, said the labor group, while the AF of L was making industrial education a reality. But even while legislation was taking form, the labor organization continued to grope for its own concept of trade education. Like the NAM, the AF of L believed in versatility and mobility at the same time, contending that the all-round workman had the greatest potentiality for resisting the tether of specialization. Yet the unionists rejected manual training—the system especially geared to general skills and the opportunity for advancement. For years and years, said one AF of L member, we asked the schools for industrial education and they gave us, instead, manual training; we need an education which combines theory and practice.[76]

In 1915 the AF of L was still exploring and refining its position —a position still flexible enough to be interwoven with a Dewey-like critique of the proposed dual vocational system.* The report of the Committee on Education for that year took business to task for trying to establish separate industrial education schools in order to serve their own interests, rather than the interests of the children: "We hold the child must be educated not only to adapt itself to his or her particular calling they are to enter later in life, but they should be educated for leadership as well; that they should have the power of self-direction and of directing others; the powers of administration as well as the ability to assume positions of responsibility."[77]

The rhetoric of mobility here was more marked than was usual in the organization's documents on education, enough so to be puzzling. Was it opportunity within the labor movement itself, the rapidly developing career-paths of "business unionism," which lay behind such educational demands? If so, the AF of L spokesmen were not ready to develop this rationale fully. In any case, they had joined the industrial-education debate with a strong traditional faith in public education and a considerable fear of business-dominated trade schools. Although this public-education ideology was not a sufficient base on which to construct a trade-training philosophy, they did not have time to ponder first and act later. They joined the divergent forces pressing for federal action, even while they explored the rhetoric of trade education. As one delegate of the AF of L remarked, "We cannot stop the trend in the direction of this kind of education in

---

* The 1915 report is so different from others that one wonders whether internal differences in the AF of L are involved. The earlier industrial-education committees were headed by John Mitchell; although he was missing from the 1915 committee, other staunch Gompers supporters were members.

the school; but we can, if we cooperate with the educators, have it come our way."[78]

National Interest and a National System of Industrial Education

During the Progressive era, the Bureau of Labor published two massive reports on industrial education which illustrate not only the increase in the number of the industrial education programs, but how ideas about industrial education were changing.[79] The 1892 report had stressed manual training in colleges, in private and public schools; technical schools and European-style trade schools were also discussed, and a few American ventures were listed—the New York Trade School, the Pratt Institute, the R. Hoe Printing Company's corporation school, and Philadelphia's Industrial Art School, which the report notes was unique for receiving a state subsidy. Finally, it listed a melange of mechanics' institutes, specialty schools, design schools, etc., which were said to resemble European trade schools.

The 1910 report displayed more sureness in the face of the diverse industrial-education institutions, and showed two changes from 1892: manual training had become less important, and trade education—private, philanthropic, and especially public— was growing at a great pace and taking a wide variey of forms.

Government participation was the new and vital element in industrial education, and was pioneered, not surprisingly, by the state government of Massachusetts. Having already introduced drawing and manual training in the public schools, the state moved one step further by establishing the famous Douglass Commission of 1906 to look into an even broader industrial education program. The Douglass Commission report marked the beginning of vocational education legislation, and, in a more subtle sense, it marked a summation of the industrial education debate. It added little new to the discussion, but picked up many of the diverse themes of the last century. Pleas of a philanthropic nature were interwoven with remarks on the need for skilled labor; appeals for "industrial intelligence" based on "principles" were combined with calls for more democratic education and a new interpretation of work in social terms.[80] The Commission recommended the introduction into the elementary schools of industrial "instruction and practice" consistent with both cultural and industrial standards. It recommended that high schools offer mathematics and science courses related to local industry, and that separate industrial schools be established for working youths over fourteen. Lastly, the report proposed a state commission to oversee industrial schools, to relate the separate industrial-school system to the public schools and at the same time give it a continuity of its own.

The Massachusetts Commission of the following year turned out a quite different kind of report.[81] It subtly avoided the philanthropic and mobility-oriented aspects of the previous report and launched a fairly direct appeal for trade training, discussing the questions of time and place for such training. Each of the Massachusetts reports, however, reveals an important point; the first, that a broad industrial education movement was bound to call on many of the ideologies which had been developing for the past century; the second, that among these, the trade school ideal was dominant, and undoubtedly would be the major factor in shaping legislation.

The same approach was characteristic of the National Society for the Promotion of Industrial Education when it was formed. The work of the Massachusetts Commission had indicated the growing feeling that industrial education needed governmental support, and the NSPIE was organized with just this purpose in mind. Strictly speaking, the National Society for the Promotion of Industrial Education was primarily an eastern rather than a national group, but this was natural, since industry and the interest in industrial education had grown earliest and most rapidly in the East. The co-initiators of the NSPIE were also eastern men. Charles R. Richards had been trained at the Massachusetts Institute of Technology and had become a teacher of manual training at Columbia. James P. Haney was, in 1906, the director of art and manual training for the New York City school system. In June of that year, the two men called a meeting of interested business-men and educators, and within a few months the larger organi-zation was formed; representatives assembled from the South and Mid-West as well as the Northeast, and baptized their new So-ciety with Theodore Roosevelt's blessing.

The membership of the group was as diverse as was industrial education itself in the first decade of the century. The first board of the Society included Milton Higgins, the Worcester manufac-turer; Anthony Ittner of the NAM; Charles Richards, by now director of Cooper Union; Robert Woods, of the famous Boston settlement house; Frederick W. Taylor; Jane Addams; Frederick Fish, president of American Telephone and Telegraph; Samuel Donnelly, the secretary-general of the Arbitration Board for the New York Building Trades; the president of the Women's Edu-cational and International Union, the heads of several technical high schools, a banker, a principal of an industrial arts school, the secretary of a New York municipal improvement organization, and the president of a southern education association. Henry Pritchett of M.I.T. was elected president, and M. W. Alexander of General Electric was made vice-president.[82] With the exception of radical political groups, which were clearly not represented, the Society managed to make bed-fellows out of as diverse a collection of Progressive era spokesmen as one could imagine.

It took little guessing to foresee that the Society would remain a collection, rather than becoming a unified group. President Eliot of Harvard spoke to them, repeating his creed of separate educations. President Van Hise of the University of Wisconsin presented his new conception of the university as a service organi-zation. Georg Kerschensteiner told them of German continuation schools. Businessmen harangued on efficiency; pragmatists warned about the dangers of industry. Rhetorically, the NSPIE was a free-for-all, but providing a platform was an important part of the Society's function. The founders realized how broad industrial education was, and saw a need to bring diverse spokesmen together, to meet and if possible understand each other well enough to work for common legislative goals.

Yet some points of view clearly dominated the organization. Many, probably a majority, of NSPIE members were devoted to the ideal of trade training, to the problem of how the skilled worker could contribute to industrial efficiency. This orientation led the group into comparing American to European trade-training systems, for although interest in European industrial education was far from new—manual-labor advocates, kindergartening leaders and industrial-drawing proponents had all drawn on European notions—the trade-school pioneers had been particularly interested in European programs and their relation to economic progress.

At first, much of the interest in Europe had centered around a comparison of immigrant laborers with native-born workers. Such was Colonel Richard T. Auchmuty's theme in his inauguration of the trade-school crusade in the late 1880's, when he argued that institutions like his New York Trade School would restore American youth to their rightful position as skilled workmen, a position which was taken from them by better trained and wily Europeans.[83] For Auchmuty, American negligence and immigrant labor unions were the main problem, but it did not take profound reasoning to extend the fear of competition from immigrant labor to a fear of competition from skilled foreign labor.

The question of America's position in world trade, like that of competition with immigrant labor at home, began to gain public attention in the 1890's. In the last quarter of the century, the American economy was undergoing an important change; exports were becoming greater than imports, and the proportion of manufactured goods within exports was becoming greater than that of agricultural. Here was a change that most early advocates of industrialization could not have prophesied; one that revitalized the old arguments and gave them new meaning. Once again Americans heard expansion lauded in the name of self-sufficiency, for the sake of a usefully employed populace. Once again, fears of growing industrialization were voiced, but now mixed with suspicion of the giant businesses and a loathing for America's imperialistic ventures. And once again, Americans were turning to England, to an increasingly industrialized Europe, and parts of Asia as well, and asking whether this was the future which America wished for itself.[84]

Americans still looked to England for a picture of their own industrial future, but England seemed to be in a state of relative manufacturing decline (an ill omen to some Americans); newly industrialized countries provided a more inspiring model. It was Germany which captured the public eye:

England and France appear to us like two rich, long established and somewhat old-fashioned commercial houses. . . . Compared to them, Germany and the United States are like young pushing firms who have their own way yet to make. . . . Already their achievements have excited the alarm of their staid rivals, and they might look forward joyously to more brilliant triumphs in the future, if each were not worried by the presence of the other.[85]

Any brilliant triumphs or ultimate victory over the German rival apparently would depend in great part on the skill of American workingmen. In the last decade of the nineteenth century and the first decade of the twentieth, treatises on French design-schools and Russian manual-training fell far back in the shadow of voluminous and ponderous descriptions of German industrial education. No American group, however, chose to take over German industrial education bag and baggage; even the NAM, in its love affair with the German continuation schools, had managed to avoid some of the most nationalistic implications of Kerschensteiner's system; and reports to the American government were at great pains to point out the democratic nature of German industrial education, although there were suggestions of some uneasiness with the German system as a whole.[86]

Given such a groundwork, many members of the NSPIE embraced German industrial education with élan, interpreting as they went. Frank Vanderlip, for example, pointed out that unlike countries such as Germany, America had never competed abroad on the basis of "superior handicraft." Thus far, the United States had relied on its mechanized production, its natural resources, its "genius for business organization and a well-trained corps of engineers"; but Europeans were already adopting American devices and business methods, and her supply of raw materials would not be inexhaustible. The United States needed to take a lesson from Germany, which was building a great industrial system without natural resources and without the advantage of native "ingenuity"; Germany had banked on one factor—a well-trained and skilled working force.[87]

Vanderlip was joined by other NSPIE members in his praise of the German system. Charles Eliot lauded the system of "sorting out" children according to their abilities and occupational interests, rather than relying, as did Americans, on an ability to do everything. James Van Cleave, president of the NAM, reiterated that group's interest in German progress and noted that the United States would have to work to keep up with her rival. Even Jane Addams, with her considerable reservations about industrial efficiency, found good in the German system, interpreting it as an extension of a German philosophic commitment to human development: ". . . I suspect that they have developed those fine, technological schools in Germany in very much the same spirit as they developed legislative protection for the workingman. . . . Germany has waked up to the fact that human welfare is a legitimate object for Governmental action. . . ."[88]

The NSPIE was, of course, doing its best to wake up America to the same fact, and within a few years of its establishment the Society's goals were crystallized. In its view, the forms of industrial education would have to remain various, for no one system would be acceptable to all; and support would have to be public, for only a large and well-financed system could really meet the problem. At first, it seemed to the NSPIE that the states could handle the matter, but by 1911, discouraged with the progress of state legislation, the Society decided to extend its campaign to the federal level.[89]

By the time the NSPIE began its federal lobbying, several attempts had already been made to pass industrial education legislation. Beginning with the Davis Bill of 1907, a series of bills for secondary-school industrial education were introduced before Congress. The political history of these bills is complex, but one fact stands out; as in the case of the NSPIE itself, the federal bills were backed by a variety of groups with distinctly different goals. The Davis Bill of 1907, the Davis-Dolliver Bill of 1910, the Page and Page-Wilson Bills of 1912, and finally, the Smith-Hughes Bill of 1917, all sought to provide several kinds of vocational education. One of the major problems in the achievement of legislation was the participation of agricultural-ists. All of the bills included support for not only industrial, but also agricultural and home-economics education. But in addition to high school agriculture courses, agricultural educators were promoting legislation for agricultural extension which they con-sidered clearly more important than the high school courses, if a choice had to be made.

Amid a host of political complications, the supporters of the Smith-Lever Bill for agricultural extension and the supporters of secondary vocational-education legislation reached a "gentleman's agreement"; the Smith-Lever law was given support by both groups, and, to insure secondary-school legislation, a Commission on National Aid to Vocational Education was created.[90] The Commission took only a few months to report: there was no dearth of material, and Commission member Charles Prosser was happy to supply NSPIE information. Shortly after the report was issued, Senator Hoke Smith, true to his word, joined Representa-tive Dudley Hughes to sponsor the recommended vocational-edu-cation bill. The sponsors worked closely with the NSPIE, which proceeded to gain support from various segments of the popula-tion. Questions were still at issue, especially that of the proposed

Federal Board for Vocational Education, but the Society was able to muster approval. Nevertheless, passage was slow; it took several pleas from President Wilson, reminding the Congress of the importance of skilled workers to national preparedness, to help the bill over its final obstacles. But within a year after the Smith-Hughes Bill was passed, all of the states had accepted its provisions, making themselves part of a federal system of vocational education.

The Smith-Hughes Act was clearly a victory for those industrial-education advocates who had supported the trade-training ideal. The legislation provided for the federal government to share the cost of teachers' and supervisors' salaries in the area of vocational education. Plans for state programs were to be submitted to the Federal Board for Vocational Education, the very creation of which was an achievement for those who wanted trade training pure and simple. In addition, the plans for trade and industrial education were limited by the provisions "that the controlling purpose of such education shall be to fit for useful employment; that such education shall be of less than college grade and shall be designed to meet the needs of persons over fourteen years of age who are preparing for a trade or industrial pursuit or who have entered upon the work of a trade or industrial pursuit. . . ."[91] A further provision allayed the trade unions' fear of a flooded labor market by restricting evening industrial education to studies which would be "supplemental to the daily employment."

There was little in the Act to bring joy to the hearts of social reformers, philanthropists, or mobility enthusiasts. One small sop was offered them in the description of part-time schooling, which could include courses "to enlarge the civic and vocational intelligence" of youths from fourteen to eighteen years of age; otherwise, the legislation was aimed at insuring classroom instruction for job preparation, combined with a goodly proportion of "practical work on a useful or productive basis."

The structure of the Smith-Hughes Act had interesting implications; its generalities and efforts to include diverse interest groups left a great deal of room for some groups—especially business and labor—to negotiate on matters pertaining to specific programs.* At the same time, the limitations of the Act made it more difficult for educators outside the professional vocational-education fold to have a significant voice in shaping industrial education. Both the permissive and limiting aspects of the Act, however, had to find their concrete realization in specific programs, for in giving initiative to the states and a guiding function to the Federal Board, the legislation assured the essentially regional and local character of trade and industrial education.

By the time of the First World War, the ideological and institutional alternatives on which local communities could draw in developing industrial-education programs were, indeed, complex. Overlaying the variety of philanthropic and mobility-oriented schemes which had emerged during the nineteenth century were the trade-training ideals which proponents of industrial efficiency, craftsmanship, business advancement and labor protection had helped to develop. The trade-training advocates (and critics) not only drew on the older ideals, but interpreted them in contradictory ways. The goals of industrial efficiency fitted neatly into rationales which stressed the need to develop the nation's resources, but spokesmen who had reservations about the consequences of industrialization—particularly the Deweyan industrial arts advocates whose interest in craftsmanship drew heavily on older themes—also made use of the industrial-efficiency vocabulary. Likewise, the idea of craftsmanship was knitted into the industrial-education rationales of antagonistic groups, such as the NAM and the unions, while, for different rea-

---

* The Federal Board was made up of the Commissioner of Education, the Secretaries of Agriculture, Commerce, and Labor, and three citizens, one each to represent agricultural, manufacturing, and labor interests. The states had the choice of forming separate vocational boards or placing vocational education under their general boards of education. Local industrial education programs usually developed advisory boards on which labor and business representatives served.

sons, neither group was able to solve the problem of mobility which the craftsman image entailed.

The complexity of given social settings added another dimension to these already overlapping and intertwining perspectives. The trade-training rationale, for example, was developed most fully in the Northeast; but the problem of developing a trade-training program might take on a radically different character where both the youths to be educated and the outlanders against whom the students were to be protected had other origins and another character. Again, the differences between the industrial-education positions of the large and small business organizations was great, even though that of a given industry in a given town might also be influenced by the character of that community—the other groups it contained and their ideological approaches. Hence, despite the importance of federal legislation in crystallizing and supporting the trade-training ideal of industrial education, the states, cities, and towns would have to grapple with the national issues anew. The public school systems could choose whether or not to participate in the Smith-Hughes program, but even this choice might be less important than how those who developed the program incorporated and reinterpreted the broad issues of industrial education.

Part II

INTERPRETATION AND CHALLENGE

5

Industrial Education
in Geographic Perspective

Before the turn of the century, industrial-education spokesmen paid relatively little attention to geographic setting. Leading industrial educators tended to take for granted the geographic locations for their activities (inasmuch as industrialization had been primarily a northeastern phenomenon, it was natural that interest had been centered there) so that their educational ideals had a universal cast; the major pre-Civil War spokesmen grappled with the relation of the honest workman to Industry, not industries. Even the manual-labor ideology, which had at first considered the qualities which geographically mobile ministers would need, was turned into a prescription for education for all men. When Horace Mann took the growth of Massachusetts manufacturing into account he departed from the universalizing tendency, but his ultimate rationale rested on broader needs and rights to common schooling.

A similar tendency can be seen among the industrial-education spokesmen who emphasized mobility. In point of fact, geographic mobility was often as important to achieving success in the scientific or engineering worlds as social mobility, and the scientific and engineering educators acknowledged this implicitly when they spoke of the far corners from which they would draw leadership. Yet their ideal of training for leadership was geared to a national rather than a geographically specific setting. Calvin Woodward, himself speaking from the booming manufacturing city of St. Louis, paid little heed to differentiation in American manufacturing.

The proponents of trade training, on the other hand, displayed the interest in geographic differentiation which had characterized the national-resources argument since the early years of industrialization. Coxe and Carey had devoted much of their polemic to the question of differentiation within the American economy, for, to them, national growth seemed to depend on the proper division of labor among agricultural, commercial, and manufacturing sectors. The late nineteenth-century proponents of industrial development were no less specific in their prescriptions; in their eyes, manufacturing growth demanded an efficient use of human resources which only the proper division and training of labor could effect. Trade-training proponents translated the argument into their own terms: the skilled workman's virtues derived from his particular competence, not from the "character" or "principles" which earlier industrial educators had stressed.

The promoters of trade training were especially conscious of the relation between skill and setting because many of them were involved in specific industrial endeavors. Although the NSPIE itself began with a rather provincial northeastern perspective, it was not long before the drive to gain national support for industrial education forced the group to take a broader view. Southerners and midwesterners joined the society, and distant state governments had to be reached. The trade trainers found themselves asking what role industrial education would play in the promotion of manufacture in each of these settings, and the NSPIE embarked on a series of city surveys to answer the question.

Had the older breeds of industrial educators taken a similar look at the difference between industrial-education settings, these spokesmen would have discovered that their respective creeds lent themselves to geographic interpretation, for the realization of industrial education involved adjusting its more universal themes to both the objective and symbolic characteristics of particular settings. In the South, industrial education was interpreted in regional terms markedly different from those of the Northeast; the southern problem was a double one—how to gear industrial education to a predominantly agricultural economy, and how to reconcile northern concepts of industrial education to the problems of mobility in that biracial society. The experience of industrial education in Burbank, California—a small western city with one very large manufacturing firm—provides an example of urban as opposed to regional approaches to industrial education. Here one can also ask about industrial education as seen from the viewpoint of a particular kind of manufacturing activity, rather than as a part of industry in general.

The Regional View of the South

The Theme of Southern Industrialization. Insofar as "the most striking feature in the history of American manufacture is the enduring strength of the Northeast," the South has been a stepchild of American manufacture.[1] Agriculture was the strength of the antebellum southern economy, and it was on the basis of agriculture and natural resources that southerners strove to establish manufacture after the Civil War. By the early part of the twentieth century, southern states were contributing a high percentage of workers to the nation's wood and textile industries; North Carolina and Tennessee, for example, began to make significant contributions to furniture manufacture. As tobacco processing began to be mechanized, the South added still another industry, but the predominance of agriculture continued; only after 1930, with a marked increase in mechanization and intensive cultivation, did the proportion of people in agriculture take a rapid downward turn. Ironically, after the peak year of 1930, when about 20 per cent of the regional population was employed in industry, southern manufacturing also declined. Subsequent developments were discouraging; in 1950 in Mississippi, only 10 per cent of the workers were engaged in manufacture. The South's comparative lack of success in industrializing was only underlined by the continuing talk of industrialization.

Well before the Civil War, the South was concerned about disproportions in her economy. Southerners had shared in the national effort to make America self-sufficient by developing native manufacture; Scotch-Irish, northern European, and New England immigrants to the South helped to establish some manufacturing concerns; but, by the mid-nineteenth century, most southern manufacture was still associated with the large plantations. William Gregg, the best known of the early southern manufacturing boosters, had chided the South on its slow development, picturing the South as a land of potential, with a transient and indolent population, content with skimming off rich top soil and moving west. The result of this pattern, he said, was a complete economic dependence on the North, an increased and fruitless embitterment toward the North, and a growing number of impoverished southerners. He warned that the South should not expect to give herself entirely over to manufacture, but that to gain prosperity in agriculture, "without a high state of perfection in the mechanic arts, is a thing next to impossible."[2]

In the years preceding the Civil War and for many years afterwards, southerners like Gregg thrashed out those issues which had been grappled with on the national stage in the earlier years of the century. The Massachusetts textile mills had particular appeal for Gregg; he saw in them a way by which the South, with money but little technique, with labor but little skill, could both industrialize and solve its poverty problems. At the same time, however, Gregg was mindful of the South as the home of the yeoman farmer and advocated an enlarged role for the honest mechanic; at "every village and cross road" craftsmen were needed to set up shops. At this same village level the quality of life itself needed improvement, through better homes, roads, fields—as well as better craftsmanship.

By the end of the devastating Civil War, both factory and neat country town were still far from a reality. Progress toward manufacturing was made during the Reconstruction era, with renewed attempts to attract immigrant labor and efforts to encourage northern investment, but the great manufacturing crusade awaited the withdrawal of the northern troops and the emergence of a new generation of developers. The heyday for promotion of southern manufacturing finally came in the eighties.[3] By 1880, the cotton mills of the South were prospering; the depression was over; northern and English money began to flow into the region, and the South shared in the nationwide real-estate boom. A new political climate favored the manufacturing partisans; many of the older southern leaders were disappearing, and those who remained often joined the growing class of indus-trialists. The promotion of southern manufacture depended on a rather delicate balance of forces. The new white leadership needed the vote of the still-enfranchised Negroes; yet it was politically impossible to support any important role for Negroes in the New South. In consequence, the new leadership remained silent on the Negro's role in manufacture. A few, following the lead of Gregg, suggested the use of Negro labor in industry, but the most common image of an industrial South ignored the racial factor.

The boosters of manufacturing faced another problem from the small farmers, especially those who did not own land. The new plantation owners easily adopted the aims of the New South, for they were businessmen to whom more railroads, more scientific cultivation, and more manufacture would be a boon; but the small farmer, whose suspicion of business and railroading was being heightened by growing agrarian movements, had devel-oped a positive hatred for all the symbols of an urban-industrial culture. The southern manufacturers tried to meet this problem by reiterating Gregg's claim that the South would have to turn from a mere political solution to her problems and, through a partnership of agriculture and manufacture, gain her rightful place in the national community.[4]

The development of cotton mills in the South was one of the most dramatic instances of southern industrial development, and here the two viewpoints of the boosters were evident. For at least the first generation of textile men, the purpose of the mills was in part philanthropic, to take the rural and mountain folk away from their homes and give them better housing, a superior social environment and a higher income. At the same time, the boosters bowed to the yeoman farmer and his suspicion of industry. Southern mills were not to be antithetical to the field, but part of it; and, indeed, the mill-in-the-field was more than an ideological creation. Textile firms were established in villages all over the South; northern and southern investors, cotton merchants, local merchants, and other small investors, contributed; a mill so often seemed crucial to city development that the little towns vied with each other, first starting mills and then looking around for funds. Northern machinery agents and manufacturers would frequently come to the rescue, for they had reason to support the South's endeavors.

It was during this drive for expansion that Daniel Augustus Thompkins, one of the major figures in southern industrial education, became involved with the mills. Thompkins was born in 1851, in Edgefield County, South Carolina, where his father was a prosperous planter.[5] Young Thompkins served that "practical apprenticeship common to the more serious-minded sons of the plantation," and he was, according to his biographer, especially fond of the blacksmith's shop. But Thompkins found his higher education disappointing, compared to the mechanical lessons at home. Although the University of South Carolina still retained some of its prewar glory, Thompkins was restless studying Latin and oratory. Only his engineering professor inspired him, and the young man soon determined to go into engineering. Since there was no place for him to study in the South, he headed for Rensselaer Polytechnic Institute in Troy, New York.

Thompkins was as serious-minded in the North as he had been at home. While his fellow students frittered their summers away, the southern youth spent his vacations in the local Troy mills, gaining practical experience in machine shops and iron-making processes. Through his pursuits he was able to meet A. L. Holley, one of the pioneer engineers of the Bessemer process, who not only advised Thompkins, but hired him when he graduated. Work for Holley was, however, disappointing; Thompkins was confined to a desk doing drafting and secretarial work, when what he really wanted was to learn the iron business from the bottom up. This dissatisfaction led him to seek a position with the Bethlehem works where, after beginning as an apprentice he was able to spend a minimum period at the drafting board and then move on to a machinist's position. The depression of the seventies, however, was preventing the mills from expanding, and they offered scant opportunity to Thompkins. He therefore accepted an unusual opportunity to go to Germany as the representative of a Philadelphia firm, to help install and instruct the operation of that company's equipment.

On his return, Thompkins was no longer a novice in the mechanical world; yet instead of accepting one of the many offers in the North, he returned to his native region—Charlotte, North Carolina. He went in two capacities, as a "missionary" and as an agent for the Westinghouse Company. As a missionary he was determined to preach the message that the South was "the cradle of manufactures," an area which had been destined to play an important role in manufacture and which now must regain its deserted path. As a Westinghouse agent, Thompkins was to sell machinery, install it, and make repairs.

Let us step back from the narrative at this point, to underline some of its implications. Here was a boy from a well-to-do planter's family who sought an education not available in the South. The southern schools of the postwar years were in decline; the universities were on the verge of becoming a part of the Reconstruction struggle, and, what is more, such schools had never been technologically oriented. The only outstanding institution of higher learning available to southern youth was the Johns Hopkins University, with its emphasis on research. In addition, the kind of education which Thompkins sought was just beginning to go out of style in the North, where the mechanical engineers were withdrawing from mechanical occupations. The fact that Thompkins had to fight to stay off the drafting board and in the shop was symptomatic of the changing profession, and his choice of the older rather than the emerging ideal was indicative of the small place engineering arts had found in the South. Indeed, when Thompkins returned to the South there was virtually no place for him. The South had yet to develop those career ladders for engineers which were under way in the North. And it was not obvious that the northern pattern could be emulated.

No clear path from the plantation to entrepreneur-engineer had been developed in the South, and the route from mechanic to industrial leader (the hobby-horse of the engineers in the era of the self-made man) was most problematic. The irony of the southern situation was that no sooner had the New South leaders established themselves than they were threatened by the insurgent Populists, and no sooner had industry gained a foothold than northern capital made of the South a "colonial economy."[6] If, during the eighties, the southern manufacturers and engineers were able to construct a career rationale for their occupation, by the era of the (northern) trusts, the career of a southern engineer had distinct limits. Historically, the southern engineer was forced to skip and modify much of the self-made-man pattern: Thompkins began as a salesman, rather than in a shop or an engineering office.

Thompkins seemed to like his new job, and it gave him plenty of time to crusade. He exhorted the South on the need for manufacturing "experience," blamed the sentimental and inefficient

The Ontario Institute for Studies in Educat.
102 Bloor Street West
Toronto 5, Ontario   July 10,

1	David Snedden & Education for Social efficiency	WW	10.25
1	Industrial Education: American Ideals & Institutions	WW	7.75	14.40

INVOICE

BM BURNS & MacEACHERN LIMITED
62 RAILSIDE ROAD, DON MILLS, ONTARIO, CANADA
TELEPHONE: 447-5131

244

⌐ Michael B. Katz
The Ontario Institute for Studies in Educat.
102 Bloor Street West
⌐ Toronto 5, Ontario ⌐ July 10,

1	David Snedden & Education for Social Efficiency	WW	10.25	
1	Industrial Education: American Ideals & Institutions	WW	7.75	14.40
			18.00	PH 38
	Less 20%		3.60	
				1478

TERMS: — NET 30 DAYS — ADD BANK CHARGES TO OUT-OF-TOWN CHEQUES old guard for resisting manufacturing and not realizing that "a gentleman and a mechanic may be combined in one man."[7] He preached the united efforts of manufacture and agriculture, and while he preached he practiced; with part of his inexhaustible energy, he began a cottonseed-oil campaign, helping to found a southern company to resist the Cotton Oil Trust, to bring better and more professional engineering to the construction of cotton-seed-oil plants. Not content with this venture, Thompkins moved into cotton milling. When still a student, he had decided that mills were the solution to cotton-growing competition, that they would cure poverty and idleness, and even give productive farmers an added outside income. While Thompkins had the Westinghouse agency he was also doing free-lance engineering work, which soon gave him enough business contacts to start a cotton-mill-machinery company. Thompkins and his company, says the biographer, rejuvenated Charlotte: townspeople began to take their hats off to businessmen. Apprenticeships were established at the Thompkins Company, and Thompkins himself encouraged the boys to continue their schooling.

The North, Thompkins decided, had gained an industrial advantage by education, by training skilled labor. The South, he insisted, needed state universities which were equal to northern universities, state agricultural and mechanical colleges on the level of Rensselaer and M.I.T., good public schools, and trade schools to teach special skills. By the 1890's, Thompkins had become a crusader for technical education not unlike that advocated by the northern trade-school partisans; his interest in mobility was combined with the conviction that industrial education should be geared to particular trades. Since the occupations which most interested Thompkins were those connected with the mills, he soon focused his efforts on the establishment of special textile schools.

Thompkins took his plea for publicly supported textile schools to state leaders such as Benjamin Tillman, and Thompkins himself was active in helping these schools get started.[8] When South

Carolina's Clemson College began to consider a textile department, Thompkins went to New England and Europe to discover the modern techniques. Unfortunately, the English expert whom Thompkins brought back to work for his company and head the Clemson department when it was established was snapped up (tellingly) by the new Lowell textile school, and the slow-moving Clemson trustees irritated Thompkins. Southern youths, he said, were going to study in northern schools and remain with northern firms; the southern mills needed skilled workers who could produce fine goods, enabling the region to diversify its cotton manufacture, to free itself from dependence upon production of coarse fabric. Thompkins also preached that community prosperity would result from schools, telling his farmer audience that by enabling their sons and daughters to obtain expert training, the schools would assure southern, rather than northern or European, management of the mills.

After a Thompkins Company man was installed at the head of the new Clemson department, Thompkins expanded his crusade by prompting the North Carolina Legislature, planning the textile department for the North Carolina State College of Agriculture and Mechanics, catalyzing Missouri into establishing a textile school, and pleading with the people of Texas and Louisiana to do the same. Thompkins' ideas altered little. He insisted that youths must be offered both apprenticeship and technical education, so that those who did not go on to technical education would have a trade, while those who did continue would profit from their practical experience. He wrote texts for the schools, and he continued his campaigns for cottonseed-oil manufacturing, textiles, home building, railroads—the whole gamut of southern reforms related to manufacturing. He was, however, no "reformer" and scorned the appellation; looking upon the factory as an educative force, he saw no need for reforms such as child-labor legislation.

Thompkins' conception of industrial education was consistent with, indeed grew out of, the premises of the New South. Broadly stated, he held that there was nothing wrong with the South which emulation of the North would not cure. He granted that the South had made some serious mistakes, slavery and the rejection of industrialization among them, but he insisted that if the region would build up manufacturing and establish public schools, trade schools, and higher schools to train a skilled working force, it would be able to compete with the North. He granted that the South was also fundamentally different from the North; that the South had a broad agricultural base with which southerners would have to deal and from which laborers would have to be drawn. Yet he insisted that if farmers' sons were trained as skilled mechanics, the region would be every bit as prosperous as the North.

This rationale reflects part of the industrial and industrial-education ideology of the South, the basic tenets of which were present in William Gregg's statements in 1845. But Gregg added another argument (a secondary theme in Thompkins' own rhetoric); namely, that part of the industrial future of the South rested on the revitalization of local communities—the scientific attitude toward farming, the moral attitude toward householding and work, and the incorporation and fostering of mechanical skills, exemplified by a blacksmith and tailor in every country town. This concept of community reform and education constituted the alternate ideal for the world of southern industrial education in its relation to southern agriculture.

The concept of education and industrial education as a part of southern community revitalization was especially attractive to northern reformers and philanthropists. Amory Dwight Mayo, a New England minister, was one of the early postwar figures in these crusades; his work of the 1880's reflected a consciousness of national (northeastern) industrial-education principles plus a special effort to adapt northern solutions to the South. Mayo felt that the basic problem of the South was the need for a "general awakening of the mind" among the masses.[9] He argued that industrialization was the first step in the awakening, that the salutary effects of the factories could already be seen with respect to the poor whites, and that someday, perhaps, too, Negroes would also be able to participate in industry. At the same time, Mayo noted, industrial training could not be fully effective without a good general education, and such an education was not really possible without a solid social basis. Industrial education was no problem for the (northern) boy, who was "reared in an intelligent and enterprising community"; he could benefit from trade training after only a "moderate amount of schooling." But the southern youth, Mayo argued, did not have even the basic mental stimulation with which to begin.

Mayo reproved southerners for their poor use of land-grant funds, but praised the few fine examples of southern industrial education—Hampton and Tuskegee, Johns Hopkins (for "valuable work" in science and industrial training), and the St. Louis Manual Training School under Calvin Woodward. Mayo's admiration for Woodward is significant; while Mayo considered Woodward as a southern educator, Woodward was espousing a theory that *he* held to be non-regional and, Woodward aside, clearly geared to industrial development in the North.[10] Though Woodward was developing a system aimed at helping the talented to get ahead, Mayo saw manual training as an opportunity to reach the lowly worker at the elementary-school level. Manual training was, for Mayo, part of a total education reform of the common schools, which if improved by such programs as manual training, kindergarten, and physical education, could provide the base on which genuine trade-training, in the higher elementary grades and high school, could be built.

Mayo's recasting of manual training went one step further, for he not only advocated artisan training before more highly skilled or technical education, but he wanted the home involved in industrial education. The basic problem of the South was, in Mayo's eyes, the southern home, the center of the southern community; industrial education could prosper only if the home, community, and school ideals were coordinated:

And the more all this industrial work is kept in close connection with the home life of the parents, the better it will be. . . . We are convinced that any system of such instruction which leads these incompetent families to shirk their own plain duty and cast upon the schools this great burden, will be a disastrous mistake. Especially in the industrial department, where the home should be the center of discipline in the spirit of labor and training in common things, there should be nothing in the school-house to give the impression that this defect is excusable. Thus, every step in this direction should be taken after full consultation with the more influential people and combined with some effort to wake up the shiftless, ignorant, and vicious class to a desire for instruction and cooperation with the school.[11]

The feature which distinguishes Mayo's argument from the complex of arguments in which Woodward engaged—with Edward Everett Hale and Gustaf Larsson—is clear: Woodward, Hale, and Larsson quarrelled over the relation of the school shop to a farm home that was mostly a thing of the past; Mayo confronted the farm home as a thing of the present, and rural life as a grueling reality. Mayo made no distinction between agricultural and industrial education in his plea, and one can readily see why. His first concern was to develop southern character to the point that youths could take productive, honest positions in the shops, farms, and homes of their communities. Although he also expected some youths to move to city factory work, others to seek more advanced training, he was sure that "the masses of laboring men and women" would never become "skilled laborers." For these masses, the answer was an elevation of intelligence to meet the "new conditions of labor"; industrial leaders would be found only among those who could receive higher training.

The Problem of the Races. The industrializers of the New South, and some of the philanthropists like Mayo, treated industrial education without great attention to racial distinctions. Daniel Thompkins was obviously unconcerned with Negroes in his textile-school scheme; Mayo was more apt to talk of the southern masses than of the two southern races. It was impossible, however, for the two major southern themes—that of industrializing an agricultural economy and that of coping with two separate populations—to remain totally distinct. One can see this more clearly by moving to the question of Negro industrial education, for the southern Negroes too had to consider their relation to the changing southern economy.

The labor history of Negroes in both North and South was important in developing an ideology for southern Negro industrial education.[12] The contrast between the pre-Civil War occupations of southern and northern Negroes was significant; slavery was the greatest difference, but not the only one. In the larger plantations of the South, an extensive division of labor had led to artisan work for some of the slaves; men were made coopers, masons, carpenters, and, on plantations where machinery was used, might become "engineers," if not actual factory hands. Town slaves often had greater freedom in developing their skills, and the much debated hiring-out system gave some slave artisans independent status. By contrast with these southern workmen (leaving aside for the moment the matter of dignity of labor for an enslaved people), the position of the Negro artisan in the antebellum North was less favorable. Since the turn of the century, when the Quaker brethren had begun to help Negroes settle in northern cities, the competition between white and Negro artisans had increased, and, aggravated by widespread prejudice among immigrant artisans, had led to patterns of discrimination, exclusion from unions and shops, even race riots. Economically, the Civil War improved the situation of neither the southern nor northern group. Negro artisans in the South were deprived of their patronage, their business contacts, and their protection against hostile white artisans. The Negro artisans of the North, and those who were gradually moving up to join them, still found opportunities for skilled work limited.

The extent to which these differing industrial conditions were taken into account was an important dimension of the Negro industrial-education discussion. For example, late eighteenth-

century philanthropic groups blurred distinctions between northern and southern industrial opportunity and advocated industrial
education for both Negro groups as a means of "preparation";
the American Convention of Abolition Societies declared that
southern Negroes needed industrial education to prepare them
for abolition, while northern Negroes needed to learn ". . . mechanic arts which will keep them most constantly employed and,
of course, which will less subject them to idleness and debauch-
ery, and thus prepare them for becoming good citizens of the
United States."[13] This concept of "preparation" remained the
most fundamental one in the rhetoric of Negro industrial education, but in the years before the Civil War several new factors
had entered the picture, greatly influencing the meaning of such
rhetoric.

First, by 1840 much of the overt philanthropic effort for both
general and industrial education of southern Negroes had to be
abandoned, shifting the setting for Negro-education debate to
the North. In the meantime, the northern Negro community itself was changing, developing a middle class with its own educational ideals. What resulted, therefore, was a complex situation
in which philanthropic discussion of industrial education was
centered in the North, the matter of industrial education for
southern Negroes vanishing in the shadow of the more pressing
question of abolition. At the same time, industrial education for
northern Negroes was examined with mixed feelings by a group
which had gained certain economic success; industrial education
was still associated primarily with pauperism, and middle-class
Negroes strove no less than middle-class whites to avoid the
charity stigma.

The discussions which took place in the (northern) Negro
conventions before the Civil War reflected the mixture of middle-
class and philanthropic strains. The major issue in these educational discussions was the theme of separation versus integration,
but one should also keep in mind that concepts of opportunity
here were regional, the northern Negroes striving for a place in

terms of their own economic chances. The manual-labor idea was raised early in the convention movement; since manual-labor schemes were often forwarded by abolitionists, it was a short step to advocating manual labor for Negroes. Negro youth, argued one convention report, needed manual-labor schools "so as to catch up in the great race we are running."[14] Part of the "catching up" would be done by improving homelife, building character, and giving Negroes the confidence they needed for their climb. But, the manual-labor advocates argued, Negroes also needed specific job training.

Manual labor for occupational training was a far cry from what Theodore Weld had intended manual labor to be; the Negro convention group was actually hammering out its own conception, centered on the issue of mobility. Many features of Weld's manual-labor scheme were included; the Negro proponents mentioned the advantage of being able to work one's way through school, the physical health which came through work, the need to harmonize the activities of mind and hand, of thinking and doing; but all these considerations were blended with an overt struggle to rise. The manual-labor schools, the same convention reported, needed a "more thorough plan," one which included literary instruction, scientific agricultural courses, "theoretic mechanics and engineering" as well as "a series of workshops under skillful and systematic instruction." These schools were to be of "high intellectual grade," offering surveying, engineering, natural philosophy, and mathematics, as well as instruction in specific trades leading to "marketable skills."

While some Negro convention members were promoting industrial education for mobility, Frederick Douglass, also active in the convention movement, was advocating industrial education for an essentially different end. While Douglass was still a southern slave, and not legally allowed to learn to read, his master had given him a trade. Douglass had fled to the North, where in the freedom of a New England town he now found himself being denied the right to work with his skilled hands. Douglass' perspective on industrial education, therefore, was not one of mobility but one which sought to establish for the northern Negro the opportunity to work at a trade: ". . . At this moment [said Douglass] I can more easily get my son into a lawyer's office to study law than into a blacksmith's shop to blow the bellows and to wield the sledge hammer."[15] It was for this goal of enabling Negro youths to pursue honest trades that Douglass importuned Harriet Beecher Stowe to establish a Negro "industrial college," where such youths could receive an adequate training. But Douglass' proposal fared no better than the manual-labor schemes suggested during the conventions. The convention movement ultimately rejected manual labor on the grounds that, by offering Negroes a separate kind of education, such schools prevented rather than contributed to improving Negro status.[16] Douglass' scheme foundered on Mrs. Stowe's lack of support, but it foundered in a deeper sense on the industrial conditions of the North itself. As the ideal of the honest workman had evolved at the very time that the independence of the artisan began to be threatened, when it was becoming apparent that the new factories would need few skilled workers and more "hands," Douglass' version of the honest Negro workman evolved in the face of increasing immigrant competition for the few "respectable" manual occupations that Negroes had been able to pursue.[17] Douglass' concept, then, was directed to establishing industrial preparation for a world of decreasing opportunity. The same logic was followed by Booker T. Washington in the South and eventually—most ironically—by southern white trade-school proponents.

The Negro industrial-education schemes which emerged in the South after the Civil War drew ideas from the New South, from earlier philanthropic movements, and from the honest-worker and mobility discussions of the previous era. From the New South (and its ideological predecessors) the educators drew the concept of the unity of agricultural and industrial progress, especially through the type of community revitalization which

Reverend Mayo envisioned. That this concept also had its roots in religious-philanthropic work can be seen in the ideas of Samuel Chapman Armstrong.

Armstrong, who had been raised in a missionary family, founded Hampton Institute shortly after the end of the Civil War. He drew inspiration for this project from a manual-labor school for natives he had once seen in Hawaii, and, in ways, the school he established came close in idea to the school which the Negro manual-labor advocates had proposed. Yet Armstrong's desire to reach Negroes still on the land gave a different cast to his concept of leadership. Hampton was to train ". . . selected Negro youths who should go out and teach and lead their people, first by example, by getting land and homes; to give them not a dollar that they could not earn for themselves; to teach them respect for labor, to replace stupid drudgery with skilled hands, and in this way to build up an industrial system for the sake not only of self-support and intelligent labor, but also for the sake of character."[18]

Like other industrial-education schemes which stressed leadership, Armstrong's system did not place the greatest emphasis on actual skills. Although the crafts were taught (as opposed to the exercise system which Woodward was to develop), the guiding purpose of industrial work was to develop leadership—missionary leadership. This strain of thought continued in the work of Booker T. Washington, himself a student at Hampton. Washington was, if anything, more concerned than Armstrong to lead his people through a fundamental reform of Negro home and community life. At the same time, Washington added another dimension—the training of honest workmen that Frederick Douglass had espoused.

The reform of the home and community clearly came first for Washington. Both he and his students tell of the struggles he had to convince Tuskegee youths to return to their rural communities to reimmerse themselves in that primitive way of life in order to improve it.[19] Washington's impulse toward this goal drew considerable support from the developing philanthropic reform movements which succeeded Mayo's pioneering attempt; for southern educational reform was adopting the community-improvement ideal. Washington allied himself as much with these philanthropic movements as with the business ideals of the New South; he and the head of Hampton worked together with various funds and helped to shape the policies of the especially important General Education Board. When agricultural extension work began, Washington threw Tuskegee's energies behind it.

It was Washington's concept of trade training, rather than the community endeavors, however, which ultimately received the most attention—and criticism. The criticism, usually launched from an urban and northern perspective, took Washington to task for his lack of interest in mobility. Yet this same lack of interest in mobility was part of Washington's own particularly southern vision. Although he often spoke in general terms about the "stage" of the Negro race and the education appropriate to that stage, Washington interspersed such language with continual pleas to stay in the South.[20] Washington embraced the New South faith in the region's progress, in spite of the fact that it was a faith which covertly excluded Negro participation in manufacturing development. The Tuskegee leader's New South, partly, perhaps, in acknowledgment of this exclusion, became the New South of the Negro craftsman, a New South which was in essence the Old South.

Washington's creed of trade training was, indeed, directed away from mobility; he was little interested in manual training, less interested in book-study, and as positively scornful of the older professions as any promoter of industrial education. Yet he did not wholly dismiss the question of higher education. He told a Fisk University audience, for example, that industrial education, like literary education, developed the "strong mind" which college men needed, the kind of strong mind which had been required to build a Corliss engine; at another time he remarked that Negroes would have to become not only carpenters but architects who could plan the work for the carpenters.[21] But all in all, Washington did not seem to have a very clear conception of a route to success for the mechanic. To the extent that he did have one, it referred to the businessman-craftsman rather than the engineer-entrepreneur or the engineering expert.

That the favorite route of mobility for Washington was through the small business was evident in his founding and promotion of the National Negro Business League. He cheered the members on with stories of how men had started as junk dealers and ended up as prominent citizens, and the Business League members reciprocated; their proceedings were one long procession of eulogies of Washington and testimonies of success. One small excerpt from a speech at a 1914 meeting of the League, however, said more than all the testimonials:

This is a day of progress, a day of combinations, a day of big things, a day of Trusts! . . . Now, if I am not mistaken the Business League's object is to build up in this country some more trusts, some more corporations, some more big Negro combines (Laughter and applause) to give the democratic party, the republican party, and Mr. Roosevelt's party something to do. (Renewed laughter and applause.)[22]

In the face of such a sadly ironic situation, Washington's ideology was wide open to attack, and that attack came, of course, from W. E. B. DuBois. DuBois' criticism heralded a shift of Negro-education rhetoric to reconcentration on mobility, and presaged yet another shift in geographic perspective—to an essentially northern view which took into account the character of northern industry. DuBois had many criticisms of Washington; his anti-intellectualism and penchant to assuage southern white sentiment seemed callous and ignoble to the northern-bred and Harvard-trained Negro spokesman. One must remember, however, that both of these men wished to train leaders; for DuBois, however, leadership was not confined to the philanthropic and missionary model which had been developed so fully in the

South, but rather drew on leadership from the northern universities where, even in the new Negro institutions, trade education had not made much progress.[23]

If DuBois' leaders were missionaries, they were to be university-trained missionaries; if they were to forward trade education, it was to be trade education which made carpenters into men, not men into carpenters. DuBois insisted the college would have to make sure that industrial teachers were culturally enlightened so that when they reached the student, they would be able "to teach him and his family what life means." DuBois stressed this broadening, character-developing aspect of trade education partly because he realized that the more traditional craft opportunities were disappearing. Washington, in his view, was misinterpreting the kind of education necessary: "*Negro youth are being taught the techniques of a rapidly disappearing age of hand work.* The training had undoubtedly good physical and mental results, but if used as a means of livelihood it will command the poor and decreasing wages of tinkers and repairers; and those who follow these methods will be completely shut out of modern machine industry."[24]

Like W. T. Harris, DuBois looked to a modern trade-education, based on a solid general education and aimed toward the greater intellectual demands of modern industrial life; like Calvin Woodward, DuBois wanted able Negroes to rise to positions of leadership. Yet, even in the nineties, DuBois questioned the possibility of their leadership in the manufacturing world, given contemporary trends. He shared Washington's interest in Negro enterprise, but noted that, as Negroes were learning business techniques, business itself was changing in the direction of large enterprise in which the Negro would not be "so readily admitted to positions of direction and cooperation."[25]

The blocked mobility which DuBois pointed out persisted as a basic problem in the North; in the South, the blocks became immense. Between the last decades of the nineteenth century and World War I, Negro mechanics in the South were able to hold onto some of their traditional occupations, even starting businesses; but a combination of many factors—white unions, mechanization, and ever-present prejudice—made the position of Negroes less and less secure. Nor was the picture for manufacture in general more bright; while the Negro businessmen debated whether to go-it-alone or try to become a part of the white business world, Negro manufacture remained generally small. The situation in the educational world was also disheartening; although Tuskegee and Hampton remained strong central institutions, the concentration of funds in these schools seemed ultimately to be made at the expense of industrial education on the local level.

The other major hope for industrial education for the Negro was the land-grant colleges, and here, too, progress was slow. Before passage of the second Morrill Act, which forbade discrimination, only a handful of Negro schools (including Tuskegee and Hampton) shared in the funds. Even the increased number of colleges after 1890 was not sufficient, for the level of elementary education for Negroes remained so low that "the Land-Grant colleges for Negroes were in 1916 largely Land-Grant high schools."[26] With so little to build on and with so much resistance from the white community, higher technical education for southern Negroes was little more than a dream. Howard University began an engineering program during World War I; it was not until 1949 that Tuskegee offered such a degree.

A conference on the Negro in business, engineering, and technical fields held at Howard in the middle forties highlights the difference in timing between southern white and Negro institutions. "In the field of engineering, in the South today," said one speaker, "there are thirty-one accredited engineering schools for white people, with 25,000 students in them, and not a single Negro in one of them. Moreover, we have not a single accredited engineering school for Negroes, and yet our entire civilization is built around civil, mechanical, and chemical engineering."[27] Before wartime expansion, even those Negroes trained in northern engineering schools had few places to turn. In short, the southern Negro engineer of the 1930's was in precisely the position that Daniel Thompkins was in 1880. For both, the career ladder in the industrial world was a problematic affair, and the lack of regional schools serving the needs of technological education made the pursuit of such a career even more difficult.

In the face of the racism which had grown more and more militant toward the end of the nineteenth century, the educational reflection of circumscribed mobility was not surprising; more curious was the fact that some white southerners began to see industrial education for Negroes as itself threatening. Northern philanthropists such as those on the General Education Board had seen a healthy element in educational rivalry—white admiration of Negro efforts at industrial education would be a way for the Negroes to gain respect. The example of a white reporter's reaction to a local Negro school exhibition of industrial-education work could be cited; the reporter was filled with admiration, noting that the school had been aided by northern philanthropy: "Bethany school children, you had better look to your laurels or the little blacks will beat us!"[28]

The rivalry, unfortunately, was not always of such a playful nature. "Many of the same men who assured us, ten years ago," wrote Edgar Gardiner Murphy in 1904, "that industrial education is the only education the negro should have, are now ready with the assurance that for fear the industrial development of the negro will clash with that of the white man, this form of negro training is the most dangerous contribution that has thus been made to the solution of our Southern problems."[29] Though speaking out of concern for his own reform interests, Murphy tapped a trend, one which was evident in the outlook of the president of the Georgia Institute of Technology. In his plea for southern trade schools, President Hall pointed to the results of Negro trade training:

When the colored race all become skilled bricklayers, somebody will have to carry the mortar. When they all become plumbers, who are going to be the helpers, the men who carry the tools? When they become scientific farmers, who are going to be laborers? Are Southerners, we Southern whites? No. We have settled that question long ago, but unless we have trade and industrial schools, our boys will have to carry the mortar for somebody, even if they have to emigrate to do it.[30]

As if having to compound the irony, the Georgia educator added that while building up their own trade schools, the whites would not, of course, neglect the needs of the "weaker race."

This interest in establishing trade training for white southerners increased the southern effort to gain governmental support for industrial education. Any crusade for industrial education in the South, however, had to take agricultural interests into account; indeed, had to gain the good will of agricultural partisans. As the state superintendent of the Virginia schools explained to the NSPIE (during a 1915 survey of Richmond), there was little enough money for education. "Under such circumstances as these," he continued, "the Virginia cities with one voice invariably speak to the rural situation as the wounded Sir Philip Sidney spoke to his wounded ally . . . 'Friend, thy necessity is even greater than mine.' "[31]

Given the paucity of funds for southern education, and the intimate relation of agricultural and industrial interests, it is understandable that industrial-education legislation was ultimately shepherded through the Congress by a southerner who straddled the worlds of agriculture and industry. In the early part of his career, when he was already a leading Georgia lawyer, Hoke Smith had supported Henry Grady and the proponents of the new industrial South.[32] Between the eighties and the nineties, however, Smith seemed to have come to the realization that southern political fortunes could not be based on the support of industry alone, and he turned his attention to agrarian reform, particularly control of the railroads. He maintained a careful balance, staying within the Democratic fold with the industrialists, but going far to meet the disgruntled farmers. His work for Cleveland's election netted him the post of Secretary of the Interior, a job he held until the split between Cleveland and the Bryanites could force even an intrepid balancer out of the political picture. Smith made good use of his ten-year political retirement; he went back to practice in Atlanta, where he became active in civic affairs, particularly in education. He served on the Board of Education, worked to establish manual training in the elementary schools, and supported the effort for "a distinct technological course" in the boys' high school of the city.

Smith's ideal of industrial education, as much as it was developed, lay somewhere between manual-training and trade-school goals. But this man was not an educational theorist; rather he was a promoter of southern progress. He advocated industrial education for the sake of boosting and revitalizing southern cities; he crusaded for agricultural education to invigorate and strengthen the agriculture sector. When shifting political winds enabled Smith to return to office, he was elected on a Progressive platform supporting railroad reform, child-labor legislation, penal codes, corporation control, Negro disenfranchisement (that peculiarly southern addition to the Progressive program), and education. In 1911, Smith became a United States Senator, and he soon headed the important Committee on Education. From this post, he promoted his agricultural-extension bill, making sure it was passed before the industrial-education legislation. Then, as agreed, Smith turned his attention to secondary-school industrial education. Here Smith was true not only to his word, but also to his southern commitments; in the resulting Smith-Hughes Act, agricultural and industrial education stood side by side.

The Urban View of a Manufacturing Town

While industrialization of the South was a long and drawn-out struggle, the industrialization of the West, particularly of California, was on its surface a short and brilliant success story.[33] In the West, as opposed to the South, industrialization did not occur in a solidly agricultural economy; between 1910 and 1950, the Far West had the smallest proportion of agricultural workers in the country, with the exception of New England and the Middle Atlantic states.

Urbanization had begun early in California. Of the two major cities, San Francisco was built up first, during the gold rush, and became the state's leading manufacturing city by the early years of the twentieth century. The earthquake of 1906, however, hurt the city's development and seemed to offer just that opportunity which the boomtown of Los Angeles needed in order to capture first place. Los Angeles expanded almost in spite of itself: the development of the railroads, the efforts of General Harris Gray Otis, real-estate speculation, the oil rush, the weather, the film industry—each in turn added to the irresistible magnetism of the Southern California city. The early immigrants to Southern California—wealthy speculators and older people looking for a luxurious retirement spot—had come from the East. By the 1920's, Americans of average means were being drawn from the middle section of the country to settle in Southern California. And during the Depression the area became a haven for dispossessed workers, especially the hard-hit farmers of the Southwest.

One of the peculiar characteristics of the region was that, unlike the South or the Middle West, urban and rural communities were not clearly delineated; large-scale business agriculture was typical, but wealthy Los Angeles residents, gentlemen farmers, also engaged in the lucrative pastime of citrus farming. Nor was it easy to draw lines around the major Southern California city. There was, to be sure, a city of Los Angeles, but there were also a host of neighboring communities which, as the population increased, tended to merge into each other. The extent to which each of these cities was a city, or, as happened to many of them, was destined to become a part of metropolitan Los Angeles, was an aspect of the region's problem of self-definition.

Such considerations were part of the background against

which Los Angeles made a determined effort to make itself into a manufacturing city. Two steps, early in the century, helped to assure this goal. One was the acquisition of enough water to support a large urban and manufacturing center—an acquisition involving an extremely bitter fight with the neighboring Owens Valley. The other step was the building of a port (a feat of great geographical imagination, since no appropriate site was available in the city itself), from which to market the rich natural resources of the area.

Indeed, until World War II, Los Angeles industry relied in great part on processing its natural resources. Manufacture was slight and small; some was connected with products such as oil, some with the film industry, which also had its technological side. Southern California was also beginning to develop textile and furniture factories, but aircraft manufacture became its first major industry.

The history of the Southern California aircraft industry, like the history of Los Angeles itself, was the American success story written large. Aircraft builders had always liked the area; even in the early experimental years, tiny shops had been started in California.[34] When the World War I aircraft boom came, California shared the industry's leadership with the manufacturing areas of the East and Midwest. Aircraft production foundered at the end of the war, but some California firms survived, and more and larger companies were gradually added. In the late 1920's, when aircraft building moved from individual ownership to large corporations, California concerns followed the pattern. Another change in the industry was particularly beneficial to the region; with her lack of manufacturing facilities, Southern California could not compete with eastern cities in the building of the delicate engines. Engine and airframe building, however, were gradually being separated, and Southern California, with its fine weather and inexpensive requirements for plant building, seemed ideal for the airframe work.

The Los Angeles area, then, was in a most propitious situation when the aircraft expansion of the late thirties began. Yet, with all the advantages of the region, the aircraft manufacturers had one distinct problem to face; despite the fact that airframe production was primarily an assembly process, it still required that about 15 per cent of the labor force be skilled.[35] In the "scramble for aircraft workers" which had begun even before the war, Southern California was at a disadvantage; because of the Depression, eastern firms could draw on a vast pool of (then unemployed) skilled workers which the Los Angeles area had never had. Like eastern firms, the Southern Californians leapt into the business of "stealing" workers, but there were few workers left to steal by the time the war began.

California's real advantage came in the realm of unskilled labor, for the southwesterners who had moved into the area during the Depression offered an immediate pool from which to draw, and more workers could easily be drawn from that section by the high wages the industry was to offer. As wartime production moved toward astounding heights, the farm source was itself exhausted; aircraft, like other defense industries, was forced to draw unskilled labor from offices, from kitchens, from schools —indeed, from rocking chairs. Yet there was one pool from which the industry conspicuously did not draw; since before the war period, Negroes had been moving to Southern California, and rumor of wartime wages had increased this migration. Their lack of participation in aircraft production grew so noticeable that government investigation ensued, but despite pressures for fair hiring practices, the proportion of Negroes in aircraft manufacture was, by 1943, still small; most of those employed were doing maintenance work; a minute number were employed in actual manufacture, though the proportion of Negro non-maintenance workers was higher on the West Coast than in some other areas.[36]

Probably the most striking new group to be recruited into aircraft manufacture were the women. At first, the companies resisted the idea of hiring them. But when the male labor market began to be strained, women seemed to the manufacturers the next logical group to hire. Women had always held a small but significant proportion of jobs in the manufacturing world, although in specific industries, factors such as the available working force and technology affected their employment. And women workers customarily had been concentrated in low-skilled jobs— one of the major reasons why so little attention was paid to them in industrial-education discussions.*

In the wartime aircraft industry, the general shortage of labor pushed women up the working ladder. Indeed, this trend gave birth to some rather high hopes about the role that women might play in aircraft manufacture.[37] Such hopes were sadly misplaced; the labor shortage lasted only with the war. More important, perhaps, was the fact that if women were to become aircraft mechanics or aeronautical engineers, some ideological groundwork would have to be laid among the women, as well as in the industrial world at large.

If the aircraft industry's conception of a labor force did not include women, it did include the variety characteristic of manufacture in general. A quick overview of the aircraft career literature gives a sense of the timing and character of this conception. In the 1920's and 1930's, aircraft proponents were struggling to establish a more professional attitude toward the industry. In the twenties, when "gypsy" pilots still abounded and men were building planes in their backyards, we find two air-force officers trying to convince would-be flyers that flying required special training and that those interested in aircraft might also consider

---

* Although beyond the scope of this present study, the problem of industrial education for women is an intriguing one. Women were mentioned occasionally in pre-Civil War discussions, but were virtually excluded from consideration in the mobility-oriented schemes of the science-and-technology educators (at least, inasmuch as these discussions were directed toward the success ideal, rather than toward the more general public-education version of manual training). With the rise of trade education, the question of training women for industrial work began to be given serious attention.

ground jobs.[38] "Hundreds of thousands" of aircraft mechanics
would be needed when commercial flying really became established, the officers declared. What is more, mechanics being in
greater demand would probably command higher pay than
pilots and would be in a position to either start shops—for many
large aircraft companies were begun this way—or become pilots
who would truly understand their planes.

Clearly, these authors felt unable to convince either their audience or themselves that the glories of being an aircraft industrialist quite competed with the glories of being a pilot. Aviation
career books of the thirties still showed concern that flying would
outshadow ground jobs, but distinctions between ground jobs
were becoming finer. Curtiss-Wright personnel director Charles
Matoon, writing in the late thirties, now warned his readers not
to be taken in by the glamour of the aircraft mechanic, not to
ignore other ground jobs which could lead to either technical
specialization or to an administrative position. He noted the
variety of commercial, service, and technological positions, and
pointed out that few men were involved in the actual making of
a plane. For those who still wished to do mechanical work, he
recommended the long route of study and apprenticeship. It was
possible, Matoon conceded, to begin as a helper or "cleaner" and
work one's way up to being a licensed mechanic; but the self-
trained, half-trained men were the first to be dropped and were
less likely to attain a mechanic's position. At best, he warned, the
job of mechanic was limited, for specialization was affecting the
mechanical aspect of aircraft work; the era of the "old-fashioned,
self-educated, all-around mechanic" had passed.[39]

None of these themes was new, for the evolution of aircraft-
career ideals between the twenties and the forties was a speeded-
up version of the development of manufacturing ideals in general.
First came the era of the honest workman, then the era of mobility, and finally, the era in which mobility was being circumscribed and delineated, in which the development of expertise
was being encouraged and in which the higher technological

reaches were now accessible only to those with formal engineering education. The curious feature of the aircraft picture is that, because the industry's growth was so rapid, the succession of career ideals overlapped and often were present concurrently. Indeed, one can still find men in the American aircraft industry who have spanned its whole history.

One Company's Interpretation of Industrial Education. In the context of the booming Southern California aircraft industry, the Lockheed Corporation was an aircraft success story itself.[40] The firm was originally begun by the Loughead brothers, who, typically for the industry in the twenties, started by building planes in small shops. By the late twenties their enterprise had grown; they moved the company to Burbank, a small city not far from Los Angeles, and then sold the firm to a large Detroit corporation. The Detroit group had done its purchasing at an inauspicious moment. The Lockheed Company collapsed completely during the Depression; by the early thirties, there was little more to buy than a promise, although the new owners, Robert Gross and those he had rallied behind him, were optimistic.

After a few years of relatively modest production, the revitalized Lockheed Company began to find itself a market. It was in 1938, however, that the real change occurred; Great Britain gave Lockheed a twenty-five million dollar order. Suddenly this company, only a few years from the bankruptcy court and just becoming a moderately successful medium-sized firm, was thrust into really large manufacture. The next few years intensified the situation, as the United States added its orders to those from overseas.

One of the company's most immediate problems was that of a labor force. During its development in the thirties, Lockheed had looked to the Los Angeles vicinity for labor. Only a limited number of men in nearby communities seemed to offer a promising source of labor. Many of these men had had experience with mechanical work, and it seemed, therefore, relatively easy to teach them factory skills. In any case, this local source was soon combined with the stream of southwestern immigrants to California, many of whom also were from rural backgrounds. In addition, as production expanded, Lockheed changed its policy with regard to hiring women, thus drawing on a new pool. Because the company had difficulties in finding skilled labor, its earliest problem was that of converting a large number of unskilled people into competent factory workers.

The new Lockheed Company had had an interest in employee training from its early years; by the mid-thirties, it had approached the local public schools, and by 1937, when the company's Educational Department was established, an arrangement had been reached with the Burbank school system.[41] Hundreds of employees enrolled for the first courses; when the war started the number quickly rose to the thousands. How the small city school system could support such activity was a problem which the federal government had foreseen for such small units. When war became imminent, a National Defense Training Program had been established, so that local communities could draw on federal funds in a way comparable to the Smith-Hughes Act. Indeed, the defense vocational program utilized much of the Smith-Hughes structure, but the former program differed from its peacetime counterpart in that funds for the war emergency came solely from the federal source and could be used in purchasing equipment. Although the federal government had some requirements concerning the recruitment of trainees, the programs, especially in the early years of the war, were shaped by local advisory boards.[42]

Given this federal support, the Burbank and Lockheed program expanded at an enormous rate; indeed, it was as though the entire city were converted into an emergency training school. At the same time, the company engaged in informal training in the plant. Such training had to fall in great part on the shoulders of the supervisory personnel; as a part of the National Defense

Training Program, training courses for foremen and supervisors were developed, so that the crucial on-the-job teaching could be as effective as possible. In order to meet this increased need for supervisory personnel, skilled workers who had been in the industry were rapidly promoted to higher positions, leaving a skilled labor gap which was extremely difficult to fill. As the shortage of skilled labor increased, the company, like others in the industry, simply increased the division of labor further; large-scale training of skilled workers was out of the question.

The company's apprenticeship program, established in 1939 in conjunction with the local machinists union, was never intended to train large numbers of men. Inevitably, a sort of craftsman-aura surrounded such a program; the California apprenticeship agreement itself, drawn up in the same years, required a course of studies to be mapped out "to the end that the apprentice shall receive instruction and experience in *all* branches of the trade, as is necessary to develop a practical and skilled mechanic versed in the theory and practice of said trade."[43] Yet, the latent function of the Lockheed apprenticeship program—a function acknowledged by union and management alike—was not the training of all-round craftsmen, but training for supervisory positions and (a trend which developed into a pronounced function in recent years) for technical work related with the company's experimental programs. In one early company memo, for example, supervisors were warned that apprentices were a very special group which had to be treated with special care; again, supervisors were told, these all-round craftsmen would soon be supervisors and inspectors themselves. Four years of careful training in cooperation with the local schools was a great investment for the company. A man with so much training—almost as much as an engineer, according to one company person—was far more useful in higher positions. In addition, the number of apprentices was always tiny compared to the total plant employment; there were fewer and fewer places in the factory itself for all-round men, and even by the early forties they were being used in either special jobs or in field service and the sales end of the business.[44]

Apprenticeships were a joint venture of the company and organized labor; in fact, from the standpoint of active promotion, apprenticeship was *the* form of industrial education for the union. The machinists happily recommended their men for teaching positions in the public school program and to serve on the various advisory committees which such programs required. But the public school training was clearly a part of the company training effort, and mass training schemes did not, as apprenticeship did, fit in with the older ideals of the union.

The International Association of Machinists, which represented the Lockheed workers, had been founded in Georgia at the end of the 1880's.[45] The original machinists' group saw themselves as southern gentlemen and craftsmen; since many members were drawn from the Knights of Labor, the union even eschewed strikes at first. Such an image, however, could not be long maintained; the IAM grew, gathering northerners into its ranks, men who worked in shops where the division of labor was far greater than that of the South. In the early years of unionization, the machinists' predominant problems were already becoming clear; the craft was being subdivided at a rapid pace, and the changes within machinists' work combined with changes in other trades and industries were leading to jurisdictional conflict.

Both the division of labor and jurisdictional factors helped to shape the union goals. Through a most difficult process of continued redefinition, the machinists developed new categories to correspond with the changing shop conditions, categories which stretched the conception of machinists' work as far as possible without altogether abandoning a sense of craft. By these redefinitions, the IAM moved slowly toward industrial unionism and toward territorial claims which not only rivaled those of other craft unions, but eventually those of the CIO affiliates.

Organization of the aircraft industry, which began in 1933, was from the beginning fraught with jurisdictional disputes. After a series of particularly bitter battles between the United Auto Workers (CIO) and parts of the West Coast industry, the Lockheed Corporation came to an arrangement whereby their plants would be organized by the more conservative machinists. But the machinists had barely gotten a foot in the door, when they were faced with the immensely increasing number of unskilled aircraft workers and a subdivision of work which carried the former trend to an unanticipated extreme. In order to maintain any place at all, the local machinists had to direct most of their educational energies toward recruiting members and giving them a sense of belonging to a laboring group.

The Burbank local, however, also spent time propagandizing for apprenticeship. It is significant that while the union newspaper of the war years rarely mentioned the public school program and only occasionally mentioned the private aircraft schools in the area, the paper did pay heed to the apprenticeship program. Aircraft workers should not expect to go back to the days when every worker served an apprenticeship, the union paper editorialized, but there was no reason, either, to return to the earlier aircraft days when no one served an apprenticeship!

In the rush during the past twenty years by management of industry to place every job on a production basis, and to subdivide the work that less and less skill would be required for more and more work, the advice of organized labor was disregarded and the national emergency proved that serious shortages of certain classes of skilled labor resulted because no apprentices had been training to prepare for the several trades. The apprenticeship program had been abandoned.[46]

Despite its willingness to support apprenticeship programs, the union did not display interest in other training activities until toward the end of the war, when the labor group began to urge its members to prepare themselves for the possibility of displacement, to seek additional training so that they would be able to find work in related field jobs like aircraft or engine mechanic.[47] Yet, the local had still not thrown its energies behind a program with the public schools, and it was not until many years after the war that it sought such a cooperative teaching arrangement.

At best, the public school could not fill all the needs of the booming aircraft industry. When it came to the problem of training higher-level technical and engineering employees, the company had to call on the resources of higher educational institutions, and these the city did not have. This training of technicians and engineers, though not the most immediate concern, grew more and more important during the later years of the war and was to become a key educational problem for the company in the postwar period.

One way of meeting the wartime need for technical people was simply to extend the division of labor to a higher level, establishing intensive training courses for draftsmen and junior engineers, who could relieve the professionals of part of their burden.[48] Intensive courses, such as those Lockheed established with the California Institute of Technology, could not, however, solve the entire educational problem. Those aeronautical engineers who could be recruited had to be acquainted with the company's products and processes, but, in addition, it was necessary to draw engineers from a variety of specialties, both to meet the need for genuine professionals and to supply the variety of special skills needed in aircraft design. The main emphasis of Lockheed's cooperative engineering-training programs, then, was upon "converting" civil, mechanical, electrical, and other engineers into men who could relate their specialties to aircraft.

As had been the case in earlier discussions, company educators were concerned that mechanical engineers be familiar with the vertical order of skills in the field. In fact, in the early years of the company's engineering program there was an effort to have the men attend trade extension courses at the local high school; the criticism of two Lockheed educators—that the engineering schools did not give men sufficient practical understanding—suggests that the theoretical-practical debate played some part in their educational ideology.[49] Yet, as in the engineering world in general, Lockheed's attempt to integrate higher and lower skills was clearly limited; engineers were, after all, professionals, and the training of professionals was a university—and company—concern.

One added problem in recruiting and training professionals was that of defining their role in management. The revitalization of the Lockheed Company came at a time when the craftsman-entrepreneur stage of the aircraft industry was nearly passed; by the time the company was becoming large, it was no longer looking solely for managerial talent but for technical experts as well. The company was, therefore, put in the position of having to sell a professional ideology to its engineers; that is, in order to meet the need for experts, the engineers had to be convinced that they would do best as experts and would be able to improve themselves through this route. At a 1941 conference on supervision at Lockheed, the two "ladders" were discussed. One, the ladder from foreman up to chief engineer—the management ladder—would draw people into management who had a working familiarity with the industry. The other was the professional ladder, and one company administrator urged the engineers not to confuse the two: "Our present procedures are aimed to give greater opportunity, scope and recognition to the exceptionally qualified designer. As a rule, such a man can make no greater mistake than endeavoring to climb the administrative ladder. Few men are really qualified in both fields . . . ."[50]

By the war period, then, the company had reached the stage where rungs on the technological ladder were fairly clearly marked, following, in general, the model of mechanical engineering, even though no such ladder could remain static, and it would continue to change with the changing character of the industry.[51]

The City's Viewpoint. As with the recruitment of workers, the geographical range of Lockheed's educational activities was pragmatically defined, varying according to the institutions available or the number which could be created or converted to meet training needs. Lockheed's educational perspective was not confined to the city of Burbank; nor, on the other hand, did Burbank ever see education primarily in terms of Lockheed. Indeed, this small city had an independent spirit.

The early history of Burbank followed a pattern common in Southern California.[52] Americans began to buy the Spanish lands about midcentury. In the early seventies, a New England dentist named David Burbank—who had a penchant for raising sheep and selling real estate—purchased some of this property himself. The routing of the Santa Fe Railroad through the district brought a little town into being, and in the course of the succeeding land boom, the Providencia Land, Water, and Development Company bought a good deal of the area. In a gust of wishful thinking, the Providencia Company plotted out a whole community, including ranches and homes, with the railway running through the center of town. In 1888, the land company failed; the small furniture factory which was Burbank's only industry closed its doors, and the little boomtown went back to raising sheep and growing grapes.

For twenty years the city underwent modest expansion. When Los Angeles began plans to tap the Owens Valley water supply during the first decade of the new century, the San Fernando Valley (in which Burbank is located) underwent another land boom and the town's promoting spirits were raised again. Burbank, the "Panorama City," would be an ideal residential city for the expanding area the city boosters claimed; so they went to work to improve transportation links with neighboring communities. But Burbank was not anxious to become incorporated into Los Angeles. On the contrary, the Burbank city fathers expanded the civic boundaries, included more of the neighboring farm lands, and invited the Valley farmers to join them, rather than the threatening metropolis. At the same time, Burbank was not content to be a residential community. Rather, its whole character was shaped around two poles, one being its residential ideal, and the other being its desire for industry.

The first symbolic step in the industrial direction came in 1917, when the town leaders induced the Moreland Truck Company to locate in Burbank. The town's population expansion of the twenties—from a mere 2,000 to 16,000—added to the conviction that industry would prosper. The city (according to town historians) shed its "rural ways" during the twenties; the Jergens Company opened a branch soap factory, and a china concern was started. Most of these light-industrial firms were located along the railroad, but on the outskirts of town a rather different kind of enterprise, a movie company, was also started. Soon Warner Brothers decided to locate in the same area, and an enterprising townsman, seeing the possibility of a new business center (the original one was by the railroad line) began a second center not far from the movie lots. A last section of town, also distant but on the railroad, was built up when first Lockheed and then the United Aircraft and Transport Company established their respective factory and airport. Burbank now had an aircraft center as well; it was 1929, and the industrial vision was close to realization.

With the Depression, the Moreland Truck Company closed; Lockheed reached the verge of extinction; and the community drew in its belt, started public relief and public works. Yet the earlier hopes still burned bright, and by the mid-thirties things began to look up. The Warner Brothers opened a new sound stage; Lockheed's employment rose to over one thousand; the Disney studios were opened in 1939—and then the aircraft boom began. By 1940, Burbank had a population of over 30,000; at the peak of war production it had nearly 60,000 residents. At the same peak, Lockheed was employing more than 90,000 people. It is obvious that no community could undergo such a transition without a strain, and part of the strain in the case of Burbank was due to its original dual ideal. All during the twenties, local literature had continued to promote "the upbuilding of industry and home life." As one booster explained, Burbank was ideal for industrial location because of the "high class of employees, for 95 per cent are white, and over 50 per cent are home owners. . . ."[53] This image persisted during the Depression, city promoters pointing to the harmony of middle-class homes and variegated industry. Yet one such brochure suggests that home and industry could be most easily harmonized if industry were of a particular type. After lauding Burbank's various industries, the brochure added: "Many cities have great industrial enterprises. Few attract outstanding craftsmen. Burbank is one of the few."[54]

There seems little question that the town fathers did not envision the kind of giant industry which Lockheed brought into their midst. If they had, they surely would have grabbed at the chance to promote the town on the basis of the new industry. Yet, in the late 1930's, the city newspaper was upbraiding the local merchants: other cities were developing themselves, the paper said, despite Burbank's great population and industrial expansion, the town was sitting back. "This is not said to belittle Burbank's business center. It is said with the thought that there must be something wrong when a community is growing so tremendously industrially, in population and home building, when the business center does not grow proportionately. . . ."[55]

Each of the two goals in the Burbank ideal had a series of attributes clustered around it. Industry meant progress and flexibility on the part of the community. Homes meant stability, order, church, culture—homogeneity, equality, and opportunity all at the same time. The goals of homeowning and industry did not necessarily blend, as the boosters wished them to, and efforts to develop the non-industrial aspect of the city were not always successful. In the 1920's, one developer tried to get the University of California to locate a southern branch in Burbank. From the 1930's on, attempts were made to establish a junior college in Burbank; and in 1951, there was an unsuccessful effort to locate a new state college there. One can rewrite, in imagination, the city's history as it would have been had such an institution been located in Burbank, but with or without a university, the homeowning ideal remained vital. Nowhere can this be seen more clearly than in the public school system, for in a community whose stated ideal was to harmonize industry and home, industrial education played a surprisingly small role. To understand this state of affairs more fully, one must look from the general ideals of the city to the school system itself.

The Burbank schools of the 1920's, like the community itself, were small but growing. The ideal of the school system was precisely in line with that of a wholesome, hearty American community. "For over ten years," said the superintendent, "our chief ambition has been that the Burbank schools shall become the best on earth in character education."[56] What "character education" meant to the school leadership seemed to be a combination of old-fashioned schooling with a fair dose of progressive education. "By almost unanimous agreement today among our educational thinkers," noted a 1927 publication of the schools, "our first objective should be to help each individual child to become a truly social individual." The "social" individual, however, seemed primarily to be one who understood his role as a citizen; there was little discussion of social problems in the philanthropic sense, except for such ventures as the "opportunity room" for Mexican children. The establishment of an adult school in the early thirties simply extended the hours of traditional day school curriculum.

In 1934, however, the scene was more profoundly altered by the election of a new superintendent, a man particularly committed to the character-development end of progressive education. The school publication was suddenly filled with descriptions of "units" on post-office building, Indian life, cooking, and the rest.[57] The superintendent waxed enthusiastic on the "creativity" which such projects would develop, the help they would be in learning to use leisure time, and—especially—the influence they would have on the youngsters' moral development. This mode of individual development, he insisted, would also provide the best method for teaching fundamental skills. On the high school level (Burbank was soon participating in a regional effort for progressive curriculum reform), attention to the individual's development would help him to choose the proper college course, or, if he were going to work, would help him to "meet people in the community who are influential in their particular service."

As one follows the superintendent's discussions through the thirties, it becomes clear that he was meeting increased resistance to his child-centered curriculum; he spoke over and over of how much the new view of education could contribute to the teaching of fundamentals; he constantly assured the Burbank parents that their own interests would be taken into account, as well as those of the children.[58] Perhaps the war saved the superintendent from an early confrontation with dissatisfied parents, for there was a marked change in his rhetoric as the city swung into defense production. Talk of creativity fell by the wayside, while the goal of citizenship education took on new importance. Vocational education moved into the limelight, especially the vocational training upon which the adult school was embarking. Regardless of these changes, however, war conditions ultimately made the superintendent's ideas even less acceptable to at least one segment of the community.

One must picture a small city in which the question of school adequacy for citizenship and training in fundamentals was suddenly given a whole new meaning by rather profound changes in the social and industrial sphere. No massive social disorder was engendered, of course, but the long-time residents of Burbank still refer to the war period—when the "new people" came in—as one of considerable difficulty. One veteran Burbank citizen recalled what it was like during the change in the plant shift, when all the young men, single men who often lived outside the community, came racing down the main street in their cars. All the aspects of this picture must be taken into account to understand the position of the Board of Education, when, around 1943, they voiced what amounted to a repudiation of the superintendent. Juvenile delinquency, the Board declared, was becoming a more and more important problem for the community; home life was faltering; sometimes there was too much money around, sometimes, too little; children were overindulged, underdisciplined, and generally neglected. The public schools concerned themselves with developing the child's ability to express himself when, in fact, the need was for not only basic studies, but the type of disciplinary training which would develop character and build an upstanding Christian citizenry.[59]

The city's partisans of home life had responded to the complexities of a changing city; in 1945, the superintendent retired, and a new gentleman, whose philosophy was obviously more congenial to the School Board, took the post.

Inasmuch as the school ideals from the twenties on had included progressive aspects, industrial arts had found a place in the curriculum. Whether the school ideology could also include vocational training did not seem to be an issue until the mid-thirties, when industrial expansion and public interest had both increased. The Lockheed Corporation had taken an aggressive interest in the public school curriculum, as far as the adult program went.* By the war years, the city also contained dozens of smaller aircraft-related manufacturers, many of whom did subcontracting for the Lockheed Company.

From a 1939 survey, one Burbank vocational educator concluded that 158 out of 160 industrial executives and businessmen wanted the schools to offer "an efficient program of instruction in all basic trades. . . ."[60] One might guess that the community's smaller manufacturers were in the vanguard of the demand for vocational education, following the pattern of the early years of

---

* Veterans of the aircraft industry point out that even in the 1930's, mere high school graduates were generally unemployable in the factories—that the industry tried to recruit slightly older people, and, therefore, emphasized education past the high school years.

the century, when the National Association of Manufacturers pushed federal legislation, while the National Association of Corporation Schools was far from enthusiastic about government support. In Burbank's development, however, it was Lockheed which actively promoted at least an adult program of vocational education, while, with some exceptions, the smaller firms only cooperated with the trend. Why this was the case is not easy to answer, but perhaps the story of one smaller firm will shed some light.

This company's original owners were two men, who, in the late thirties, began to make aircraft parts in a small shop not far from Burbank. The shop was soon moved into Burbank itself, and the enterprise expanded rapidly. At the peak of wartime production it employed several thousands and, like Lockheed, was forced into the use of "green hands" and mass-production techniques. Yet, according to one of the small firm's veterans, mass-production methods were even less compatible with his company's work than that of Lockheed. Skilled workmen, he explained, were essential to the production of intricate aircraft parts. From the firm's earliest years, the emphasis was on highly skilled men; it recruited experienced machinists from the area and also, until the war, brought in men from automobile and machine companies of the Midwest and East to teach the special skills needed.

Likewise, education for such an enterprise could not be on a mass-production basis. The parts company, this spokesman explained, focused on on-the-job rather than school training. Even the school programs of the war period did little good, he noted; Lockheed could afford to lend machinery to the schools, but these machines were not necessarily best for the smaller firm's learning purposes. The training of skilled workers, he continued, was best done in the shop; in the early fifties the company inaugurated an apprentice program, which was, after all, the best way to learn. Yes, he admitted (to a question as to whether the larger firms, as many persons commented, did the training and the smaller firms gleaned the results), the company did gain some trained men from the Lockheed Company, but one must understand that skilled work was a relatively small part of their concern, while it was the primary function of the smaller firm's business.

It was primarily under the urging of the Lockheed Company and the State Bureau of Industrial and Vocational Education, then, that the School Board began to consider the question of trade training in the late thirties. But whatever small-scale plans may have been contemplated were soon swept aside in the demand for defense workers. Federal money came in to subsidize a vast adult training program and to establish the large training shops which the programs required. Although the school also had several vocational teachers employed for the purpose of teaching the high school boys, this concern had to be secondary; the shops were used on a twenty-four hour basis for adult workers, and the vocational program for the youth could hardly take priority.

However, high school boys did become a part of the massive training program in an interesting fashion. As the manpower situation became more critical, "Boy-power" projects had been established in public schools all over the country; through Burbank's wartime "work-experience" program, five or six hundred local youths went to work in defense industry, primarily, of course, aircraft. But after the war emergency was over, the work-experience program became much smaller; the entire high school vocational program seemed to go into a decline. The machinery was there, yet it is questionable whether the spirit was also present, despite the fact that the school literature continued to promote a well-balanced high school program, preparing students for the world of work as well as for college. Industrial education courses continued, though in diminishing variety. Slowly but surely the vocational teachers left or retired, and were replaced, if at all, by industrial-arts teachers. More than one Burbank educator described the remaining work-experience program as a way of providing the vocational training which the school system it-self could not offer.

In retrospect, the local inhabitants often explained the decline of trade-training interest in the following manner: although the aircraft industry was of great importance to Burbank and many Burbank citizens earned their livelihood in that industry, as parents they had higher ambitions for their children; both the skilled workers and the city's professionals wanted their sons to reach at least the professional level. In support of this theory, one Burbank educator recalled that even during the war, when many high school boys were working in the plants, the suggestion that they make such work a career was greeted with "raucous hooting."

The mobility explanation was not the only one which Burbank citizens could offer, however. One educator, who had ultimately moved from the city's vocational program to a college position in the industrial arts, pronounced the common theory false. Burbank, he argued, was truly devoted to industry—the early invitations to the Moreland Truck Company, the interest in trade training during the thirties, and the present importance of industry all bore this out. Nevertheless, the school system had to make some surface concessions to the tastes of part of the community. The schools had to restyle "vocational education" as the more general "industrial-arts education," because with the latter rubric they could gain more public support. What actually went on in industrial-art classes, the educator continued, was little different than what went on in the vocational classes—that is, the teaching of work skills. In addition, the educator noted, part of the explanation lay in the fact that Burbank shared in the statewide enthusiasm for junior colleges which developed after World War II. Then, everyone thought that vocational education would be moving into the junior colleges, where indeed, it belonged.[61] Burbank, he concluded, made a grave mistake in not establishing its own junior college.

Local Ideals and the Educational Map. The question of a junior college for Burbank was first raised in the 1930's, and it was repeatedly raised until the early 1960's, when Burbank formally joined the Los Angeles City College system. From the Burbank standpoint the issue of a junior college was complex, involving the many financial factors which taxpayers are wont to discuss, but for us the most interesting feature of the debate was the question of the division of labor between educational institutions in the area.

Despite the fact that Burbank had maintained her civic independence, the town had gradually become part of a vast metropolitan area, stretching unbroken for hundreds of miles. It was inevitable, therefore, that the Burbank junior college debate should involve not only a definition of Burbank as a community, but its relationship to the large community with which it was geographically merged.[62] This question was apparent in a 1944 meeting at Burbank in which the Board of Education, representative Burbankers, and educators from surrounding communities met to discuss the city's educational scheme.[63] The community feeling in favor of a higher educational institution was an important point made in favor of such a college, but other representatives seemed to feel that a Burbank facility would only duplicate those of nearby communities, lowering the educational level of all. The only virtue of the proposal, it seemed to some, would be if Burbank were to offer courses not available in these other schools. The meeting rejected the possibility of an intercommunity post-high school system; the pride of the individual communities seemed too great for such a step.

Part of the conflict at this meeting resulted from the presence of educators from neighboring junior college systems, especially nearby Glendale, which stood to lose at least some of their Burbank students if the city built its own college; in other matters, community pride had never actually prevented the sharing of educational facilities. Indeed, since the development of its vocational adult school program, Burbank had played a considerable role in the area's efforts to supply post-high school education. In the forties and fifties, the adult school offered one of the largest apprenticeship programs in the state, drawing youths from Burbank and many other communities, and serving both local and more distant industrial needs. Burbank adult educators feared that a junior college in the city would absorb much of their vocational training function, but Burbank never built its college. Another junior college was built even closer than Glendale, and most of the adult school apprenticeship work (particularly that of Lockheed) was transferred to this third college. In essence, the junior-college decision had eliminated a good share of the city's vocational-education activities.

The entire junior-college debate can be seen as the community's effort to draw an educational map—a map on which the careers of Burbank students could be charted in a way consistent with the symbolic valuations the community placed on industry and culture. The degree to which the community's ambiguous ideal subtly penetrated this debate was remarkable; one spokesman could argue that Burbank ought not to build a junior college because the Los Angeles colleges offered a fine vocational and general program; another spokesman could argue that Burbank should build a school because California students liked to attend colleges close to home. In the face of its own communal ideals, it was impossible for Burbank to draw the kind of map implicit in Lockheed's educational planning, one which included both a highly specific sense of educational function (every kind of school from the lofty CIT to the most modest welding school could be called on if the occasion demanded) and a wide geographic sweep (from the East Coast engineering schools to the local adult school). Yet, even the Lockheed and Burbank perspectives taken together do not exhaust the industrial-education activities of the area; a brief glance at some nearby educational institutions reveals how Burbank's students and aircraft industry figure in other educational maps, indeed how Burbank and Lockheed figure in a temporal and geographic palimpsest of educational conceptions.

Let us turn first to Pasadena Junior College; it was a fairly popular choice for Burbank students, and the contrast between Burbank and Pasadena conceptions of education is enlightening. Pasadena would have had difficulty in promoting itself as that average American community which Burbank chose for its hallmark. It was distinctly wealthly from its early years. Built up by New Englanders in the 1880's, Pasadena's style revolved around retired millionaires, culture, and gracious living.[64] The gracious living was facilitated by a large number of servants, Negroes and Mexicans, who by settling either with or near their employers, or in another section of town, gave the community two distinct and disparate social classes. The fact that middle-class people also eventually settled in the community did not seem to inspire Pasadena to style itself all-American and homogeneous in population. It did, however, remain primarily residential until after the war, when light industry began to locate there. Strangely, in contrast to Burbank, Pasadena had offered industrial education for many years.

The Pasadena schools were geared to include manual work and to take into account a diverse population. In the late nineteenth and early twentieth century, manual training and sloyd were given a prominent place in the curriculum. These served as a prelude to establishing a genuine vocational high school, and the presence of the Throop Institute (later CIT) encouraged this endeavor. By the mid-twenties, Pasadena had also added a junior college which included a vocational curriculum. The appointment of a "full-time researcher" for the public schools during the twenties, helped to assure that diverse student abilities and interests would be taken into account, and the theme of suiting education to occupation was continued by a superintendent in the thirties, who stressed the need for vocational training "for the pupils who are non-academic in interest and ability."[65] Under the leadership of John Sexon, the junior college also carried out this basic ideology, for the college was to meet the needs both of terminal students and of those who were university bound.

As early as 1931, the Pasadena Junior College had included an aeronautics curriculum, to prepare students for the area's aircraft industry. The school soon recruited a local expert, a gentleman who had established his own small aircraft factory and airport in Pasadena, to teach the subject, and under his guidance, aeronautical work soon became one of the school's major vocational areas. The emphasis on production in the aircraft curriculum remained primary. Two kinds of programs were offered; one was aimed at developing technical people, men with a solid background in drafting and design. The second had the object of training all-round aircraft mechanics, men who could go to the assembly plant rather than the drafting room. There was little effort to train men either as ground personnel or as pilots; these latter jobs, according to a teacher in the aircraft department, constituted separate skills, suited to the airport rather than the factory.

The Pasadena aircraft program looked to the whole Los Angeles area for its students, and then looked to particular factories, Lockheed among them, for employment of these students. Another school which followed a similar recruitment pattern was the Los Angeles Trade and Technical College, originally the Frank Wiggins Trade School, which was founded by the city of Los Angeles in the middle 1920's.[66] In type, it was a classic trade school, whose aim was "distinctly vocational"; it developed a wide variety of programs geared to the needs of Los Angeles industry and business, and from the very beginning drew Los Angeles area students in large numbers. Although often called a high school, until its official conversion to a junior college in 1949, the trade school drew mostly high school graduates or students in that age group. The first course related to the aircraft industry was established in 1928—a course in aircraft sheetmetal work; in 1932, the art department added aircraft drafting, and by 1936, the first aircraft mechanics teacher was hired. The aircraft department continued to expand, reaching, like other such training programs, great proportions during the war years.

During its first decade, the Frank Wiggins aircraft program trained people chiefly for production work. Almost all the students, a veteran teacher remarked, went to the factories; the more talented moved into supervision, but only a few went on to higher technical study. After the war, however, the aircraft department took a somewhat different direction. It had always been interested in training skilled workers, but it seemed to these aircraft educators (as it did to many others at the end of the World War II) that the future for aircraft mechanics lay not in the factories (except in small numbers), but in maintenance work. The emphasis of the trade-school department, then, became the training of licensed mechanics, men who would work for the airlines or for a variety of business concerns, where the all-round aircraft mechanic (sometimes, indeed, still even in the flyer-mechanic combination) was in growing demand. Here was an institution, then, which drew students from all over the Los Angeles area and sent them first to aircraft factories (Lockheed was one of the major employers of the schools' graduates) and later to other kinds of aircraft employers.

Finally, let us turn to an institution which evolved in yet another way in relation to the area's aircraft industry. The Northrop Institute of Technology was originally a company school which the Northrop Company, like Lockheed, had developed to train wartime production workers. After the war, the school was sold to one of its educational directors and was converted to an institution for training both licensed mechanics and quasi-engineers. The hallmark of the school's engineering ideology was its practicality, its intensive two-year course in aeronautical engineering; the students studied during the entire year and spent all their time on technical subjects. This preparation, one Northrop educator noted, enabled graduates to go directly to industry, to begin their work immediately without the company's having to "lead them by the hand," as was necessary with most regular engineering graduates. Although liberal-arts courses were important, he continued, aircraft companies such as Lockheed seemed to appreciate the Northrop approach. The boys already knew what they wanted when they came to Northrop, he said, and the school had only to acquaint them with the specific industrial opportunities and to give them training especially geared to these opportunities.

Northrop continued to expand its engineering program, adding several new curricula, but not surprisingly it eventually added a liberal-arts section, and rapidly moved in the direction of academic accreditation and the awarding of bachelor degrees. This was sign of the times, said the Northrop educator.

It was also a result of the fact that the Northrop ideology was geared to mobility; the graduates had always been expected to rise through the engineering ranks, just as the graduates of orthodox engineering schools. The school was never set up to train mere technicans, the educator insisted, but always to train men with an understanding of engineering dynamics; even the aircraft maintenance engineering course, with its inclusion of aircraft mechanics training, had prepared men for high-level positions on both the technological and commercial ends of the aircraft industry.

The geographic scope of the Northrop Institute was even wider than that of the Los Angeles Trade and Technical College or the Pasadena Junior College aircraft program; yet, all, at least at some point, included both Burbank and Lockheed in their educational maps, and all were to some extent included in the perspectives of either the city or the company. The important factor, however, was that each of these educational conceptions —the aircraft schools', Burbank's, Lockheed's—changed in time, including new career ideals and dropping others which no longer seemed viable. One could figuratively pick up any of these maps and plot a course of study and work for a given individual at a given time. Each was adaptable, and yet based upon a particular conception of occupational education and of progress.

As the experience of this complex of institutions suggests, the process of knitting national industrial-education ideologies into the formation of policy for given settings in given times is sufficiently subtle that one cannot predict the course which a given school system or community might take on the basis of nationally voiced ideals alone. Yet it seems quite possible that if one were to develop a typology of the regional, state, and urban communities which have undertaken industrial education efforts—giving special attention to not only economic and social structure but to the symbolic character of the locale—an understanding of these communities, combined with a broad analysis of the institutional and ideological character of American industrial education, could lead to a more systematic picture of the fates and possible fates of industrial-education programs.

The types of ironic reversal of industrial-education ideals which we have encountered in our examination of the southern interpretations and those of Burbank bear out the importance of geographic perspective. The southern interpretation of industrial education for morality, mobility, or the acquisition of trade skills was intimately linked with both the relation of industry to agriculture and the biracial situation. The juxtaposition of morality and work skills took on a special meaning where impoverished rural communities predominated; industrial education for mobility was given a new twist where access to manufacturing leadership was blocked or limited; and the ideal of trade training for the "average American boy"—the darling of the northern trade-training advocates—became problematic in its application where there was no average between black and white and the very appellation "workman" was a doubtful distinction.

The examination of Burbank affords an example of analysis in seemingly more microcosmic terms—a particular town within a particular region, a particular population with particular civic, educational, and industrial goals—yet this urban interpretation of industrial education could be subject to the same kind of questions as the regional setting. In Burbank, the philanthropic ideology played little if any role, for neither the vision of industrial expansion nor the vision of a homogeneous, comfortable community left scope for uplift or reform. The ideal of mobility was subject to subtle differentiation, depending on the particular industrial perspective or the particular community members involved. The trade-training ideal found a temporary home in a variety of institutions, more of them outside the city limits than within. Indeed, the comparison of educational facilities and ideals in communities surrounding this manufacturing town suggests both the range and differences in posture which are possible within the same region; one Burbank citizen compared his community to a New England factory town—a kind of analogy which suggests ways in which the differential urban interpretations of industrial education might be further explored.

The question which the study of particular settings raises continually refers one back to the broader national picture of which they are a part, for although the major industrial-education ideologies were well established by the early years of the twentieth century, continued change on the large economic, social, and political scene posed new challenges to each of the accepted rationales. In the following and final chapter we are going to turn again to the major industrial-education ideals to ask how their partisans have handled them in recent critical periods. The local and regional perspectives do not disappear but constitute a counterpoint to this broader national picture.

6

The Reassessment
of Industrial-Education Ideals

In the hundred years of industrial-education discussions beginning with the 1820's, the goal of industrialization itself received
remarkably little challenge. The major elements of the manufacturing ideal—the expanding economy, the increasing importance
of factory workers, the changing nature of industrial opportunity
—were simply taken for granted by most industrial-education
spokesmen. There was little explicit attention, for example, to the
economic depressions which were taking place while the manual-
training or trade-school ideologies were being formulated. Even
industrial educators with the greatest reservations about the manufacturing world—the philanthropists, the social reformers, the
socialists—geared their remedies to that world.

Given this general acceptance of industrialization, we are
prompted to ask what happened to industrial education in the
1930's when, it would seem, the notion of industrialization was
subject to its greatest trial. First, however, we must look to the
arguments of the twenties, for the educational reaction to leisure
and apparent prosperity in that decade forms a curious continuity with the response to unemployment and impoverishment

during the Depression; the arguments for leisure education during the twenties and the counterarguments of the vocational educators were a prelude to the treatment of these issues during the Depression—the new views of leisure education, the educational plan for national recovery, and the reactions of vocational educators themselves.

The last and final section of our study will consider the contemporary industrial-education debate, one which is marked by not only the persistence of the three basic industrial-education ideologies, but a particular interest in national goals and in the relation between industrial education and these goals. By turning to the recent literature on industrial education and to the legislative hearings which proposed to reevaluate the national system of vocational education, we can locate some of the key questions for American industrial education of the future.

Prosperity and Depression

Industrial Education in the Twenties: As soon as the Smith-Hughes Act had been passed in 1917, the new vocational education system went into operation. Teachers and administrators helped in the training for defense industries; plans were laid for the occupational training of war veterans; new areas of interest were opened by the need for foreman training which wartime expansion had made so evident. Beneath and beside these special concerns, vocational educators were beginning to build broad foundations; during the decade of the twenties, they would have to construct a professional house from the beams and floorboards which the Smith-Hughes legislation had provided; specific programs would have to be planned to meet the federal prerequisites; programs would have to be implemented taking a variety of local needs and interests into account; the requirements for vocational teachers and administrators would have to be established, and the profession would have to be defined in relation to other teaching specialties.

Despite the fact that the ideological groundwork for vocational education was established, however, vocational educators were not to be left in peace to spend their first professional decade elaborating practical policy and working out ideological refinements. The traditional criticisms of the machine age had begun to take on a particular intensity during the economic boom of the twenties, and as fears about unemployment, growing leisure, and moral turpitude increased, industrial education, too, was subject to an implicit challenge. In the course of these discussions, old fears about the working class took on new life; workers, said some, would be debased through enslavement to machines; workers, said others, would be deprived of their jobs through mechanization, would be thrust out into idleness and a menacing lack of moral discipline.[1]

In the face of these fears, it is not surprising to find that educators and philanthropists placed considerable emphasis on the uplifting power of education: indeed, the modern adult-education movement stepped into the breach precisely as the lyceum movement had in the previous century, to assure that the workingman would become a whole and responsible human being. Although there had been wide and varied educational activities involving adults in both colonial and pre-Civil War America, the modern adult-education movement developed as part and parcel of the Progressive era, with roots, like the era itself, in the last decades of the nineteenth century.[2] Although the adult programs of this era were intimately related in their purposes, they had no broad ideology and no central social organ by which to coordinate their programs. Evening programs in the public schools, for instance, had been developing since the public schools themselves, offering a variety of courses reflecting the current trends in public education. University extension arose in the context of the developing relation of the university to its community, while ventures such as the Chautauqua movement and the workingmen's colleges spanned both formal and informal educational worlds.

Curiously enough, the achievement of institutional unity (to the extent that this ever existed in adult-education activities) did not come until the 1920's, that is, until after the glow of Progressive reform had dimmed. But adult education was one reform movement which was able to draw on the very imagery—of the machine age, of leisure—which marked the twenties. Two important developments also contributed to the crystallization of adult education in this period. The first was the great expansion of evening schools which had occurred in connection with the Americanization movement. Some of the motives which had inspired the movement were of a character which repelled the more idealistic adult educators, yet the fact remained that Americanization classes had given adult education a widely acknowledged role in the public schools.

The second circumstance which promoted the development of adult education in the twenties was the founding of a national adult-education organization through the efforts of Frederick P. Keppel, president of the Carnegie Corporation.[3] Keppel's concern that the numerous adult activities had no over-all coordination led the corporation to sponsor a series of meetings which resulted in the formation of the American Association for Adult Education in 1926. The make-up of this group was significant, for in choosing representatives the corporation had favored public figures who had shown interest in the issues of adult education rather than teachers and administrators who had worked in the area. The involvement of important persons helped to bring the adult-education debate to greater public attention, but the costs were considerable; critics continued to charge that the movement was the captive of its philanthropic sponsors and was distinct from the realities of public adult education.

One of the most articulate of the adult-education spokesmen during the 1920's and 1930's was Eduard C. Lindeman. Lindeman had come into adult-education work through rural sociology and rural-reform activities and had acquired a more urban viewpoint when he joined the *New Republic* staff and became a disciple of Herbert Croly. Lindeman's 1926 treatise, *The Meaning of Adult*

Education, showed how deeply at least some of the progressive tenets, especially Croly's interpretation of them, came to mark Lindeman's thought.

He opened his small volume by describing a recent trip to Denmark and his discovery of the Danish folk high schools, which he felt could provide a guide to American education. To Lindeman, the Danish institutions demonstrated the possibility of developing the whole individual without ignoring the importance of economic security. Americans, he argued, needed to apply the ideas they had learned about making education meaningful to a program of life-long learning, one which would enable adults to face the society's fragmented and complex structure. Adult education needed to be geared to social participation and individual fulfillment; Americans would have to become acquainted with the principles that underlay their technological society so that they could apply the method of intelligence to that society; they would also have to learn to understand its political principles, so that all Americans, especially those in the working class, could contribute to democratic action, to temperate and thoughtful political decisions. In addition, Americans needed to develop individual creativity through participation in the arts from which an "indigenous folk expression" would develop: Americans should take as a model the Danish farmer (a man whom Lindeman actually met and who became a kind of symbol for him) who labored in his fields and then went home to paint pictures, pictures which he would not sell for anything!

Lindeman's suspicion of materialism and of the industrialized world which seems to have promoted such an attitude was not far from the surface. For him, the factory had nothing to teach men, and education for work was merely a gross necessity of life: "Vocational education," he said, "is designed to equip students with the proper means for arriving at their selected goals. Adult education goes beyond the means and demands new sanctions, new vindications for ends."[4]

All the adult-education spokesmen did not join Lindeman in

this stance. James Earl Russell, for example, not only a major figure in the American Association for Adult Education but the long-time head of Teachers College, had a strong and catholic commitment to vocational training. Russell was one of those in the adult-education movement who sought to harmonize the goals of vocational and cultural development, of work and leisure-time activity. He felt that education had failed to give Americans a sense of the proper value of work, particularly of non-professional work:

There will not be great improvement in the quality of service until the public demands better service and is willing to pay for it; to bring the public to an appreciation of good service and to an understanding of what is a just economic wage is adult education. To create in the worker a love for his vocation, to make him feel the elbow-touch with other men in occupations in other countries, to introduce him to the romance of industry and to give him the ability and the desire to spend his leisure in a way befitting his manhood—that is adult education. Perhaps the most significant opportunity of adult education is the chance of exhalting in the public mind the division of labor, particularly in those fields in which manual labor is at a premium.[5]

It would be difficult to imagine a statement which more fully combined the participation-in-the-industrial-world aspect of Progressive thought (Russell virtually repeated an earlier statement of Dewey's) with the conclusion that one must have trade training for adults.

While Russell, with his particular eclecticism, represented an intermediate position in the adult-education discussions, trade-training advocates stood at the extreme of the spectrum—the opposite extreme from Lindeman. It is not surprising that advocates of trade training claimed adult education as their rightful territory, for, you will recall, the Smith-Hughes Act, though allowing federal aid for certain non-vocational courses in the curricula of high-school aged youth, provided that adult evening classes be confined to "instruction . . . which is supplemental to the daily employment."

Who should know the meaning of this phrase better than Charles Prosser, who had fought the battles of NSPIE, served on the National Commission for Aid to Vocational Education, and had then, at least briefly, served as the executive director of the Federal Board for Vocational Education.[6] Prosser and his friends were fully aware of the critique implied by many of the new adult educators; indeed, *Vocational Education in a Democracy*, which he wrote with Charles R. Allen, came out in the same year as Lindeman's little treatise. Taken together, the two books sounded like the first clash of swords in a duel.

Prosser and Allen's own classic dealt thoroughly with the question of the "iron man." First, the authors restated what they took to be the position of leisure educators, namely, that the concept of the "iron man" had led to such great specialization and to such unbearable monotony of work that educators needed to center their energies on education for non-work time. Prosser and Allen felt that the leisure educators implied that education for work would take care of itself. Next, Prosser and Allen attacked the idea that the modern factory was a monolithic mass; it was a highly complex business, they said, requiring more skill, wider knowledge, and greater flexibility and responsibility on the part of the workers than any industrial endeavor in history. In addition, there were still a vast number of small shops in this country which required a wide range of skills, and there were still traditional trades where mechanization had made little impact. Even if mechanization were complete, the authors parried, America would still need men to design and build its "iron man." And again they argued; this was an age of science and invention; since industry continually changed, the country would always need changing skills:

When the advocates of no training for wage earning, but all training for leisure see all this shift and flux and see nothing else, they feel justified in the educational policy they propose. In any event, they certainly have the better of the argument with those enthusiasts who, in the face of the foregoing facts, still look to the all-day preparatory school as a solution of the problem of mass training for the workers of a changed and changing mechanical world.[7]

Prosser and Allen were wielding a two-edged sword; they were just as anxious to defeat the proponents of the traditional day-training school as to defeat the advocates of education for leisure. The two authors had little use for mixing vocational and general studies; rather, they felt that general education should come first and that afterwards, when the student was out in the world of work, he should pursue his vocational training.

In arguing with the leisure educators, Prosser and Allen placed special emphasis on the point that vocational education could take place in a variety of settings, some formal and some informal. Ideally, the authors stated, the evening schools should confine their part of adult vocational teaching to the related subjects, and actual shop training should be done in the plant—with vocational teachers going to the factory to do their teaching. All such adult courses, wherever offered, should be short and functional, geared to the specific needs of the workman, teaching him the specific skill which he wished to learn. Indeed, said the vocational educators, the very fact that he wished to increase his skills made such a course meaningful, and (here, Lindeman might have been made aware that the progressive-education argument could cut both ways) educators who tried to cram unwanted moral or intellectual lessons down the throats of these workers did not realize that they were adults.

Just as an anti-materialist and anti-technological attitude lurked not far beneath the surface of Lindeman's argument, an anti-intellectual attitude was near the surface of Prosser's. Wealth, Prosser and Allen insisted, was the basis of leisure; therefore, Americans would have to establish adequate vocational education if they wished time for enjoyment. What citizens actually did with their leisure time was entirely their own business; if one gave the children a "genuine interest and pleasure in reading wholesome if simple things" and gave them a taste for "recreation" and "some deep-rooted hobby," adult leisure time would be used well enough. Who, asked Prosser and Allen, were these "scholastics" who called on "abstract pseudo facts" to impose a selfish, academic conception of education on the workers? "Are they all to read Shakespeare and Milton? Commune with the philosophers?"[8]

This symbolic debate between Lindeman and Prosser, with its valuable critiques on both sides and its profound attitudinal disparities, represented an extreme of alienation between vocational and other forms of education, an especially important extreme when one realizes that the intent of most industrial education of the succeeding hundred years was to bring together the mind and the hand and (at least on the part of the philanthropists) to bring mutual understanding between the worker and the thinker. And although the trade-training perspective from which Prosser spoke was only one possible industrial education stance, it was a position gaining powerful institutional backing from the growing Smith-Hughes system.

The Depression Years. The terms of the leisure versus work-education debate which were established in the twenties continued relatively unaltered during the Depression; that is, each group could point to the Depression and say, You see, this proves that we need more leisure (or vocational) education. At the same time, however, each group was subject to a considerable challenge; it was not at all clear that unemployment was the same as leisure nor that leisure activities could solve the problems of an economically and emotionally depressed population. Nor, on the other hand, was it clear that vocational education had much meaning when men could not get jobs.

Lindeman, for example, became head of one of the WPA leisure programs, and, though not much more interested in work-time activity than he was in the twenties, he did refine his ideas in terms of the Depression; leisure was now "the privilege and the reward of those who do useful work," a kind of "freedom" which came from fulfilling one's work obligation to society. Thus,

Lindeman was really looking forward to a post-Depression world in which jobs, and therefore leisure, would increase. On this account, he was particularly concerned that the Depression interest in recreation, in mere "play and playgrounds," not be confused with genuine democratic recreation for adults. Indeed, he insisted, physical recreation and nature study could be as valuable as serious political and intellectual discussion, if each activity were seen in the context of a social meaning. In the same sense, said Lindeman, the learning of manual skills could help to replace values lost in modern industry—the ability to work for "esthetic ends." "We may now utilize our leisure for purposes of developing those once essential skills which are still capable of furnishing us with a sound education."[9]

For James E. Russell, the midway spokesman in the adult education camp, shop skills could not simply become non-utilitarian; to no one more than Russell did the Depression cause concern and basic puzzlement:

For forty years I have been preaching the necessity of making vocational education—one type of adult education—a constituent part of our educational system. I have urged it, not merely as a means of aiding individuals to give the best service of which they are capable but also because it seemed to me the surest way of training good citizens. . . . It is the irony of fate that I had not foreseen the time when thousands on thousands of my fellow citizens are unable to find work, no matter how competent or how willing to give of their best. It may be the conservatism of age or the disillusionment that follows to confident conclusions drawn from faulty premises that makes me hesitant in predicting the future.[10]

Many adult educators must have shared Russell's disillusionment, and yet during this very period vocational education was, as Russell had hoped, being given a place within the adult-education fold. One factor which surely contributed to this state of affairs was the growth of the NEA Department of Adult Education.[11] Here, public school adult-educators could organize their own sentiments, threatening to form (as they eventually did) a counter-organization to the lofty and philosophic American Association for Adult Education. Caught between these camps, the AAAE developed a policy statement which stressed the "balance" between cultural and vocational subjects, a "balance" which became the watchword of much adult education ideology.

Lyman Bryson of Columbia's Teachers College, the first professor of adult education, reflected this commitment to "balance" in his 1936 textbook. Together with a variety of forms of adult education, Bryson included occupational training; it was this form of adult education, he said, which had always had the most support (from the public and educators in general, if not from adult-educators):

However much one might criticize this as a crass and limited conception of public responsibility for the teaching of adults, it should also be said that occupational training can be made education in its broadest sense. A motive which is strictly pragmatic and derived from one's needs on the job is as good a motive for leading an adult back to educational experience as any other. If occupational training is narrow, if it does not lead on, under guidance, to training which applies to the whole range of an individual's possibilities, that is the fault of the teacher and not of the subject studied.[12]

Although Bryson was willing to accept Prosser's concept of the evening industrial school as a "fragmentary extension" of the regular school, as "a sort of repair station to which busy workers can go for specific answers to quite definitely understood and clearly stated problems," such an activity was embraced in a progressive context. The job of educating a young man to "become a better mechanic," said Bryson, involved not only concrete skills, but an attitude toward workmanship, an understanding of his relation to his own work and the work of others.

In formulating its "balance" theory, the AAAE was responding not only to the growth of adult vocational education, but also to the educational trend of the Depression, which was giving vocational education a prominent place. The adult-education group was quite fearful that the new federal activities would distort adult-education goals, that the aim of improving the quality of American life would be drowned in a series of ad hoc and mere locally-oriented programs.[13] Such fears were not unfounded, for the federal education efforts of the Depression were actually taking adult-education activities out of the hands of small groups of devotees and making such education a form of national policy. The efforts of adult educators to promote their own perspectives within the context of these nation-wide programs were not totally successful, and the role of education in these ventures was ambiguous.

For example, although no place had been provided for education in the Civilian Conservation Corps plans and there was an evident lack of interest in education on the part of the CCC military administration, the Labor Department introduced hobby-activities and vocational guidance into the camps, and the Commissioner of Education, George Zook, soon developed a program of voluntary vocational and academic classes. It was not long before the adult-education potentialities of the CCC were perceived; educational director Clarence S. Marsh spoke of the camp programs as the basis for "a great American folk-school movement" which would grow out of America's "native culture" and which would suggest "new ways of bridging the gap between school and job."[14] Other adult educators, such as Frank Earnest Hill, also saw in the camps the beginning of a new basis for education; CCC classes were true adult education, he said, because they were voluntary. The experience of the camps in vocational and cultural education, Hill insisted, pointed to an answer for that long worrisome problem of out-of-school youth: "Perhaps a particular type of education is needed for the younger group. And perhaps the public school systems can act as centers for the new venture—a venture using a freer method and a different personnel than their own, and tying closer to the life of the farm, factory, and office."[15]

Hill's suggestions for "A freer method and a different personnel" implied a rather far-reaching critique of the established education system. Perhaps the critique might have been ignored had it been voiced by peripheral groups of utopians alone, but the penetration of such idealism into governmental planning, especially in the work of Harry Hopkins and his social-work colleagues, made the challenge quite a real one.

Reform-minded social workers of the twenties had shared the concern of many Americans that the apparent prosperity hid a host of social problems: in a 1929 address to the national social work organization, the editor of *Survey* had warned, "We have need in America today for prophets to write new parables of the new times we live in—of men out of work in the midst of prosperity, of year-round households and broken working time, of mechanical contrivance and social disintegration. . . ."[16] As the social disintegration of the twenties gave way to the greater disintegration of the thirties, social workers came to the fore, struggling to adjust their traditional techniques to mass unemployment. One of their persistent concerns was that social work, especially case work as opposed to community work, had been ignoring the needs of youth, that now American youths were puzzled and frustrated because the normal economic order had been so disrupted.

As early as 1933 the Federal Emergency Relief Administration, in cooperation with the Federal Board of Vocational Education, had begun to attack the "youth problem" by providing funds for vocational education classes; the establishment of the Apprenticeship Training Program was another step in this direction. Yet New Deal reformers were also looking for more revolutionary solutions. While FERA was still in its early stages, Mrs. Roosevelt, Secretary of Labor Perkins, industrialist Charles Tausig, and others were laying plans for the National Youth Administration. As director of the New Deal relief activities, Hopkins was also concerned. When the NYA was established in 1935, Hopkins appointed Aubrey Williams as head, and Williams, a social-work administrator, gathered other social workers to help with the program.

Not surprisingly, the agency had a rhetoric of rescue and up-lift: "Now, I am frank to say," Hopkins declared, "that my sym-pathies . . . are with the people at the bottom of the heap."[17] Yet, as an earlier part of our discussion suggests, a philanthropic approach could take several forms. Philanthropists could aim at making the downtrodden man part of the current social order—making him, in industrial education terms, into an honest work-man—or they could strive to create a better or new social order in which the creation of honest workmen would be a natural consequence. The New Deal plans for education looked in both these directions: sometimes Williams suggested that fundamental social changes might come from NYA efforts, yet he felt the agency also had to cope with problems in their present context.[18]

The immediate goal which the NYA pursued was that of taking youth off the streets and out of competition in the job market. To this end, out-of-school young people were placed in a wide variety on non-regular jobs, often in government offices or shops. Although the NYA did not at first carry on vocational education itself, the temptation to move in this direction was almost irre-sistible, for the philanthropic approach which the agency took was educational in its very nature. This can be seen from the description of the NYA by two enthusiasts, Betty and Ernest K. Lindley.[19]

The "youth problem," the Lindleys said, was not only the result of unemployment but could also be traced to a lack of equal educational opportunities, an inadequacy in the number, size, and character of the nation's schools, and the fact that the young person was "completely abandoned" by society between the time he left school and the time he (hopefully) found a job. The CCC and the Federal Committee on Apprenticeship Training were both steps in the direction of a democratic solution to the youth problem, the Lindleys continued, but the NYA offered a chance for a totally new departure; one could see how meaningful NYA work experiences were to the youth, because they often came back to their shops for sparetime instruction.

Yet the educational potential of NYA projects was not yet being realized. The NYA had set up its own shops (which could be geared especially to vocational education) but these shops, which had so far been limited to the production of relatively trivial items—making bird-houses and repairing toys—were not ideal for learning purposes. On the other hand, the Lindleys noted, the vocational classes which were being made available to NYA enrollees by the public schools involved problems of their own; the youths who were to attend these classes were precisely the ones who had the least tolerance for formal classroom work.

While the Lindleys and the NYA were struggling with the traditional industrial education problems of school versus shop, the government agency was also striking out in another direction from which the Lindleys took hope. They pointed to the NYA Community Youth Centers as places where the youths could combine study, work and recreation—thereby avoiding the "isolation" to which out-of-work youth were prone. But these NYA supporters were even more excited by the Residence Centers, which provided a completely separate environment for the young people. The Lindleys acknowledged that the centers were difficult to operate; they were expensive, and low-income families who were unaccustomed to having their children away from home felt doubly deprived when their children forfeited the regular NYA wage to stay at the Centers. Yet, the Lindleys argued, these centers were an excellent preparation for society.

To illustrate their point, the authors included photographs of a group of Resident Center enrollees; the caption under one of the pictures explained that the girls shown had good food, clean surroundings, jobs which brought them spending money, and "normal good times which their overcrowded impoverished homes have often denied them." This aspect of the NYA ideal could not have been more clearly underlined. As part of the complex debate about whether home, school, or shop were the best setting for industrial education, the NYA logic of removing young people from their homes in order to provide them with a better environment was inextricably intertwined with the goal of preparing them for the working world.

Taking a quick glance backward, we can see how the idea of residence centers fits in with a whole train of thought common to industrial educators in general. The philanthropic outlook had always implied some criticism of the social conditions engendered by an industrial society. One solution, which dated from the early part of the industrial-urban era, was to remove children from poor homes in order to rescue them and perhaps improve the society as a whole; to place them in separate child-uplift institutions which their promoters often spoke of as surrogate societies. The problem involved in such proposals was that of the relation of these surrogate societies, these little societies for children, to the "real" world; the answer arrived at depended precisely on what the reformers envisioned the great world to be.

One fine example can be seen in the work of William R. George, who in the 1890's established a reform community called George's Junior Republic.[20] The Republic involved taking children away from their corrupting city environment, but unlike the work of Charles Brace, did not involve saving children through a country home; rather, George sought to reproduce the "real" world of business—a world presumably inaccessible to urban waifs. The Republic was a child-society in toto; the young folk all held jobs in Junior Republic industries; they were paid in Junior Republic money, which they could spend at the Republic's stores. All of these businesses were run by the children, who were aided or taught in apprentice fashion by a few adult advisors. If a child didn't like his job, he could leave it and seek employment in another community endeavor, and, consistent with George's laissez-faire outlook, if the Junior Republic employer did not like his worker, the lad could be fired.

George's Republic, then, was aimed at the reform of individual youth; the existing structure of society was accepted; the little society imitated the great one, with the important omission of poor homes and vice-ridden streets. The famous Gary plan suggested another type of relation. This system was evolved under Deweyan inspiration as a solution to the problems of the impoverished industrial city. The ideal of the Gary plan, Randolph Bourne explained, "is that the child should have every day, in some form or other, contact with all different activities which influence a well-rounded human being, instead of meeting them perfunctorily once or twice a week, as in the ordinary school."[21] The school included carpentry, cabinet-making, electrical work, plumbing, and shoe-making shops, a supply store, a medical office, a dental clinic, playgrounds, libraries, and art exhibits. It was, according to Bourne, "a self-sustaining child community." The work of the shops was "real"; they were run by craftsman and staffed by students in apprentice-like relation. There was no question of the activities being useless; one year, noted Bourne, the school set up a shoe shop, because so many of the children had no shoes.

If George's little society emulated the great one, the Gary system's Deweyan logic led it back to pre-industrial society, the virtues of which would have to be recaptured before a better industrial order could be achieved. The NYA Residence Centers, finally, though also calling on the experience of the past, were preparing for an America in which jobs would be available, in which leisure time would be increased, and in which men would live in a more wholesome, more just relation to each other—in which, perhaps, they would live cooperatively, as did the NYA youth.[22]

While the NYA utopians took unsure steps toward realizing their ideals, the professional vocational-educators were struggling in a different fashion. Their problem of adjusting a trade-training ideology to the lack of jobs was no mean task—ideologically nearly impossible. The goal of vocational education, they insisted, was still that of trade training, and "thru no hocus pocus of the depression can it become a finishing school for the polite amenities or a preparation for leisurely time-killing."[23] Yet, what adjustments were vocational educators, who in earlier years had shared the business-as-usual feeling so prevalent in the nation as a whole, to make to depression conditions? In 1931, the Federal Board for Vocational Education declared that vocational education could not deal with the "more general causes of unemployment," but that it might be of some help in giving training to unemployed men, thus "providing a partial remedy for the problems of unemployment in its broader social aspects."[24] Although the Federal Board report made no suggestion that the form of training be readjusted to new industrial conditions, the vocational educators were keenly aware of the limitations the Smith-Hughes Act placed on retraining programs; that very phrase—"shall confine instruction to that which is supplemental to the daily employment"—which had limited classes to the upgrading of the workman's skills, prevented federal aid to the same workman when he was out of work.

The Federal Board met this problem on one level by simply encouraging local programs to undertake retraining without federal assistance; yet the problem struck deeper than this. Could a truly skilled workman fail to find work? Trade-school pioneer Colonel Auchmuty had blamed such unemployment on the immigrants, their unions, and the lack of American responsibility for trade training; presumably the vocational educators had solved this latter problem by the thirties, by which time they were also less inclined to xenophobia and quite committed to cooperation with organized labor.

The Federal Board cast around for explanations: "Unemployment," said a 1931 Bulletin, "is an economic and social condition due to mal-adjustment of production, manufacture, distribution, and consumption of goods."[25] With this beginning point, the Board concentrated its advice on local efforts to retrain men and match them to available jobs. By 1934, however, another explanation was being emphasized: "Research and invention.—These are the two main causes of economic change."[26] What America needed, the Bulletin authors deduced, was a training adapted to technological change, a training which emphasized more "head" and less "hands."

By shifting the character of their Depression explanation, the trade trainers were moving into what was dangerous territory for them—an ideological direction which would ultimately challenge much in the trade-training ideal itself. Even Charles Prosser, with his emphasis on changing industry, had been careful to insist that formal work not become too theoretical.[27] So, as though to cover its tracks, the 1934 Bulletin also pointed to factors other than technological change which contributed to the current situation—to "freedom of competition," the government's pursuit of its "social conservation idea," the continuing "clash of interest" between business and labor unions, and racial discrimination—all playing a part in the difficulty men were having finding positions.

Yet, in the eyes of the Federal Board, there was even another dimension to the current national adversity; America paid a high price for its great economic growth. There were more "socially maladjusted people" in this country than ever before, the Board (quoting liberally from the *Readers Digest*) suggested; "crime and disobedience to law" were on the upswing; thousands of Americans were killed and maimed every year in automobile accidents. The nation could take a vital step in the direction of solving these problems, the Bulletin concluded in a rhetorical coup de grace, by providing more vocational education; the crime rate could be lowered and the many Americans handicapped by accidents could be rehabilitated.

This was really a most curious discussion on the part of the vocational educators. They seemed to be trying out each of the alternative ideologies—first that of basic technical training (educating more "head" and less "hands") and then that of vocational education for philanthropic aims (the prevention of crime). It was as though the fact of large scale unemployment forced the vocational education ideologists to shore up their own creed with ideals which in other circumstances they would have been combatting.

Educational activities during the Depression also posed a problem for educators in general, for such activities touched on the sensitive area of local-federal relationships. Movements for federal aid to schools below the university level had never gained much headway, and even with the exceptional Smith-Hughes system the trend was toward local autonomy; the states had great leeway from the first and were free to delegate many decisions to local units. In addition, the Federal Board had difficulty holding its own as a separate government agency; it was, in fact, reduced to a mere advisory board as early as 1933, with its administrative work being taken over by the Office of Education.[28] The Office of Education had never been happy with this separate national board (which was, in fact, abolished eventually) and was none too happy, as well, with the federal vocational-education efforts of the Depression years.

In the first years of the New Deal, the federal Office, especially through the efforts of Commissioner George Zook, sought a role in the national education schemes. On the whole, however, he lost out to the social-work contingent. That education should be made an aspect of relief work and that many social workers and certain educators saw the government projects as the beginning of a new education system based on "a freer method and a different personnel" did not, of course, sit well with local educators. As the decade drew to an end and it seemed possible that the national relief organizations might be expanded even further to meet mobilization and defense industry needs, local educators began a concerted attack, not on vocational education, they said, but on the policy of federal administration.

Yet the public-school educators had clearly drawn lessons from their Depression experiences; they now saw a need to re-think school programs, to make sure that state and local school systems really met the needs of youth. "This obligation," the Educational Policies Commission announced, "is not reduced if a youth withdraws from formal school before he is equipped for full-time employment. There will be no 'out-of-school unemployed youth' for federal agencies to educate, when schools everywhere extend their responsibilities to all young people until they are satisfactorily established in adult vocations."[29]

Old Themes and the Continuing Debate

The past decade, with its resurgence of interest in industrial education, has proved to be a time of trial for the national vocational-education system. Although a current of dissent existed ever since the passage of the Smith-Hughes Act, there developed no situation quite comparable to the present one in which the proponents of both the philanthropic and mobile worker ideals— ideological predecessors and rivals of the trade training ideal— have gained new positions of strength. In turning to recent expressions of each of these major ideals, we can expect to find rich examples of ideological confrontation; but we should also expect to find, as in the past century and a half, attempts to reconcile and blend conflicting ideals as well as to interpret them in terms of geographic interests and the needs of special groups within the population.

The philanthropic ideal of the honest workman has had, as we have seen, a special appeal in periods of social stress, when industrial change seems to threaten the possibility of a good life for working people; for the philanthropic ideal has always implied that honest work is essential to self-respect and social harmony and that the honesty of work is connected with its quality. Listen to some of the rhetoric surrounding discussion of the Job Corps program and remember earlier advocates of the philanthropic ideal.

A man cannot work or live in decency unless he has education and training. . . . While we are training hundreds in the advanced techniques of cybernated society, thousands of others are being left behind on the human slag heap. . . .

It [the Job Corps] is not merely a trade school. . . . The value of Job Corps is that it will sharpen the mind and the body so that the enrollees can cope with the changes imposed by a rapidly changing world.[30]

or again,

The stories of the past among the 46 youngsters at the Government's new Job Corps Center near Pleasanton are uniformly depressing.

"Family of nine . . . dad unemployed . . . getting welfare . . . finished ninth grade, quit work . . . couldn't get in the army . . . couldn't get a steady job. . . ."

. . . Although not yet having too much of a sample of the instruction at the Center, [one young man] has had plenty of food—and that, he said, is 'the best part of it; it's even better than at home.'

On the shoulder of his dark blue windbreaker—the same as worn by all the young trainees—is the Job Corps symbol: a ladder with an arrow pointing upwards.[31]

This rhetoric of uplift, however, implies the existence of jobs; while the Office of Economic Opportunity sends out pleas for cooperation from employers and looks to new openings in the job market, other Americans are concerned with the possibility that, in the not-so-distant future, the economy will simply offer no semi-skilled jobs.[32] Mechanization in its new form—automation—with its frightening prospect of enforced leisure for the lowly worker, challenges the entire honest-workman ideal and, as throughout the history of industrial education discussions, inspires many holding this ideal to propose more fundamental reconstruction of society.

No contemporary social critic illustrates this response better than Paul Goodman. In his view, nothing can replace the ideal of "a manly job that is useful and necessary, requiring human energy and capacity, and that can be done with dignity and honor."[33] Yet, Goodman argues, with the current irrational drive for economic growth there are relatively few such jobs left. No one talks about the dignity of labor anymore; the era of the self-made man is gone; the alienation of the worker from his product is an accomplished fact; and Americans are continually diverted from the genuine problem of lack of work by a screen of psychological jargon about adjustment. The few jobs to which one can bring a dignity of labor, Goodman notes, are the lowly manual jobs which the society still requires. One can, at least, be a good dishwasher; whereas, higher skilled jobs, like that of auto mechanic, run entirely counter to the prevailing spirit of planned obsolescence. Dishwashing is obviously not the answer, since in our society, dishwashers and their kind are allowed the least human dignity and are only objects of exploitation.

Goodman concludes that the solution can lie only in a fundamental reform of the social order, a recapturing of the ability (which the Depression proved we still have) to live modestly. The wealth of this country assures a basic subsistence for all, which each could earn with a small amount of honest work. Beyond that, the nation should let those who wish to work for high wages do so, but no pressure should be put on the others who might wish to strive in less material directions, to complement their meaningful work with meaningful leisure.

The Job Corps and the Goodman utopia, then, represent two ways which the proponents of the honest workman are facing the question of automation. Like the New Deal educational ventures, these efforts for economic opportunity rely mainly on the hope that the economy itself (supplemented, perhaps, by public works) and a concerted attempt to keep youth off the job market for a period of training will result in sufficient honest work for each employable citizen. On the other hand, Goodman, like many philanthropic utopians from the Jacksonian period on, looks to a more fundamental recasting of the social order.

Yet there are still other responses to the question of automation; indeed, one can reject the entire honest-workman concept, claiming that automation implies highly trained technicians, men who understand the principles underlying modern industry.

Here, of course, is the second major industrial-education ideal, and one which has received considerable attention through the recent crusade for technical education.

To contemporary proponents of technical training, it seems that the technical institutions which were so long step-children on the American educational scene have finally come into their own.[34] Such proponents note how little attention was paid to the few technical institutes of the 1890's, how slowly technical education grew, and how, despite the increase in such institutions during the second World War, there were still fewer than one hundred at mid-century—that is, before the passage of the National Defense and Education Act of 1958. By the early 1960's, the support to technical education which that Act had provided had so catalyzed the educational world that some 600 programs were now devoted to technical education.

Given such rapid and recent institutional growth, one should expect to find technical educators experiencing many ideological aches and pains. In general, the technician ideologies are very like those of the post-Civil War science and engineering educators, stressing a grasp of basic principles combined with a high degree of competence. Contemporary technical educators agree with Calvin Woodward that no mere "knacks of the trade" are adequate preparation, yet these contemporary gentlemen, though also looking toward engineering as a model, realize that technical work is somewhat less lofty than engineering. There is such an uncertainty as to where, precisely, technical work falls in the technological hierarchy, that technical-education proponents continually make fine distinctions between types of technicians, in order to avoid some of the problems to which generalizations about technical education are leading.[35]

Although the technical-education proponents are unsure of how closely such education approaches that of the engineer, they are quite certain that it is superior to that of the mere skilled worker. The education of the technician, says spokesman Ross Henninger, differs from that of the skilled worker because it emphasizes "the understanding and practical application of basic principles rather than the acquisition of proficiency on the manual side."[36] Indeed, Henninger continues, technicans' work has arisen out of the fact that engineers are becoming increasingly involved in scientific investigation, and others are needed to pursue the less experimental aspects of engineering work. Though technical education stresses the "practical" aspects of engineering, it has much in common with engineering education itself; the technician will benefit little from "manual or manipulative skills" or from "technological subject matter taught from that angle."

Although Henninger clearly leaves a niche to the skilled worker—just below that for the technician—it is but a small rhetorical step to an overt attack by technical-education proponents on vocational-education ideals. Such an attack was launched by Grant Venn in his 1964 discussion of technical education; he argued that technological change had outdated the current vocational-education system, that such education closed doors to other educational opportunities, over-burdened students with extra courses, gave the students no clear path to jobs, and provided no "logical progression from school to school and level to level." Continuing his technical-education-for-mobility argument, Venn criticized the vocational-education programs for having become too specialized, too keen on emulating shop conditions instead of stressing basic preparation—as engineering education does. In the case of engineering, he said, the problem of teaching actual industrial procedure has been taken over by industry itself, which "has accepted the necessity of spending a longer time breaking in the recent graduate."[37]

Venn argued that the blame for current vocational-education problems lay with the rigid categories and restrictions imposed by the Smith-Hughes Act; that it was a document well-suited to industrial conditions of its period, but totally out of date by now. Recent legislation—the National Defense and Education Act, the Area Redevelopment Act and the Manpower Training and Development Act—had helped break down traditional categories of job training, but cooperation would also have to come from intermediate level institutions. The American education scene, Venn noted, never allowed much room for intermediate technical institutes. Those which have been developed—the junior colleges—had taken the "road of least resistance" by making themselves into college-preparatory institutions. But there was still hope from a current trend to incorporate technical education into junior college programs, for here was the most logical place to do technical training.

In the face of these resurgent philanthropic and engineering ideologies, the trade-training advocates have, in general, stood fast; indeed, as critics have noted, forty years of profession-building through the Smith-Hughes structure has given the vocational educators a considerable base.[38] During the House of Representatives hearings on the Vocational Education Act of 1963, president of the American Vocational Association Milo Peterson's testimony on the virtues of vocational education was given in a style virtually unchanged from that used by trade-trainers of the Smith-Hughes period.[39] Yet Dr. Peterson's testimony did not give the whole picture. First, despite the continued avowal of the skilled-workman ideal on the national level, individual states and localities had long been making adjustments to the particular industrial needs of their communities and the particular ideals of their own educational frameworks. In the second place, many vocational educators had already listened to criticism, especially that levelled by technical-education proponents, and had begun to bow to and even approve of the necessity for change. We can better understand this move to compromise if we look at instances in which major educational spokesmen attempted to bridge such ideological gaps.

The House vocational education hearings themselves offer an excellent example. The first witness to testify in the 1963 hearings was Commissioner of Education Francis Keppel. The Commissioner was not in an easy position, for the peculiarly non-national character of American public education places the office in the position of channeling specialized and often contradictory sentiments. Keppel began his statement to the subcommittee with a strong endorsement of vocational education; although "times have changed," he said, America's vocational-education goals have remained essentially those outlined by the National Commission for Aid to Vocational Education in 1914: "For vocational education has only one principal purpose: to train people to earn a living. . . . It interweaves with general basic education a specialized education that permits citizens to be self-supporting, contributing members of our national family."[40]

The Congressmen were listening carefully to the Commissioner's statement and were ready with questions. Why, they asked, had the vocational-education system not been more successful in achieving its goals? There were several factors, replied the Commissioner: economic and social conditions can influence youths to leave high school; "general educators" often withhold their full support from vocational programs; and finally, there is admittedly a need to rethink the more rigid restrictions of the Smith-Hughes Act, to give the vocational-education system the flexibility it needs in the face of changing industry. With this last point the Commissioner was moving over to the technical education argument, but taking particular care that he did not shift into an attack on vocational education:

We are faced in our society with this obvious need for the "upgrading," if that is the word one should use, of skills. All of us recognize its clear relation to greater productivity and growth of the gross national product. As in all human affairs, it is hard to keep one's eye simultaneously on two or three things. I would, however, suggest that along with the trend in the vocational education movement, the educators have done remarkably well in keeping their eye on the fact that not all training is in this upper level category.

In point of fact, I think they have probably maintained the balance when others have forgotten it, because obviously we will need to have training programs in a variety of tasks and service occupations, such as shoe repair, for decades to come.

The problem of keeping these things in balance seems to be one of the most difficult we have. This is one of the reasons why I so heartily agree . . . on the importance of keeping research and report programs going constantly on the shifting nature of occupations. . . .[41]

While Keppel's testimony began with the vocational education position and expanded to include technical education goals, James B. Conant has proposed an educational scheme which includes all three industrial education ideals. Indeed, it is as though Conant, also a man in touch with a wide spectrum of American educational opinion, has divided his educational universe to make room for each industrial education approach. The more talented students, he contends, need an education especially geared to preparing them for higher, particularly professional work, an education in which science and mathematics play an important role.[42] The middle-level students need a well-conceived general education, together with an education for skilled work which the best vocational programs offer. Finally, there is a group of students at the bottom of the vocational ladder, some of whom can be raised through proper education, but many of whom cannot be turned into skilled workers by any amount of effort. It is extremely important, Conant declares, that these students not be ignored, for our high school drop-outs, our unemployed and frustrated youth, are the very soil for social unrest and juvenile delinquency. These least talented youths can and ought to be retained in school long enough to be taught "simple types of manual skills," to be taught how to dress, to comport themselves in job-hunting, to take a dignified if modest place on the job ladder.

Conant's shift to a distinctly philanthropic rhetoric when he speaks of the underprivileged becomes even more noticeable as he juxtaposes this rhetoric with the traditional skilled-worker argument. Indeed, Conant seems to have helped at least some trade-training proponents to reconcile their ideals with philanthropic ideals—those with which they have long sought to avoid identification; might we not, asks one vocational educator after noting Conant's approval of training for skilled work, also be doing a better job for our underprivileged youth?[43]

While traditional positions on industrial education have continued to blend in this way, contemporary discussion has also reflected the interweaving of themes of national growth and special local or group interest. The world wars and the cold war have given new life to the manufacturing debate. As was true in the early years of industrialization, the desire for self-sufficiency and growth have resulted in an emphasis on industrial innovation, so that within contemporary industrial education discussions the goals of self-sufficiency and technological expansion are often conjoined. No figure illustrates this combination of arguments better than the outspoken Vice-Admiral Hyman Rickover:

The shrinking of the once-broad materials base of our industrial civilization makes us, for the first time in our history, dependent on foreign countries for materials which are basic to our technical organization. . . . We shall not remain truly free and powerful unless we compensate to the fullest possible extent for the lack of materials resources within our own borders. There is one way, and only one way, in which this can be done. It is by using far more effectively than heretofore our national resources in brain power. . . .[44]

Rickover goes on to discuss the importance of a general—intellectual—education to provide the foundation for technological training. He does leave room for trade training, but, as with Conant, this is for the second, less-talented, group of students. Indeed, Rickover's argument suggests the ideological problem involved in advocating both the trade-training and engineering ideologies on the basis of national well-being. This is precisely what Commissioner Keppel was doing in his attempt to reconcile the two viewpoints before the House subcommittee; a continued increase in the gross national product, he suggested hopefully, would create "positions" to which trained people could go.[45] Yet the congressmen listening to Keppel felt frustration, for they, too, were committed to national goals and were searching for an industrial education program which suited the national needs. Was there not *one* solution, which transcended these institutional and ideological alternatives?

We know it is not a simple matter and we know it is complicated. What we are concerned about is the security of the country and the economy of the country. We are concerned that we produce the manpower the country needs, and we are not interested in getting bogged down in the squabbles that go on in the States about who is going to be running the show. . . .

We want first-class, top quality people produced to do the jobs the nation needs to have done, and the fact that it is a complicated problem is, I think, not going to solve the problem.[46]

The temper of the hearing was not favorable to the vocational educators; despite Keppel's efforts to reconcile the skilled-worker and technical-worker ideals, it seemed to many as though the vocational educators were clinging to an outmoded system, one which suited the purposes of individual locales more than those of national needs.

This same criticism could be recast and used by emergent minority groups. Clarence Mitchell of the National Association for the Advancement of Colored People, for example, made a poignant plea to the subcommittee. In essence he said: You speak of vocational education for developing the nation's skills, but, for my people, the national vocational-education scheme has become nothing more than a new form of discrimination. Look at the two vocational schools in Atlanta: the white school offers electronics, tool-and-die design, radio and television, machine shop, refrigeration and air-conditioning work, iron-working, carpentry, steamfitting, painting and decorating, blue-print reading and drafting, gas-fitting, and lead welding; the colored school offers "catering, practical nursing, dry-cleaning, and landscape gardening."[47]

The solution which Mitchell proposed was to provide national training, in terms of national economic trends, so that Negroes would not be penalized by local conditions and prejudices.

Mitchell's argument wavered, however, for his critique of the Atlanta situation suggested that trade training and higher technological opportunities should both be available.

Yet conflict between the national, mobility-oriented ideal and the local and specifically trade-training ideal, which was so evident in Mitchell's testimony, was far from confined to the area of minority groups. In one sense, the entire outcome of the vocational education hearings was a compromise between these positions, between the claims of technical-education partisans and the claims of the partisans of the skilled worker. Since this latter group consisted primarily of traditional vocational educators nurtured in a Smith-Hughes environment, it was tempting for reformers of various kinds to interpret the legislative battle in terms of the degree of victory over the vocational education "establishment." However, when one looks at the vocational education hearings and considers the continuing industrial-education discussions in their light, such an explanation seems simplistic. The testimony of spokesmen for state and local industrial-education systems, some of whom were welcoming and some of whom were resisting change, showed the question of local needs to be far more than a matter of what would happen to the American Vocational Association.

After Commissioner Keppel, Secretary of Labor Wirtz, and AVA president Peterson had all testified, the procession of state and local vocational educators began.[48] A New Jersey educator pleaded that despite the manufacturing image of his state, more agricultural-education funds were needed to meet new modes of urban agriculture. A North Carolina educator pointed to the displacement of agricultural workers, who streamed into the state's population centers without having acquired urban work skills. The Vocational Education Director of Connecticut told of the problems of his industrial and urban state and of the necessity for bringing educational and manufacturing demands into accord; it was all very well to speak of national training for engineers, he said, for engineers were mobile and could be brought into the state; but technical workers and craftsmen must be drawn from the local population, who look to industrial opportunity near home.

Of all the local spokesmen at the vocational education hearings, the testimony of the educators from Kentucky had a special irony and a special pathos. The irony was both historical and contemporary, involving the images of America as a rich land, rich first in agriculture, then in industry. The pathos is clear. Several times the congressmen asked the Kentucky representatives what use they had for an elaborate trade-education program, in view of the industrial condition of their state. Yes, the vocational educators conceded, industrial opportunities had been very limited, and until the problem was attacked on a national scale, the state would not be able to join the mainstream of American economic prosperity. Yet Kentucky did not wish to offer only agricultural education; its youth wanted industrial training. Many, especially those from the eastern portion of the state or those who were trained in advanced electronic techniques, could not find jobs in Kentucky, but at least they could go to other states to find work; they could avoid joining the ranks of the unemployed, becoming burdens to the state or its neighbors. Our people would like to stay at home and work, said the educators, and perhaps in the future they will be able to; but we must begin somewhere; "We must have a backlog of skilled people before we can ever hope to get industry."[49]

One can see from the vocational education hearings that despite the strong continuity of industrial education ideologies developed during the nineteenth century, the debate of the past fifty years has had a special character which gives it a distinctly "modern" flavor. By the 1920's, the image of the nation's industrial population was beginning to approach our own; the era of the factory-by-the-stream employing spinsters and children, the era of a boom or bust manufacture luring boys from the farm, and the period of giant industries exploiting immigrant labor, were variously becoming things of the past. The problem of the working child was changing with the growth of secondary schooling; the process of mechanization, the nature of the developing working force, and the indigenous passion for social reform had finally thrust American youth out of industry, leaving the inescapable challenge of establishing a new relation between the child and the industrial world.

In solving this problem, however, consideration of the child alone could not be sufficient. As the discussions of work and leisure or work and unemployment of the twenties and thirties suggest, ideals of work in their secular dimension have clearly shaped solutions for the school-aged child. The meaning of adulthood and self-fulfillment in their relation to citizenship and economic well-being are closely linked to interpretations of industrial education for youth, as well as the industrial reeducation or the non-industrial education of adults.

During the twenties and thirties, the industrial-education debate was usually cast in universal terms; the discussions revolved around Man, Work, and Industry as they had in the early years of industrialization. But during the past decade, the element of tension between broader national formulations and the problems of special regions or special groups has come to the fore. While spokesmen for scientific or technical education have revitalized the ideal of mobility through a nationally-oriented prescription for careers, the traditional trade trainers and locally-oriented industrial educators have reemphasized the problems connected with specific industrial settings. At the same time, the newest generation of philanthropists and reformers has looked at both solutions and is trying to interpret each from the viewpoint of the traditional philanthropic commitments to uplift and regeneration: the Job Corps strives to bring unemployed young people into the mainstream of American life; Clarence Mitchell pleads ambiguously for access to a trade training which is being criticized for its specificity; and many, from a viewpoint seriously challenging the social framework within which these educational systems must function, are sharply critical of the very concept of trade-training, claiming that it becomes a trap for the chronically oppressed poor.[50]

At a distance, these conflicting and sometimes internally contradictory positions seem to merge, for the recent spate of educational and social-welfare legislation lends a unity to industrial-education activities, making them appear part of a quest for the fulfillment of a national ideal. But on closer inspection, a plurality of national ideals emerges; rival visions of American industrialization persist; disparate ideals for industrial education endure, grounded on alternative solutions to the problems of national growth, individual opportunity, and universal well-being.

Concluding Note on the
Direction of Industrial Education

Although the problem of industrial education in the United States is really not a single problem at all but a group of problems clustering around concepts which are as general as those of "industry" or "education," time and institutional change have gradually given these problems unity; what might have seemed a collection of relatively unrelated efforts a century ago have become bound together and intertwined in their fates. The Land Grant Act, the Smith-Hughes Act, and the flood of educational and social-welfare legislation of the past decade have continued to thrust questions concerning industrial education before the public eye. The increase of multipurpose federal funding and the growth of comprehensive educational institutions have given those engaged in industrial education an increased awareness that their work lies somewhere in a matrix of industrial education activities.

The strain between the unity and plurality of industrial education was crystalized in some respect by the formation of the National Society for the Promotion of Industrial Education in the early years of the century. And inasmuch as different industrial education groups continue to confront each other, the problem of communication which the National Society defined remains a genuine one. The situation is complicated by the nature of government support; sometimes legislation is geared to one school of industrial education thought rather than another; sometimes the claims of several groups are reflected; and sometimes the legislation is so open-ended that its interpretation is left in great part to the various groups of industrial educators themselves. This open-endedness is much like that I encountered on a tour of facilities on which I was taken by one industrial education teacher. We came to a large shop filled with machinery which, the teacher sadly remarked, was no longer put to great use. It was not the machinery, but the idea which was outdated, he assured me; during the war, federal funds had made it possible to purchase the equipment, but now there seemed little place for it in the school's program.

To me this scene was symbolic—not of "waste" in the usual sense, but of the shifting interpretations and lack of communication which have characterized the industrial-education debate. The machinery was meaningless in itself, yet it could have been used by teachers trained in any of the major industrial-education traditions. The teachers might well have fought over the "meaning" of the machinery in relation to their particular endeavors, and, if the teachers had been sufficiently plentiful and the equipment sufficiently scarce, there also might have been a fight over who was best entitled to use it. It is also possible, as was literally true in this case, that no one would have taken an interest in these "iron men."

One conclusion which might be drawn is that, indeed, both the machinery of industrial education and the enterprise itself are out of date; that they are not only heading for extinction but that we would do ourselves a favor by hastening their demise. Actually, one would have to look long and hard to find someone to draw such a conclusion, for an argument against industrial education in total would seem to involve the rejection of all of the different interpretations of American industry. Instead, those who charge that industrial education is antiquated really speak from one or another of the major industrial-education viewpoints.

In the past few years the skilled workman ideal of the trade-trainers has been called backward-looking—either by partisans of mobility who are more interested in training for higher occupations, or by philanthropic spokesmen who consider the poor victimized or neglected by vocational-education programs. The promoters of philanthropic industrial education have also been called out-dated—by the trade-trainers, the partisans of mobility, or by other philanthropists, who see some philanthropic formulations as inconsistent with the dignity of modern man. The advocates of industrial education for mobility are also called obsolescent—by promoters of uplift or skilled work who see the traditional ideal of mobility as no longer suited to a modern bureaucratized society.

Yet despite such continual attacks of one upon the other, the basic industrial education positions have remained remarkably viable. It is tempting to attribute this to the fact that each is linked with a basic and itself viable vision of America as an industrial nation, as well as to the fact that the basic shape of each position has not precluded its reinterpretation. For, although the industrial education debate has been so strongly patterned as to become stale and predictable at times, the arguments have undergone gradual change—a process which I suspect will continue to keep them alive, science, automation, or the elimination of poverty notwithstanding. If past adaptability is any indicator, the philanthropic industrial-educators who thrive so well when public goals are directed toward uplift and regeneration (as they are in the current "war on poverty"), also fare well in times when economic questions are in abeyance, but social and moral questions are brought to the fore. The partisans of the mobile worker are no less accustomed to shifting with the tide; they have been dealing with the problem of circumscribed mobility since the latter part of the nineteenth century and have continued to develop educational prescriptions by which mobility can be facilitated—through more subtle types of training and through a continued raising of standards to meet and forward scientific and technological frontiers. Finally, the somewhat battered partisans of trade training seem to be making room for a reinterpretation of their ideal; even before the federal reevaluation of vocational education began, a great many vocational educators were looking toward the training of technicians. Though seemingly the approach of mobility-oriented industrial educators, this could be reconciled with an updated concept of the skilled worker. The continued growth of post-high school training reinforces this view; junior colleges and other programs that seek a midway point between high school and college-level training are easily seen as the appropriate training grounds for the new skilled worker, while in some places, college education itself can be seen in this light.

In part, the modification of industrial-education ideologies and institutional arrangements to correspond with the changing qualities of the population and with the changing character of American industrial activity takes place with relative ease, because the ideals of industrial education—following broader ideals for the nation's industrial development—are keyed to change. For the same reason, American industrial educators find the prospect of applying their prescriptions to the industrialization of other nations appealing. American industrial educators of every persuasion are already engaged in development and technical aid programs; often, the encounter not only demands a rethinking of the industrial-education solutions which emerged in the American context, but a reviewing of the entire spectrum of basic manufacturing ideals. Perhaps the challenges posed by overseas work will do as much to recast the nature of the American industrial-education debate as any aspect of industrialization encountered at home; at the very least, an increasing number of persons involved in American industrial-education activities can grapple with the problems of different peoples, speak to counterparts from other countries, and meet traditional rivals on fresh fields.

NOTES

INDEX

Notes

Chapter 1

1 See Orrin Leslie Elliott, *The Tariff Controversy in the United States, 1789–1833* (Palo Alto, Calif., 1892); Joseph Dorfman, *The Economic Mind in American Civilization* (New York, 1946), II, 531 ff.

2 Tench Coxe, *A View of the United States of America* (Dublin, 1795); see also Leo Marx's excellent discussion of Coxe in *The Machine in the Garden* (New York, 1964); and Henry Nash Smith, *Virgin Land* (New York, 1957), on the development of the agrarian ideology.

3 Coxe, *A View of the United States*, p. 36.

4 Simon N. Patten, *The Premises of Political Economy* (Philadelphia, 1885), pp. 221–22.

5 Francis Bowen, *The Principles of Political Economy*, 2nd ed. (Boston, 1859), p. 75.

6 William Graham Sumner, *Protectionism* (New York, 1888), p. 51.

7 On the ideals espoused in nineteenth-century success literature see Irwin G. Wyllie, *The Self-Made Man in America* (New Brunswick, N.J., 1954).

8 Andrew Carnegie, "How to Win Fortune" (reprinted from the *New York Tribune*, April 13, 1890), in his *The Empire of Business* (New York, 1933), pp. 91–92; cf. Thorsten Veblen, *The Engineers and the Price System* (New York, 1963); and Paul W.

Strassmann, *Risk and Technological Innovation* (Ithaca, N.Y., 1959).

9 Coxe, *A View of the United States,* pp. 30 ff.; Mathew Carey, *Addresses of the Philadelphia Society for the Promotion of National Industry,* N. S., No. 1 (Philadelphia, 1819), pp. 35 ff.; and Patten, *The Premises of Political Economy,* p. 236.

10 Francis Wayland, *The Elements of Political Economy* (New York, 1837), p. 339.

11 John Taylor, *Tyranny Unmasked* (Washington, D.C., 1822), p. 132.

12 Amasa Walker, *The Science of Wealth,* 4th ed. (Philadelphia, 1872), pp. 46 ff.

13 Edward T. Devine, *Misery and Its Causes* (New York, 1909), p. 12.

Chapter 2

1 Theodore Parker, "The Laboring Classes" (reprinted from *Dial,* 1841), in his *Social Classes in a Republic,* ed. Samuel A. Eliot (Boston, 1907), p. 52.

2 Henry K. Rowe, *History of Andover Theological Seminary* (Newton, Mass., 1933); Bernard A. Weisberger, *They Gathered at the River* (Boston, 1958), pp. 15–16.

3 See Lyman Beecher, *A Plea for the West* (Cincinnati, 1835), pp. 24–25; and on the evangelical movement itself, Whitney R. Cross, *The Burned-Over District* (Ithaca, N.Y., 1950).

4 See L. F. Anderson, "The Manual Labor School Movement," *Educational Review,* XLVI (November, 1913), 369–86; and Charles Alpheus Bennett, *History of Manual and Industrial Education up to 1870* (Peoria, Ill., 1926), pp. 182–92.

5 *Quarterly Register and Journal* [of the American Education Society], II, No. 2 (November, 1829), 116.

6 Article by H. Humphrey, *Quarterly Register and Journal,* II, No. 3 (February, 1830), 129.

7 "Manual Labor" by "A Clergyman of New Hampshire," *Quarterly Register and Journal,* VII, No. 1 (August, 1834), 64–67.

8 Peter G. Mode, *The Frontier Spirit in American Christianity* (New York, 1923), pp. 59 ff.

9 Theodore D. Weld, *First Annual Report of the Society for Promoting Manual Labor in Literary Institutions* (New York, 1833), p. 59.

10 Richard Harrison Shyrock, *Medicine and Society in America, 1660–1860* (New York, 1960).

11 *The Journal of Health*, I, No. 23 (August 11, 1830), 358; and *Journal of Health*, II, No. 7 (December, 1831), 107.

12 Richard K. Means, *A History of Health Education in the United States* (Philadelphia, 1962), pp. 32 ff.; and Norma Schwendener, *A History of Physical Education in the United States* (New York, 1942).

13 Weld, *First Annual Report*, p. 55.

14 Quoted from the *Annals of Education* (1831) in Anderson, "The Manual Labor School Movement," p. 372.

15 William Ellery Channing, "Self-Culture," *The Works of William Ellery Channing*, 17th ed. (Boston, 1867), II, 369; and his "Lectures to the Laboring Portion of the Community," *Works*, V, 151–230.

16 Merle Curti, *The Learned Blacksmith* (New York, 1937), pp. 9–10.

17 See Victor S. Clark, *History of Manufactures in the United States* (New York, 1949), I, 438–40; and John R. Commons *et al.*, *History of Labour in the United States*, I (New York, 1918), 72 ff.

18 Thomas Kelly, *George Birkbeck: Pioneer of Adult Education* (Liverpool, 1957).

19 *Commemorative Exercises at the Fiftieth Anniversary of the Franklin Institute*, (Philadelphia, 1874), pp. 39–40.

20 *Journal of the Franklin Institute*, I (January, 1826), 2–10; and Merle Curti, *The Growth of American Thought* (New York, 1943), pp. 333–36.

21 Josiah Holbrook, "American Lyceum of Science and the Arts" (Worcester, Mass., 1826), reprinted in Bennett, *History of Manual and Industrial Education up to 1870*, p. 342.

22 Nehemiah Cleaveland, "Lyceums and Societies for the Diffusion of Useful Knowledge," *The Introductory Discourse, and the Lectures, delivered before the Annual Meeting of the American Institute of Instruction*, I (Springfield, Mass., 1872), 145–60; "Review of an Address on Lyceums by W. C. Woodbridge," *American Journal of Education* (Boston), V, Series 3 (1835), 193–204.

23 See Kenneth Wiggins Porter, *The Jacksons and the Lees* (Cambridge, Mass., 1937); Hannah Josephson, *The Golden Threads* (New York, 1949); and Vera Shlakman, "Economic History of

a Factory Town," *Smith College Studies in History,* Vol. XX, Nos. 1–4 (1935).

24　Josephson, *The Golden Threads,* p. 117.

25　*Address of the American Society for the Encouragement of Domestic Manufactures* (New York, 1817), p. 14.

26　Nathan Appleton, "Labor, Its Relations, in Europe and the United States, Compared," *Hunt's Merchants' Magazine,* XI, No. 3 (September, 1844), 219.

27　James H. Lanman, "American Manufactures," *Hunt's Merchants' Magazine,* V, No. 2 (August, 1841), 122–45.

28　See Marcus Wilson Jernegan, *Laboring and Dependent Classes in Colonial America, 1607–1783* (Chicago, 1931); Lawrence A. Cremin, *The American Common School* (New York, 1951); Forest Chester Ensign, *Compulsory School Attendance and Child Labor* (Iowa City, 1921); and Paul H. Douglass, *American Apprenticeship and Industrial Education* (New York, 1921), p. 59.

29　For discussions of Mann as a humanitarian and of the participation of humanitarians in the crusade for public education, see Lawrence A. Cremin's introduction to *The Republic and the School: Horace Mann on the Education of Free Men,* ed. Cremin (New York, 1957); Frank Tracy Carlton, *Economic Influence upon Education Progress in the United States, 1820–1850* (Madison, Wis., 1908); and Merle Curti, *The Social Ideas of American Educators* (New York, 1935), pp. 104 ff.

30　See Horace Mann, "Third Annual Report, for 1839," *Life and Works of Horace Mann,* ed. Mary Mann (Boston, 1891), III, 1–52; and his "Report for 1841," *Life and Works,* pp. 92–128.

31　Mann, "Report for 1848," *Life and Works,* p. 251.

32　Commons *et al., History of Labour,* Vols. I and IV (1935); Arthur B. Darling, "The Workingmen's Party in Massachusetts, 1833–1834," *American Historical Review,* XXIX, No. 1 (October, 1932), 81–86; and compare an alternative interpretation of the workingmen's movement in Walter Hugins, *Jacksonian Democracy and the Workingclass* (Stanford, Calif., 1960).

33　Seth Luther, *An Address to the Working-Men of New England* (Boston, 1834), p. 7; see also Louis Hartz, "Seth Luther: the Story of a Working-Class Rebel," *The New England Quarterly,* XIII, No. 3 (September, 1940), 401–18.

34　Seth Luther, *An Address on the Origin and Progress of Avarice* (Boston, 1834), p. 35.

35　See Perry Miller, *The Transcendentalists* (Cambridge, Mass.,

1960); and Norman Ware, *The Industrial Worker, 1840–1860* (Boston, 1924).

36 Arthur Eugene Bestor, Jr., "Albert Brisbane—Propagandist for Socialism in the 1840's," *New York History*, XXVIII, No. 2 (April, 1947), 128–58; and Alice Felt Tyler, *Freedom's Ferment* (Minneapolis, 1944), p. 180.

37 Albert Brisbane, *A Concise Exposition of the Doctrine of Association*, 2nd ed. (New York, 1843), p. 42.

38 *Ibid.*, p. 29.

39 Horace Greeley, *Hints Toward Reform* (New York, 1850), p. 362.

40 See Anselm L. Strauss, *Images of the American City* (New York, 1961).

41 Ulines, *The State of Prisons and of Child-saving Institutions in the Civilized World* (Cambridge, Mass., 1880), pp. 112–13. For a general history of penal institutions see Harry Elmer Barnes, *The Repression of Crime* (New York, 1926), pp. 112–33.

42 Quoted from an 1823 report to the Society in B. K. Peirce, *A Half-Century with Juvenile Delinquents* (New York, 1869), pp. 49–50.

43 *Ibid.*, p. 258.

44 *The Seventeenth Annual Report of the New York Association for Improving the Condition of the Poor* (1860), pp. 37–38; also see Robert H. Bremner, *From the Depths* (New York, 1956).

45 Irwin G. Wyllie, *The Self-Made Man in America* (New Brunswick, N.J., 1954), pp. 29 ff.

46 See, for example, A. J. Hutton, "Industrial School for Delinquents," *Proceedings of the Thirteenth Annual Conference on the Education of Truant, Backward, Dependent and Delinquent Children* (1916), pp. 55–61, and discussion, pp. 61–63.

47 Charles Loring Brace, *The Dangerous Classes of New York* (New York, 1872).

48 Hastings H. Hart, *Preventative Treatment of Neglected Children* (New York, 1910), p. 18; Guy Hanna, "Vocational Training in Boys' Correction Institutions," *Proceedings of the Thirteenth Annual Conference on the Education of Truant . . . Children*, p. 3.

49 See Nina C. Vandewalker, *The Kindergarten in American Education* (New York, 1908).

50 Elizabeth Peabody, *Lectures in the Training Schools for Kindergarteners* (Boston, 1888), p. 23.

51 Reverend R. Heber Newton, "The Bearing of the Kindergarten on the Prevention of Crime," *Proceedings of the National Conference on Charities and Correction* (hereafter cited as *Proc. NCCC*) (1886), p. 55; Emma Marwedel, "Prevention of Criminal Idleness," *Addresses and Proceedings of the National Education Association* (hereafter cited as *Proc. NEA*), XXIII (1893), 372–81; and Caroline T. Haven, "The Relation of the Kindergarten to Manual Training," *Proc. NEA* (1892), pp. 443–48.

52 Joseph Lee, *Constructive and Preventive Philanthropy* (New York, 1906), pp. 202–03; also see Henry S. Curtis, *The Play Movement and Its Significance* (New York, 1917).

53 Florence Kelley, *Modern Industry* (New York, 1914).

54 John Spargo, *The Bitter Cry of the Children* (New York, 1906), pp. 190–91.

55 For example, see Robert Hunter, *Poverty* (New York, 1912), p. 209; Hannah Kent Schoff, *The Wayward Child* (Indianapolis, 1915); and Jacob A. Riis, *How the Other Half Lives* (New York, 1962).

56 Josephine Shaw Lovell, "Methods of Relief for the Unemployed," *The Forum*, XVI (February, 1894), 655–62.

57 Mary E. Richmond, *The Good Neighbor in the Modern City* (Philadelphia, 1907); and her *Friendly Visiting among the Poor* (New York, 1903).

58 Jane Addams, *Democracy and Social Ethics* (New York, 1907), pp. 34–35; and her *Twenty Years at Hull House* (New York, 1930), pp. 235 ff.; see also Kathleen Woodroofe, *From Charity to Social Work* (London, 1926), p. 95; and Ralph E. Pumphrey and Muriel W. Pumphrey, eds., *The Heritage of American Social Work* (New York, 1961), p. 258.

59 Jane Addams, "Child Labor and Education," *Proc. NCCC*, XXXV (1908), 367.

Chapter 3

1 See, for example, U.S. Bureau of Census, *Report on Manufacturing Industries in the United States, at the Eleventh Census, 1890,* Part I (Washington, D.C., 1895), p. 47; see also the debate on industrialization in Ralph Andreano, ed., *The Economic Impact of the American Civil War* (Cambridge, Mass., 1962); and Irwin G. Wyllie, *The Self-Made Man in America* (New Brunswick, N.J., 1954), on the ideology of industrial success.

2 See Richard Hofstadter, *Academic Freedom in the Age of the College* (New York, 1961), pp. 194 ff.; Dirk J. Struik, *Yankee Science in the Making* (Boston, 1948); and Russell H. Chittenden, *History of the Scheffield School of Yale University, 1846–1922* (New Haven, Conn., 1928), Vol. I.

3 John Tyndall, *Six Lectures on Light Delivered in America in 1873*, 2nd ed. (London, 1875), pp. 215, 218.

4 Daniel Coit Gilman, "Our National Schools of Science," *North American Review*, CV, No. 207 (October, 1867), 495–520.

5 Daniel Coit Gilman, *The Launching of a University* (New York, 1906), pp. 33, 335–37; and his "Handicraft and Rede-Craft," *Century*, XXXII, No. 6 (October, 1886), 837–41; see also Abraham Flexner, *Daniel Coit Gilman* (New York, 1946), pp. 16 ff.; and John C. French, *A History of the University Founded by Johns Hopkins* (Baltimore, Md., 1946), pp. 169–70.

6 Reports of W. T. Barnard quoted in Isaac Edwards Clarke, *Art and Industry* (Washington, D.C., 1898), IV, 783 *et passim*.

7 Charles W. Eliot, "Inaugural Address as President of Harvard College," *Educational Reform* (New York, 1898), p. 21.

8 Charles W. Eliot, "The New Education: Its Organization," Part I, *Atlantic Monthly*, XXIII (February, 1869), 212.

9 *Ibid.*, p. 217.

10 "President White's Remarks," in Tyndall, *Six Lectures on Light*, pp. 241–42.

11 Edward L. Youmans, ed., *The Culture Demanded by Modern Life* (New York, 1867), pp. 54–55; and Simon Newcomb, "Abstract Science in America, 1776–1876," *North American Review*, CXXII, No. 250 (January, 1876), 120–22.

12 See, for example, "The Moral Lesson of the Credit Mobilier Scandal," *Nation*, XVI (January 30, 1873), 68.

13 Jonathan Baldwin Turner, "Industrial Universities for the People," reprinted in Edmund J. James, *The Origin of the Land-Grant Act* (Urbana, Ill., 1910), p. 50.

14 Earl D. Ross, *Democracy's College* (Ames, Ia., 1942), pp. 87 ff., 108.

15 See Carl L. Becker, *Cornell University* (Ithaca, N.Y., 1943), pp. 168–69.

16 Andrew Dickson White, *Autobiography* (New York, 1905), I, 371.

17 Andrew Dickson White, "Scientific and Industrial Education in

the United States," *Popular Science Monthly,* V (June, 1874), 170–91.

18 See Struik, *Yankee Science,* pp. 93 ff., 244 ff.; and Charles Riborg Mann, *A Study of Engineering Education* (New York, 1918).

19 Palmer C. Ricketts, *History of the Rensselaer Polytechnic Institute, 1824–1894* (New York, 1895), pp. 6–7.

20 *Ibid.,* p. 93.

21 See Samuel C. Prescott, *When M.I.T. was "Boston Tech." 1861–1916* (Cambridge, Mass., 1954); and James Phinney Munroe, *A Life of Francis Amasa Walker* (New York, 1923).

22 Francis Amasa Walker, *Discussions in Education,* ed. James P. Munroe (New York, 1899), pp. 14–15.

23 *Ibid.,* pp. 59 ff.

24 Cf. the analysis in Samuel Haber, *Efficiency and Uplift* (Chicago, 1964).

25 For example, "Amateur Engineering," *Hunt's Merchants' Magazine,* LIII (July 1, 1865), 80–84.

26 See, for example, such interpretations of Edison as George Parsons Lathrop, "Talks with Edison," *Harper's Magazine,* LXXX, No. 177 (February, 1890), 425–35.

27 Robert H. Thurston, "The Mission of Science," *Proceedings of the American Association for the Advancement of Science* (hereafter cited as *Proc. AAAS*), XXXIII (1884), 227–53.

28 O. Chanute, "Scientific Invention," *Proc. AAAS,* XXXV (1886), 165–82.

29 Robert H. Thurston, "President's Inaugural Address," *Transactions of the American Society of Mechanical Engineers* (hereafter cited as *Trans. ASME*), I (1880), 13–29; and his "Our Progress in Mechanical Engineering," *Trans. ASME,* II (1881), 450–53.

30 See William H. Bryan, "The Relations between the Purchaser, the Engineer, and the Manufacturer," *Trans. ASME,* XIX (1897–98), 686–99.

31 Oberlin Smith, "The Engineer as a Scholar and a Gentleman," *Trans. ASME,* XIII (1891–92), 49–50.

32 *Ibid.,* pp. 52 ff.

33 John D. Runkle, "The Manual Element in Education," reprinted in Charles Alpheus Bennett, *History of Manual and Industrial Education, 1870–1917* (Peoria, Ill., 1937), pp. 340–46.

34 George I. Alden, "Technical Training at the Worcester Free Institute," *Trans. ASME,* VI (1884–85), 514.

35 Calvin M. Woodward, "The Training of a Dynamic Engineer in Washington University, St. Louis," *Trans. ASME,* VII (1885–86), 745.

36 *Ibid.,* 742–43.

37 Remarks of Angus Sinclair following Woodward, "The Training of a Dynamic Engineer," *Trans. ASME,* VII (1885–86), 772; see also remarks of Kent, Couch, and Sweet, following Alden, "Technical Training," *Trans. ASME,* VI (1884–85), 528–35.

38 Robert H. Thurston, "Technological Schools," *Proc. NEA* (1893), pp. 534–49.

39 For a typical engineering argument against manual training and in favor of trade education see John B. Johnson, "A Higher Industrial and Commercial Education as an Essential Condition for Our Future Material Prosperity," *Proceedings of the Society for the Promotion of Engineering Education,* VI (1898), 11–36.

40 "Calvin Milton Woodward," *The National Cyclopaedia of American Biography* (New York, 1907), IX, 469.

41 Charles Penny Coates, *History of the Manual Training School of Washington University,* U.S. Bureau of Education Bulletin No. 3 (Washington, D.C., 1923), p. 70.

42 Bennett, *History of Manual and Industrial Education, 1870–1917,* pp. 318–19.

43 Calvin M. Woodward, *The Manual Training School* (Boston, 1887), pp. 245, 252, 261–88.

44 *Ibid.,* p. 184.

45 *Ibid.,* p. 194.

46 *Ibid.,* pp. 210–11.

47 *Ibid.,* p. 171.

48 *Ibid.,* p. 54.

49 Calvin M. Woodward, "The Teacher of Tool Work," *Proc. NEA* (1890), p. 749.

50 Calvin M. Woodward, "The Relation of Manual Training School to Technical Schools," *Proc. NEA* (1888), p. 586.

51 Calvin M. Woodward, "The Opportunity and Function of the Secondary School," *Proc. NEA* (1903), pp. 60–65.

52 For example, see Alfred Bayliss, "What may be done for Manual Training in the Country Schools," *Proc. NEA* (1904), pp. 623–27; and W. D. Parker, "Some Possible Relations of Normal Schools to Manual Training," *Proc. NEA* (1897), pp. 749–52.

53 See Arthur Beverly Mays, *The Concept of Vocational Education in the Thinking of the General Educator, 1845 to 1945* (Urbana,

Ill., 1946); and Edward A. Krug, *The Shaping of the American High School Today* (New York, 1964).

54 See minutes of the Industrial Education Department, *Proc. NEA,* especially 1876; and Edgar B. Wesley, *N.E.A., The First Hundred Years* (New York, 1957), pp. 61 ff.

55 Edward Everett Hale, "Half-Time in Schools," *North American Review,* CXXXIX (November, 1884), 443–52.

56 Calvin M. Woodward, "The Function of the Public School," *Proc. NEA* (1887), p. 215.

57 *Ibid.,* 222–23.

58 For example, see William T. Harris, "Does the Common School Educate Children above the Station They are Expected to Occupy in Life?" *Education,* III, No. 5 (May, 1883), 461–75; and his "Excessive Helps in Education," *Education,* IX, No. 4 (December, 1888), 215–20; also see Kurt F. Leidecker, *Yankee Teacher* (New York, 1946).

59 William T. Harris, "Industrial Education in the Common Schools," *Education,* VI, No. 8 (June, 1886), 607–11; and his "The Educational Value of Manual Training," *Proc. NEA* (1889), pp. 417–23, and discussion, pp. 424–30.

60 William T. Harris, "The Intellectual Value of Tool-Work," *Proc. NEA* (1889), pp. 92–98.

61 Discussion following Harris, "The Educational Value of Manual Training," *Proc. NEA* (1889), p. 427.

62 William T. Harris, "Originality," *Journal of Speculative Philosophy,* I, No. 3 (1867), 127–28; and his "Vocation versus Culture," *Education,* XII, No. 4 (December, 1891), 193–206.

63 For example, see Virgil G. Curtis, "The Relation of Manual Training to Technical Education," *Proc. NEA* (1901), pp. 657–65, and discussion, pp. 673–82; and Thomas M. Balliet, "Manual, Trade, and Technical Education," *Proc. NEA* (1903), pp. 65–71.

Chapter 4

1 The struggle for acceptance of trade training by the public schools can be traced in the *Proceedings of the National Education Association* beginning with tentative suggestions in the 1870's; although the philanthropically oriented use of trade training was also argued before the NEA, by spokesmen such as Felix Adler, their biographies and histories of their educational pro-

grams provide the best sources: for example, Cheesman A. Herrick, *History of Girard College* (Philadelphia, 1927); Edward C. Mack, *Peter Cooper* (New York, 1949); and Abbie Graham, *Grace H. Dodge* (New York, 1926).

2 Cf. Charles Forcey, *The Crossroads of Liberalism* (New York, 1961); and Samuel Haber, *Efficiency and Uplift* (Chicago, 1964).

3 See Kenneth Wiggins Porter, *The Jacksons and the Lees* (Cambridge, Mass., 1937), I, 125–26; Thomas C. Cochran, *Railroad Leaders, 1845–1890* (Cambridge, Mass., 1953), pp. 79 ff.; and especially the journal *Iron Age* during the 1870's.

4 Kenneth K. Kolker, "The Changing Status of the Foreman," *Bulletin of the Business Historical Society*, XXII, No. 3 (June, 1948), 84–105; and Carl J. Cabe, *Foreman's Unions* (Urbana, Ill., 1947).

5 Frank Barkley Copely, *Frederick W. Taylor* (New York, 1923), Vol. I.

6 Frederick W. Taylor, "A Piece-Rate System," *Trans. ASME*, XVI (1894–95), 856–903; see also the discussion of Taylor in Haber, *Efficiency and Uplift*.

7 Quoted in Copely, *Frederick W. Taylor*, II, 63.

8 Frederick W. Taylor, "Shop Management," *Trans. ASME*, XXIV (1902–03), 1419–20.

9 Frank Parsons, *Our Country's Need* (Boston, 1894); and his *Choosing a Vocation* (Boston, 1909); see also Arthur Mann, *Yankee Reformers in an Urban Age* (Cambridge, Mass., 1954), pp. 126–44; and John M. Brewer, *History of Vocational Guidance* (New York, 1942), pp. 57 ff.

10 Meyer Bloomfield, "Education and Efficient Living," *Proceedings of the Society for the Promotion of Engineering Education*, XXI (1913), Part I, 36; and his *The Vocational Guidance of Youth* (Boston, 1911).

11 Hugo Münsterberg, *Vocation and Learning* (St. Louis, 1912), p. 11; and see also Margaret Münsterberg, *Hugo Münsterberg* (New York, 1922), pp. 208 ff.

12 Hugo Münsterberg, *Psychology and Industrial Efficiency* (Boston, 1913), p. 309.

13 David Howard Dickason, *The Daring Young Men* (Bloomfield, Ind., 1953).

14 *Craftsman*, I, No. 1 (October, 1901), i–ii.

15 Gustave Stickley, "Thoughts Occasioned by an Anniversary: A

Plea for Democratic Art," *Craftsman,* VII, No. 1 (October, 1904), 53.

16 Gustave Stickley, "The Use and Abuse of Machinery, and Its Relation to the Arts and Crafts," *Craftsman,* XI, No. 2 (November, 1906), 204.

17 Helen R. Albee, "The Modern Craftsman; the Question of His Livelihood," *Craftsman,* I, No. 6 (March, 1902), 44.

18 *Ibid.,* p. 45.

19 Mary K. Simkhovitch, "Handicrafts in the City," *Craftsman,* XI, No. 3 (December, 1904), 363.

20 Editorial, *Craftsman,* I, No. 1 (October, 1901), ii.

21 Isaac Edwards Clarke, *Art and Industry,* U.S. Bureau of Education (Washington, D.C., 1885), I, lxxxiv.

22 George A. Bartlett, "Free Industrial Evening Drawing Schools," *Proc. NEA* (1885), pp. 607–14; and Otto Fuchs, "Art Education," *Proc. NEA* (1885), pp. 275–83.

23 Mrs. A. F. Dimmock, "Drawing in Primary and Grammar Schools," *Proc. NEA* (1885), pp. 284–87.

24 W. S. Goodnough, "Address," *Proc. NEA* (1886), pp. 428–32.

25 Charles M. Carter, "Manual Training through Industrial Drawing," *Proc. NEA* (1886), p. 446.

26 Charles M. Carter, "The Industrial Idea in Education," *Century,* XXXVI, No. 5 (September, 1888), 680.

27 Charles G. Leland, "Hand-work in Public Schools," *Century,* XXIV, No. 6 (October, 1882), 890–91.

28 Gustaf Larsson, "Sloyd for Elementary Schools Contrasted with the Russian System of Manual Training," *Proc. NEA* (1893), pp. 599–606; and his "Sloyd an Important Factor in the Education of Boys," *Manual Training Magazine,* XIII, No. 3 (February, 1912), 232.

29 Clara I. Mitchell, "Textile Arts as Constructive Work in Elementary School," *Proc. NEA* (1901), pp. 649–50.

30 John Dewey, *The School and Society* (Chicago, 1899), p. 103.

31 *Ibid.,* p. 104.

32 John Dewey, "The Place of Manual Training in the Elementary Course of Study," *Manual Training Magazine,* II, No. 4 (July, 1901), 193–94.

33 James Earl Russell, "The School and Industrial Life," reprinted in James Earl Russell and Frederick G. Bonser, *Industrial Education* (New York, 1912), pp. 17–18; also see Nicholas Murray Butler, "The Training of a Teacher," *Century,* XXXIX, No. 6

(October, 1889), 915–16, for the earlier head's formulation; and Lawrence A. Cremin, David A. Shannon, and Mary E. Town-send, *A History of Teachers College, Columbia University* (New York, 1954).

34 Frederick G. Bonser, "Fundamental Values in Industrial Education," Russell and Bonser, *Industrial Education*, p. 46 ff.

35 John Dewey, "A Policy of Industrial Education," *New Republic*, I, No. 7 (December 19, 1914), 11–12.

36 David Snedden, "Vocational Education," *New Republic*, II, No. 27 (May 8, 1915), 40–42.

37 John Dewey, "Education vs. Trade Training," *New Republic*, II, No. 27 (May 8, 1915), 42.

38 John Dewey, "The Need of an Industrial Education in an Industrial Democracy," *Manual Training Magazine*, XVII, No. 6 (February, 1916), 412.

39 See Ira Kipnis, *The American Socialist Movement, 1897–1912* (New York, 1952); Charles Howard Hopkins, *The Rise of the Social Gospel in American Protestantism, 1865–1915* (New Haven, Conn., 1940); and Richard Hofstadter, *Social Darwinism in American Thought*, rev. ed. (Boston, 1963).

40 Frank Tracy Carlton, *Education and Industrial Evolution* (New York, 1908), p. 76.

41 Donald Drew Egbert, Stow Persons, and T. D. Seymour Bassett, *Socialism and American Life* (Princeton, N.J., 1952), II, 383.

42 Edward Bellamy, "Should Every Boy Learn a Trade?" (reprinted from the *Boston Herald*, 1892), in *Edward Bellamy Speaks Again!* (Kansas City, Mo., 1937), p. 207.

43 C. Hanford Henderson, *Pay-Day* (Boston, 1911), p. 146.

44 *Ibid.*, p. 331; see also William E. Walling, *The Larger Aspects of Socialism* (New York, 1913), pp. 257 ff., for a conservative socialist interpretation of progressive education.

45 For example, see Lee Galloway, *Organization and Management* (New York, 1909), p. 204; and Edward D. Jones, *Business Administration* (New York, 1914), pp. 249–50.

46 Edmund J. James, *Education of Businessmen* (New York, 1892), p. 11.

47 Edmund J. James, *A Plea for the Establishment of Commercial High Schools* (New York, 1892), p. 14; see also Benjamin R. Haynes and Henry P. Jackson, *A History of Business Education* (Cincinnati, Ohio, 1935).

48   See Cheesman A. Herrick, *Meaning and Practice of Commercial Education* (New York, 1904).

49   Harlow S. Person, *Industrial Efficiency* (Boston, 1907).

50   Albert James Beatty, *Corporation Schools* (Bloomington, [Ind.], 1918), pp. 44 ff.

51   Thomas E. Donnelley, "Some Problems of Apprenticeship Schools," *The National Association of Corporation Schools First Annual Convention, Papers, Reports, and Discussions* (hereafter cited as *NACS Papers*), I (1913), 131.

52   Charles P. Steinmetz, "Engineering Schools of Electrical Manufacturing Companies," *NACS Papers*, I (1913), 156–61.

53   "Report of the Committee on Public Education," *NACS Papers*, IV (1916), 243–46.

54   "Committee on Corporation Schools," *NACS Papers*, V (1917), 575.

55   "Continuation Schools—The Application of the Smith-Hughes Vocational Education Law," *NACS Papers*, VI (1918), 237–60.

56   See Thomas C. Cochran, *The American Business System* (Cambridge, Mass., 1960), p. 59; Albion Guilford Taylor, *Labor Policies of the National Association of Manufacturers* (Urbana, Ill., 1928), pp. 12 ff.; and Clarence E. Bonnett, *Employers' Associations in the United States* (New York, 1922), pp. 12 ff.

57   David M. Parry, "Annual Report of the President," *Proceedings of the Eighth Annual Convention of the National Association of Manufacturers* (hereafter cited as *Proc. NAM*), VIII (1903), 13–15, 80–81.

58   Anthony Ittner, "Apprenticeship and Trade Schools," *Proc. NAM*, IX (1904), 133–34.

59   "Report on Industrial Education," *Proc. NAM*, X (1905), 150.

60   Frederick Upham Adams, "The Dearth of First-Class Mechanics," *American Industries*, VI, No. 2 (September, 1907), 7.

61   "Industrial Education," *Proc. NAM*, XVII (1912), 162.

62   "Address of Mr. H. E. Miles," *Proc. NAM*, XVIII (1913), 226; also see Georg Kerschensteiner's own arguments to his American audience in, for example, *Education for Citizenship*, trans. A. J. Pressland (Chicago, 1911).

63   "Report of the Committee of Industrial Education," *Proc. NAM*, XIX (1914), 85–86.

64   See Philip R. V. Curoe, *Educational Attitudes and Policies of Organized Labor in the United States* (New York, 1926); and

John R. Commons, *et al.*, *History of Labour in the United States,* II (New York, 1918), 43 ff.

65 See Marguerite Green, *The National Civic Federation and the American Labor Movement, 1900–1925* (Washington, D.C., 1956); and Bernard Mandel, *Samuel Gompers* (Yellow Springs, Ohio, 1963).

66 Samuel Gompers, *Seventy Years of Life and Labor* (New York, 1925), I, 432.

67 *Ibid.*, p. 431.

68 Samuel Gompers, "The American School and the Working Man," *Proc. NEA* (1916), p. 182; note that the socialist critique of industry which still marked Gompers' rhetoric only gradually came to educational fruition, beginning with such programs as described in Louis Levine, *The Women's Garment Workers* (New York, 1924), pp. 482–504.

69 *Report of the Proceedings of the Twenty-Third Annual Convention of the American Federation of Labor* (hereafter cited as *Proc. AF of L*), XXIII (1903), 259.

70 James M. Motley, *Apprenticeship and the American Trade Unions* (Baltimore, Md., 1907), pp. 31 ff.

71 Quoted in George A. Stevens, *New York Typographical Union No. 6*, New York State Bureau of Labor Statistics, Annual Report, 1911, Vol. II, Part I (Albany, 1912), p. 333.

72 *Proc. AF of L*, XXVII (1907), 173.

73 "Report of the Committee on Education," *Proc. AF of L*, XXVII (1907), 318–19.

74 From President Gompers' report, *Proc. AF of L*, XXIX (1909), 35–36.

75 "Report of the Special Committee on Industrial Education," *Proc. AF of L*, XXIX (1909), 138.

76 Frank Duffy, "Industrial Education and What Labor Unions Are Doing to Promote It," *American Federationist*, XIX, No. 5 (May, 1912), 392–96; and Charles H. Winslow, "Labor's Demands for Industrial Education," *American Federationist*, XVIII, No. 2 (February, 1911), 115.

77 "Industrial Education—Vocational Training, Democratization of the Schools," *Proc. AF of L*, XXXV (1915), 322.

78 Remark of J. M. Lynch of the ITU, *Proc. AF of L*, XXXII (1912), 275.

79 *Industrial Education*, Eighth Annual Report of the Commissioner

of Labor, U.S. Bureau of Labor (Washington, D.C., 1893); and *Industrial Education,* Twenty-fifth Annual Report of the Commissioner of Labor, U.S. Bureau of Labor (Washington, D.C., 1911).

80 *Report of the [Massachusetts] Commission on Industrial Education* (Boston, 1906).

81 *Report of the [Massachusetts] Commission on Industrial Education* (Boston, 1907).

82 "Proceedings of the Organization Meetings," *National Society for the Promotion of Industrial Education Bulletin* (hereafter cited as *NSPIE Bull.*), No. 1 (1907).

83 See Richard T. Auchmuty, "The Needs of Trade Schools," *Century,* XXXIII, No. 1 (November, 1886), 83–92; and his "An American Apprentice System," *Century,* XXXVII, No. 3 (January, 1889), 401–5.

84 See Edward C. Kirkland, *Industry Comes of Age* (New York, 1962), pp. 282 ff.; and Harold U. Faulkner, *The Decline of Laissez Faire, 1897–1917* (New York, 1962), pp. 52–67.

85 Archibald Carey Coolidge, *The United States as a World Power* (New York, 1909), p. 203.

86 See for example Holmes Beckwith, *German Industrial Education and Its Lessons for the United States,* U.S. Bureau of Education Bulletin No. 19 (Washington, D.C., 1913), pp. 50–51.

87 Frank A. Vanderlip, "Address," *NSPIE Bull.,* No. 1 (1907), pp. 20–21.

88 Jane Addams, "Address," *NSPIE Bull.,* No. 1 (1907), p. 39; also Charles W. Eliot, "Industrial Education as an Essential Factor in Our National Prosperity," *NSPIE Bull.,* No. 1 (1907), pp. 9–14; and James W. Van Cleave, "Industrial Education from the Standpoint of a Manufacturer," *NSPIE Bull.,* No. 1 (1907), pp. 15–16.

89 See Robert Ripley Clough, "The National Society for the Promotion of Industrial Education," unpublished thesis, University of Wisconsin, 1957; cf. Lloyd E. Blauch, *Federal Cooperation in Agriculture Extension Work, Vocational Education and Vocational Rehabilitation,* U.S. Office of Education Bulletin No. 15 (Washington, D.C., 1933).

90 Layton S. Hawkins, Charles A. Prosser, and John C. Wright, *Development of Vocational Education* (Chicago, 1951), p. 81.

91 "Smith-Hughes Act (S703—Public 347—Sixty-fourth Congress)," reprinted, Hawkins, Prosser, and Wright, *Development of Vocational Education,* p. 602.

Chapter 5

1   Harvey S. Perloff, Edgar S. Dunn, Jr., Eric E. Lampard, and
    Richard F. Muth, *Regions, Resources, and Economic Growth*
    (Baltimore, Md., 1960), p. 151.
2   William Gregg, *Essays on Domestic Industry* (Charleston, S.C.,
    1845), p. 14; see also Broadus Mitchell, *The Rise of the Cotton
    Mills in the South* (Baltimore, Md., 1921), pp. 10 ff.
3   See C. Vann Woodward, *Origins of the New South, 1877–1913*
    (Baton Rouge, La., 1951), pp. 131 ff.; cf. Broadus Mitchell and
    George Sinclair Mitchell, *The Industrial Revolution in the South*
    (Baltimore, Md., 1930), pp. 31 ff.
4   See Raymond B. Nixon, *Henry W. Grady: Spokesman of the New
    South* (New York, 1943); and Henry W. Grady, *The New South*
    (New York, 1890).
5   See George Tayloe Winston, *A Builder of the New South* (Gar-
    den City, N.Y., 1920).
6   Woodward, *Origins of the New South*, pp. 291 ff.
7   Winston, *A Builder of the New South*, p. 92.
8   Thompkins' career may profitably be compared to Tillman's, since
    both men wove ideals of vocational education into their peculiarly
    southern life-styles. See Frances Butler Simkins, *The Tillman
    Movement in South Carolina* (Durham, N.C., 1926).
9   A. D. Mayo, *Industrial Education in the South*, U.S. Bureau of
    Education, Circular of Information, No. 5 (Washington, D.C.,
    1888); see also *American Brains in American Hands* (Manhattan,
    Kansas, 1888).
10 Calvin M. Woodward, "What Should be Added to the Essential
    Branches of the Elementary Course of Study to Meet the Indus-
    trial Needs of Localities," *Proc. NEA* (1893), pp. 266–68.
11 Mayo, *Industrial Education in the South*, pp. 35–36.
12 See Ulrich Bonnell Phillips, *American Negro Slavery* (New York,
    1926); W. E. Burghardt DuBois, ed., *The Negro Artisan* (Atlanta,
    Ga., 1902); and Sterling D. Spero and Abram Harris, *The
    Black Worker* (New York, 1931).
13 Quoted in Carter G. Woodson, *The Education of the Negro Prior
    to 1861* (New York, 1951), pp. 77–78.
14 *Proceedings of the Colored National Convention Held in Roch-
    ester, 1853* (Rochester, N.Y., 1853), pp. 30–32.
15 Frederick Douglass, *The Life and Times of Frederick Douglass*
    (New York, 1941), p. 319.

16 *Proceedings of the Colored National Convention, Philadelphia . . . 1855* (Salem, N.J., 1856), p. 11.

17 Frederick Douglass, "Learn Trades or Starve," reprinted in Phillip S. Foner, *The Life and Writings of Frederick Douglass* (New York, 1950), II, 223–25.

18 Quoted in Frances Greenwood Peabody, *Education for Life: The Story of Hampton Institute* (Garden City, N.Y., 1918), p. 99.

19 See Thomas Monroe Campbell, *The Moveable School Goes to the Negro Farmer* (Tuskegee, Ala., 1936).

20 See Booker T. Washington, ed., *Tuskegee* (New York, 1905), pp. 8–9; and his "Industrial Education for the Negro," in *The Negro Problem*, ed., Washington (New York, 1903), pp. 9–29.

21 Speech at Fisk University, 1895, *Selected Speeches of Booker T. Washington*, ed. E. Davidson Washington (Garden City, N.Y., 1932), pp. 37–38; and DuBois, ed., *The Negro Artisan*, p. 7.

22 *Annual Report of the Fifteenth Annual Convention, National Negro Business League* (August, 1914), p. 34.

23 W. E. Burghardt DuBois, "Of the Training of Black Men," in his *The Souls of the Black Folk*, 14th ed. (Chicago, 1924), p. 108; "The Talented Tenth," in *The Negro Problem*, pp. 62–63. For a careful analysis of the DuBois-Washington debate, see August B. Meier, *Negro Thought in America, 1880–1915* (Ann Arbor, Mich., 1963).

24 W. E. Burghardt DuBois and Augustus G. Dill, eds., *The Negro American Artisan* (Atlanta, Ga., 1912), p. 121.

25 W. E. Burghardt DuBois, ed., *The Negro in Business* (Atlanta, Ga., 1899), p. 25; see also Lorenzo J. Greene and Carter G. Woodson, *The Negro Wage Earner* (Washington, D.C., 1930).

26 John W. Davis, "The Negro Land-Grant College," *Journal of Negro Education*, II, No. 3 (July, 1933), 318–19.

27 *The Post-War Outlook for Negroes in Small Business, the Engineering Professions, and the Technical Vocations*, Howard University Studies in the Social Sciences, Vol. V, No. 5 (Washington, D.C., 1946), p. 9; see also Warmouth T. Gibbs, "Engineering Education in the Negro Land-Grant Colleges," *Journal of Negro Education*, XXI, No. 4 (Fall, 1952), 546–50.

28 Quoted in Raymond B. Fosdick, *Adventures in Giving: The Story of the General Education Board* (New York, 1962), pp. 94–95.

29 Edgar Gardiner Murphy, *Problems of the Present South* (New York, 1904), p. 79.

30 Lyman Hall, "Needs of the New South," *Annals of the American*

Academy of Political and Social Science, XXII, No. 2 (December, 1903), 269.

31 *NSPIE Bull.*, No. 20 (1915), p. 213.

32 Dewey W. Grantham, *Hoke Smith and the Politics of the New South* (Baton Rouge, La., 1958).

33 Perloff, *et al.*, *Regions, Resources, and Economic Growth*, pp. 272–73, 471–75; also see Robert Glass Cleland, *From Wilderness to Empire*, ed. Glenn S. Dumke (New York, 1960), pp. 272 ff.

34 See William G. Cunningham, *The Aircraft Industry: A Study in Industrial Location* (Los Angeles, 1951).

35 "Half a Million Workers," *Fortune*, XXIII, No. 3 (March, 1941), 96–98.

36 "Negro Employment in Airframe Plants," *Monthly Labor Review*, U.S. Department of Labor, Bureau of Labor Statistics, LXV, No. 5 (May, 1943), 888–89.

37 For example, see Dickey Meyer, *Needed—Women in Aviation* (New York, 1942).

38 Arthur Sweetser and Gordon Lamont, *Opportunities in Aviation* (New York, 1920).

39 Charles S. Matoon, *Your Career in Aviation* (Buffalo, N.Y., 1939); cf. "Airline Mechanic," *Fortune*, XXII, No. 2 (August, 1940), 45–47; and Samuel Burger, *Careers in Aviation* (New York, 1946).

40 See "Lockheed Aircraft Corporation," *Fortune*, XXII, No. 2 (August, 1940), 49–53; and Frank J. Taylor, "Merchants of Speed," *Saturday Evening Post*, CCXVIII, No. 43 (April 27, 1946), 12–13. Some of the material on which the remaining portion of this chapter is based was gathered through interviews done in Burbank and the Los Angeles area in March and April of 1965.

41 Lockheed Aircraft Corporation, "Lockheed-Vega Education Service," typewritten paper, Lockheed Training Department files (Burbank, Calif., 1940?); Lockheed Aircraft Corporation, "Report on the Status of Training," mimeo. (Burbank, Calif., 1942).

42 W. Daniel Musser, *Vocational Training for War Production*, U.S. Office of Education Bulletin No. 10 (Washington, D.C., 1946).

43 "Apprenticeship Agreement, State of California October 14, 1939."

44 Lockheed Aircraft Corporation, "Report of the Status of Training," p. 122; and Lockheed Aircraft Corporation, "Interdepart-

mental Communication Re: Apprenticeship Training" (August 28, 1940), included in "Lockheed-Vega Education Service."

45 Mark Perlman, *The Machinists* (Cambridge, Mass., 1961).

46 "Apprenticeship Training," *American Aeronaut*, II, No. 36 (February 13, 1942), 2.

47 "Training Now Will Assure Jobs," *American Aeronaut*, IV, No. 25 (November 19, 1943), 10.

48 E. V. Gustavson, "Engineers Made to Order," *Aviation*, XLII, No. 11 (November, 1943), 167; and Hall L. Hibbard, "Value Received from an Engineering Department," *Aviation*, XXXIX, No. 7 (July, 1940), 46–47.

49 Randall Irwin and Jacob Kadushin, "Training College Graduates for the Aeronautics Industry," *Mechanical Engineering*, XLIII, No. 3 (March, 1941), 190–92.

50 From a talk by B. C. Bolton, Administrative Engineer, *A Report of the Supervisor Training Conference, Lockheed Aircraft Corporation*, California State Department of Education, Bureau of Trade and Industrial Education (n.p., 1941), p. 98.

51 For an example of the problem the company faced when lines had to be drawn between management and the growing number of research scientists, see "Where Does the Lab End and the Plant Start," *Business Week*, No. 1373 (December 24, 1955), pp. 90–92.

52 *A Brief History of Burbank, California*, Burbank Chamber of Commerce Service Bulletin (1961).

53 *Your Burbank Home*, Burbank Merchants' Association (1928?), p. 15.

54 *Burbank—Its Place in the Sun*, Burbank Chamber of Commerce (mid-1930's?).

55 "Our Business Center," *Burbank Daily Review* (August 13, 1939), p. 4; see also "Adieu and Hail," *Burbank Daily Review* (December 30, 1939), p. 4.

56 *School Progress*, newsletter from the Burbank schools to parents, I, No. 1 (June 13, 1927), 2.

57 *Burbank City Schools*, published by the Burbank School System, II, No. 3 (April 23, 1934), 2; but there was no special emphasis on aviation, as in Robert W. Hambrook, *Aviation in the Public Schools*, U.S. Office of Education, Vocational Education Bulletin No. 185, Trade and Industrial Series No. 53 (1936).

58 *Burbank City Schools*, VI, No. 2 (April 25, 1938), 2.

59 "Minutes of the Board of Education of the Burbank Unified

School District" (November 17, 1943), July, 1943–June, 1944 Volume of the Minutes (typescript, Office of the Board of Education, Burbank, Calif.), p. 104.

60 "Vocational Work Urged for Burbank Secondary Schools," *Burbank Daily Review* (April 20, 1939), pp. 1–2.

61 Cf. Melvin Lewis Barlow, "A History of Trade and Industrial Education in California," unpublished Ph.D. dissertation, University of California, Los Angeles, 1949.

62 For a discussion of symbolic locales and urban life, see Anselm L. Strauss, *Images of the American City* (New York, 1961), especially Chapter IV.

63 Burbank Board of Education, "A Summary of the Conference on Educational Planning," mimeo. (Burbank, 1944).

64 Carey McWilliams, *Southern California Country* (New York, 1946), pp. 144 ff.; and National Commission for the Defense of Democracy of the National Education Association, *The Pasadena Story* (Washington, D.C., 1951).

65 Pasadena City Schools, Superintendent's Annual Report, *81 Years of Public Education in Pasadena* (Pasadena, Calif., 1955), p. 37; see also John A. Sexton and John W. Harbeson, *The New American College* (New York, 1946).

66 Franklin R. Johnson, *A Brief History of the Los Angeles Trade-Technical Junior College and the Frank Wiggins Trade School* (Los Angeles, 1954).

Chapter 6

1 For an example of the fear that mechanization will result in dangerous idleness, see George Barton Cutter, *The Threat of Leisure* (New Haven, Conn., 1926).

2 See C. Hartley Grattan, *In Quest of Knowledge* (New York, 1955); see also Edward George Hartmann, *The Movement of Americanize the Immigrant* (New York, 1948).

3 Malcolm S. Knowles, *The Adult Education Movement in the United States* (New York, 1962), pp. 190 ff.

4 Eduard C. Lindeman, *The Meaning of Adult Education* (New York, 1926), pp. 47–48; see also Robert Gessner, "The Seeker, A Biographical Sketch," Eduard C. Lindeman, *The Democratic Man,* ed. Gessner (Boston, 1946).

5 James Earl Russell, "The Educational Paradox: An American

Solution," *Journal of Adult Education,* I, No. 3 (June, 1929), 243–44.

6 Layton S. Hawkins, Charles A. Prosser, and John C. Wright, *Development of Vocational Education* (Chicago, 1951), pp. 148–50.

7 Charles A. Prosser and Charles R. Allen, *Vocational Education in a Democracy* (New York, 1926), p. 79.

8 *Ibid.,* p. 100.

9 Eduard C. Lindeman, *Leisure—A National Issue* (New York, 1939), p. 19.

10 James Earl Russell, "Looking Ahead," *Journal of Adult Education,* VI, No. 4, Part I (October, 1934), 480–81.

11 Some grounds for my speculation can be found in Knowles, *The Adult Education Movement,* pp. 159 ff.

12 Lyman Bryson, *Adult Education* (New York, 1936), p. 36.

13 "Emergency Education: How It Will Effect the Adult Education Movement," *Journal of Adult Education,* VIII, No. 1 (January, 1936), 73–74; see also "Unemployment and Adult Education," *Journal of Adult Education,* III, No. 1 (January, 1931), 5–36; and Harry A. Overstreet, "Capturing the Depression Mind," *Journal of Adult Education,* IV, No. 1 (January, 1932), 8–15.

14 Quoted in Harry Zeitlin, "Federal Relations in American Education, 1933–1943," unpublished Ph.D. dissertation, Columbia University, 1958, p. 80.

15 Frank Earnest Hill, *School in the Camps* (New York, 1935), p. 72.

16 Paul U. Kellog, "Unemployment and Progress," *Proceedings of the National Conference of Social Work,* LVI (1929), 101.

17 Quoted in Zeitlin, "Federal Relations in American Education," p. 227; see also Searle F. Charles, *Minister of Relief: Harry Hopkins and the Depression* (Syracuse, N.Y., 1963), pp. 47 ff.

18 George P. Rawick, "The New Deal and Youth," unpublished Ph.D. dissertation, University of Wisconsin, 1957, p. 199.

19 Betty Lindley and Ernest K. Lindley, *A New Deal for Youth* (New York, 1938).

20 William R. George, *The Junior Republic* (New York, 1910).

21 Randolph S. Bourne, *The Gary Schools* (New York, 1916), p. 15.

22 Cf. Thomas Minehan, *Boy and Girl Tramps of America* (New York, 1934), in which the old alternative of the "street" is now interpreted in Depression terms.

23 Franklin J. Keller, "Vocational Education for Leisure," *Proc. NEA* (1934), pp. 797–98.

24 *Annual Report of the Federal Board for Vocational Education* (1931), p. 9.

25 "Vocational Training and Unemployment," *Federal Board for Vocational Education Bulletin,* No. 159 (1931), p. 1.

26 "Vocational Education and Changing Conditions," *Federal Board for Vocational Education Bulletin,* No. 174 (1934), p. 13.

27 Prosser and Allen, *Vocational Education in a Democracy,* pp. 301 ff.

28 Hawkins, Prosser and Wright, *Development of Vocational Education,* pp. 159–60; and Rawick, "The New Deal and Youth," pp. 178 ff.

29 Educational Policies Commission, *The Civilian Conservation Corps, The National Youth Administration, and the Public Schools* (Washington, D.C., 1941), p. 56.

30 Vernon R. Alden, "Planning for Education's Forgotten Men," *Saturday Review* (May 15, 1965), pp. 68, 85.

31 "Job Corps Center: Where Youth Find Hope," *San Francisco Chronicle* (May 16, 1965), p. 2.

32 For example of a widely read statement on the subject, see Donald N. Michael, *Cybernation: The Silent Conquest* (Santa Barbara, Calif., 1962).

33 Paul Goodman, *Growing Up Absurd* (New York, 1960), p. 26.

34 Ross G. Henninger, *The Technical Institute in America* (New York, 1959), pp. 8 ff.

35 See Lynn A. Emerson, "Technical Training in the United States," Appendix I in *Education for a Changing World of Work,* Report of the Panel of Consultants on Vocational Education, U.S. Office of Education (Washington, D.C., 1963).

36 Henninger, *The Technical Institute,* p. 19.

37 Grant Venn, *Man, Education and Work* (Washington, D.C., 1964), pp. 32–33.

38 For an attack on the vocational education "establishment," see Edward T. Chase, "Learning to be Unemployable" (reprinted from *Harper's Magazine,* April, 1963), in *Vocational Education Act of 1963, Hearings before the General Subcommittee on Education and Labor,* HR, 88th Cong., 1st Sess. (hereafter cited as *VEA Hearings*), pp. 642–49.

39 *VEA Hearings,* pp. 231–44.

40 *Ibid.,* p. 68.
41 *Ibid.,* p. 102.
42 James B. Conant, *The American High School Today* (New York, 1959); and his *Slums and Suburbs* (New York, 1964).
43 Earl T. Beddell, "Vocational Education for Divergent Youth," *American Vocational Journal,* XXXVII, No. 1 (January, 1962), 30–32.
44 Hyman G. Rickover, *Education and Freedom* (New York, 1959), p. 56.
45 *VEA Hearings,* p. 182; cf. Frederick Harbison and Charles Meyers, *Education, Manpower, and Economic Growth* (New York, 1964).
46 Congressman Brademas' statement, *VEA Hearings,* p. 158.
47 *Ibid.,* p. 618.
48 *Ibid.,* especially pp. 392–93, 456, 494, and 555 ff.
49 *Ibid.,* p. 561.
50 See, for example, Patricia Sexton, *Education and Income* (New York, 1961).

Index

259